TISSUE INTERACTIONS DURING ORGANOGENESIS

Documents on Biology

Edited by **Etienne Wolff,** *Collège de France* and **Th. Lender,** *Faculté des Sciences d'Orsay*

E. Wolff *Tissue Interactions During Organogenesis* (Volume 1)
H. Lutz *Invertebrate Organ Cultures* (Volume 2)
G. Feher *Electron Paramagnetic Resonance With Applications to Selected Problems in Biology* (Volume 3)

Other volumes in preparation

TISSUE INTERACTIONS
DURING ORGANOGENESIS

Edited by

Etienne Wolff

Collège de France

GORDON AND BREACH Science Publishers

New York   London   Paris

Editorial office for the United Kingdom

Gordon and Breach, Science Publishers Ltd.
12 Bloomsbury Way
London W.C. 1

Editorial office for France

Gordon & Breach
7–9 rue Emile Dubois
Paris 14ᵉ

PREFACE

Documents on Biology

A CHARACTERISTIC of our times is the publication of an enormous number of scientific papers throughout the world. However, due to new developments, they soon become outdated and incomplete. To keep pace with the increasing amount of knowledge, teaching programs are having to be constantly revised and there is a growing demand for the publication of recent work at a student level.

This new series, *Documents on Biology*, is intended to meet these demands, and it is hoped that it will prove equally valuable to undergraduates and researchers who wish to keep up to date with advances in other aspects of biology. Each volume will attempt to draw together the most recent work by specialists in a particular field of biology, and the authors, through their own wider knowledge and experience, will be able to present the most relevant points without unnecessary detail.

Volumes on particular animal groups, by raising problems of basic zoology, will give the student a firm foundation which is essential before he can successfully tackle the problems of physiology, behaviour, experimental embryology etc. Other volumes will concentrate on one specific problem, such as regeneration, drawing together related work in different groups and treating the subject comparatively.

Though the subject matter has been made easier for the student, it is hoped that this will not deter him from thinking for himself. Rather, it is hoped that he will be stimulated to work further, so that, with the help of the author, he will acquire a higher and more valid level of knowledge.

It is with these aims in mind that this series has been established, and so that modern trends in biology are available to the student, lecturer, research worker and those who work outside the field of biology alike.

Etienne Wolff
Th. Lender

CONTENTS

INTRODUCTION

Etienne Wolff

Collège de France, Paris, and C.N.R.S., Nogent-sur-Marne

SOME BIOLOGISTS are inclined to consider "organizers" as common-place factors, without specificity. As such, they would merely initiate certain reactions, in the same way as the activating factors of an un-fertilized egg.

This view is reinforced by recent research in molecular biology. In the processes of differentiation, all interactions take place within the cell between the chromosomal genes and the cytoplasm, mediated by specific or non-specific RNA. What role do inducers of external origin play in these intracellular cycles? Can the whole process be considered as a "closed system" and, if the inducers do play an active part, are they simply "push-buttons", mere triggering devices, which release a series of chain reactions, and do they themselves play no part in differentiation?

It must be accepted that they act somewhere in the chain of nucleo-cytoplasmic transmission. We do not yet know exactly at what point they act in these cycles, but investigations on metabolic inhibitors, such as those of BRACHET and DENIS (1963), BRACHET, DENIS and DE VITRY (1964), and DENIS (1966), show that the inducers probably act at the point where a gene DNA becomes transcribed into a messenger RNA. There is no doubt that all developmental processes in an organism proceed by means of pre-established genetic mechanisms, both in the inducer and in the competent cell. Molecular biology has been particularly valuable in showing that most problems of development reduce to genetic problems, thus providing a link between embryology and genetics.

If it is postulated that the inducers act at gene level, then their role must be that of an activator or, in the terminology of molecular biology, a derepressor of the transcription of a cistron into messenger RNA. This question is still not resolved, nor is the way in which inducers act within the cell; however, much important research in experimental embryology over the last twenty years has demonstrated how they act on tissue masses. Several of these investigations have been carried out in our laboratory, and will be described in this book.

The role of inducers cannot be underestimated: they are the specific initiators of differentiation, and this specificity will be considered in detail in the present work. Some recent investigations in experimental embryology, which will subsequently be described, show that the inducers differ qualitatively and have different modes of action. A simple finding borne out by a wealth of evidence, is sufficient to substantiate this hypothesis: the primary inducer of the central nervous system does not directly bring about differentiation of either cartilage, kidney, liver, or lungs. These various organs have specialized inducers which do not generally act on another organ, and when these inducers do produce differentiation of a foreign tissue, they often leave their own particular mark on it.

For several reasons the concept of organizer and inducer has become a little discredited over the last twenty years. The first criticism is that the concept appears to have a metaphysical significance; some consider that it evokes teleological ideas involving factors of unity or totality. It should incidentally be noted that, even as first conceived by SPEMANN, the organizer did not have this interpretation. Even so, it is still better to replace the idea of a single organizer by that of specific inducers which separate development into distinct processes of differentiation.

A second argument is that investigations into the nature of the primary inducer (or inducers) have long been disappointing. The fact that many living tissues or tissue extracts are capable of inducing differentiation in amphibian primordial organs seemed to indicate that inducer substances were widely distributed in nature and had no specificity. The admirable biochemical research of TIEDEMANN, which followed the basic and decisive work of TOIVONEN and YAMADA, has refuted this belief.

A third argument is our present ignorance about the chemical nature of most inducers. We can answer this by saying that there are several instances of morphogenetic substances whose chemical nature is fairly well defined; for instance, in reproductive organogenesis there are the sex hormones, whose exact structure is known, and the primary inducers of primordial organ differentiation, whose chemical nature has been partly elucidated by Tiedemann and his associates. However, most inducers have not yet been isolated as definite chemical substances. Is this a valid reason for underestimating their role or contesting their existence?

If a filter or dialysing membrane is placed between the inducer tissue and the competent tissue, the latter differentiates; when a secretion of the inducer tissue is collected on a glass slide, or an extract of inducer tissue is prepared, both of these are found to have the same activity as the living tissue; can it then be denied that morphogenetic substances have been collected by these procedures? If the latter have a definite action, specific for a determined tissue on an undetermined primordium, can we still speak of a non-specific action, like that of a trigger mechanism set in motion by no matter what impulse? Even if some day it is shown that the inducers act as derepressors, this still does not exclude their having a specific activity.

It is certainly difficult to isolate inducer substances and characterize them chemically, as we are dealing with infinitesimal quantities of inducer tissue and even smaller amounts of inducer substances. Even the most refined techniques of modern biochemistry cannot altogether solve the problems of extraction, fractionation, and isolation of inducers. We should blame technical difficulties rather than doubt the existence of these substances. With improved methods, such as those of immunochemistry which are discussed in the last chapter, these problems may well be tackled in the near future.

The concept of inducer substances is further criticized on the grounds that it is difficult to characterize them chemically, and that the action of a defined chemical substance is substituted for that of a living tissue. The phenomenon of induction is thought to result, not from the action of a single substance, but from molecular interactions between juxtaposed tissues. Some consider that these interactions arise from molecular orientations at the interface between two tissues, and others that linkage phenomena between complementary molecules are involved, as between antibodies and antigens. Modifications of membrane permeability have also been suggested. These hypotheses are plausible, but they substitute obscure or unknown mechanisms for known reactions, even though the latter are not yet fully elucidated. In all instances, the passage of molecular modifications from one cell to another is envisaged. Why should inducers, which are known factors, not have an activity which is postulated for unknown factors? The chemical nature of vitamins and hormones remained unknown for a long time, but their existence was not doubted, and their physiological properties and specificity of action were still investigated.

To study the mode of action of inducers on a receptor tissue, the nature of the differentiations which they produce, the conditions under which these are produced, and lastly the chemical constitution of the inducers, is one problem. To elucidate the intracellular mechanisms of differentiation, the messengers by which an activated gene orders the synthesis of specific proteins and other substances elaborated in the cell, is another problem. The two sets of investigations are complementary. In both, inducers play a part. They even establish a link between the two, since the cycle of intracellular reactions begins at the time and point where an inducer has exercised its effect. It can be said that the concept of inducers is as necessary and as well established as that of enzymes. We are inclined to attribute a role of prime importance to the latter in differentiation, and this is justified. However, we tend to minimize the importance of the former—and yet they are at the origin of all differentiation.

Tissues possessing inductive properties do not exercise their action in one direction only. They are not exclusively inducers. There is no hierarchy of embryonic primordia, where some are exclusively inductive and others exclusively receptive. A tissue induced by another can in turn become the inducer of a third: it can even have an inductive action towards its own inducer. We shall see many examples of this. That is why we prefer the idea of interaction between embryonic tissues to the concept of induction. It is this which explains the title given to this book. It does not exclude the existence of substances with a specific action which, if preferred, could be termed morphogenetic substances or, to use a more general term, differentiation substances.

Specificity of action of inducers

The specificity of inducers can be interpreted in several ways. It in fact corresponds to several modes of action which recent research in experimental embryology has clarified.

Firstly, the natural inducer is the only possible one and cannot be replaced by another tissue: this is a case of strict specificity, of which we shall see some examples. One such is the notochord-neural tube system in vertebrate differentiation. There are also instances where the natural inducer can be replaced by a small number of other rudiments; these are generally tissues whose origin is related to that of the natural inducer. This is so for the secondary inducer of the liver: the natural inducer, the hepatic mesenchyme, is not the only one capable of producing hepatic differentiation; other mesenchymes, usually from neighbouring organs, can replace it. But we shall see that not all mesenchymes inducing hepatic cords are capable of provoking complete differentiation of this tissue (LE DOUARIN, 1964). Thus, in one sense, specificity is relative to the nature of the inducer. The latter may have a *strict* or a *partial* specificity.

In a second type of interaction, the inducer provokes a specific differentiation: the differentiated tissue then carries the imprint of the inducer. Differentiation is orientated by the inducer, not by the competent tissue. Let us take an example from the work of BISHOP-CALAME (1966). When a ureter is placed in contact with lung mesenchyme, the latter, instead of differentiating pulmonary structures, forms secondary urinary canaliculi. This differentiation of the competent tissue, i.e. the pulmonary mesenchyme, bears the mark of the inducer.

Lastly—and this is a third possibility—the inducer has a precise but non-specific action. We shall see instances where the competent tissue reacts in accordance with its own potentialities, determined by its genetic capacities and not following the directives of the inducer. This is what happens, for example, when pulmonary epithelium is placed in contact with metanephric mesenchyme. The latter, instead of producing bronchial ramifications, forms secondary urinary canaliculi. It could be said that, in this case, the determination of the competent tissue is stronger than the order given by the inducer. There are thus degrees of specificity in the nature or action of inducers. It is these two points of view that we shall principally be dealing with in the chapters which follow.

The chapters in this book were the themes of seminars held at the College de France, Paris, in 1967. Chapter 1 draws together the work of Professor HADORN and his colleagues in Zurich. The remaining chapters provide some explicit examples of relevant work carried out, mainly in the bird class, by several researchers at the Laboratory of Experimental Embryology of the College de France, Paris.

References

BISHOP-CALAME, S. (1966). Etude expérimentale de l'organogenèse du système urogénital de l'embryon de poulet. *Arch. Anat. Microscop. Morphol. Exp.*, **55**, 215–309.
BRACHET, J., and DENIS, H. (1963). Effects of actinomycin D on morphogenesis. *Nature*, **198**, 205–206.

BRACHET, J., DENIS, H., and DE VITRY, F. (1964). The effects of actinomycin D and puromycin on morphogenesis in amphibian eggs and Acetabularia mediterranea. *Develop. Biol.*, **9**, 398–434.

DENIS, H. (1966). *Activité des gènes au cours du développement embryonnaire.* Desoer.

LE DOUARIN, N. (1964). Etude expérimentale de l'organogenèse du tube digestif et du foie chez l'embryon de poulet. II. Etude expérimentale de l'organogenèse hépatique. *Bull., Biol. Fr. Belg.* **98**, 589–676.

CHAPTER I

DETERMINATION,
PRELUDE TO DIFFERENTIATION

Etienne Wolff

Collège de France, Paris, and C.N.R.S., Nogent-sur-Marne

WHAT IS the first effect of an inducer on a competent tissue? In general, all differentiation is preceded by a remarkable condition, difficult to define objectively, which is termed *determination*. The only characteristic that distinguishes a *determined* primordium from an undifferentiated one is a *prospective* character. It is on the way to becoming differentiated; its future is in some measure decided, although there is as yet no visible morphological modification. HADORN (1965) proposes the following definition of determination: "Determination is a process which initiates a specific pathway of development, by singling it out from among various possibilities for which a cellular system is competent".

A determined tissue is generally orientated irreversibly in a particular direction. It should be added, however, that there can be several degrees of determination, and that it can be more or less complete. When the presumptive ectoderm of an early stage gastrula has received induction from the chorda-mesodermal tissue, it is orientated towards neural differentiation. Although this differentiation is not yet visible, if the ectoderm continues to develop, it cannot produce anything other than a part of the nervous system. Thus determination represents a prospective value.

The determination of an organ is quite a complex problem. It implies first the determination of the inducer, and secondly, the determination of competence, as the competent tissue can only respond to the inducer at a certain stage and in a certain situation. It is only then, when the inducer acts on the competent tissue, that the latter becomes determined. These

1

processes are probably motivated by different genes. The determination of the inducer often precedes the stage where it can exercise its activity; the latter must go through a stage of maturation. For example, the primary organizer of amphibia, the chorda-mesoderm, is determined at an early stage, that of the "grey crescent", but it has to develop up to the stage of gastrulation before it can exercise its inductive functions.

Competent tissue must also undergo maturation. This is seen very clearly in the case of the gastrula ectoderm which only responds to inductive action at a particular developmental stage; it is incompetent and un-responsive until the beginning of gastrulation. Furthermore, if the ectoderm is allowed to develop beyond the gastrula stage, either in the embryo itself or in culture, it loses its competence in a few hours. In certain cases, competence itself results from an induction. This can be seen, for example, in Planaria, where the marginal body fimbria is only competent with respect to the cerebral inducer, and can only respond by forming eyes. The cerebral inducer, as LENDER (1952) showed, is completely inactive in the caudal marginal regions, while it is active in the anterior region which normally bears the eyes. But the competence of this area becomes established during development, following an induction whose nature is still unknown, but which is probably also due to the brain. Whether by maturation or induction, the competent tissue must acquire a certain determination before it can respond to an inductive action.

Determination is thus a complex phenomenon; it is a sort of predifferen-tiation, a differentiation which remains invisible using present histological methods. It has not yet been characterized by biochemical criteria. It is possible that more highly developed techniques will reveal more definite characteristics of determination. Biochemical modifications are certainly involved. A model can be found in sexual differentiation. As has been demonstrated in our laboratory, *biochemical determination* becomes estab-lished in the reproductive glands before their morphological differentiation. It is manifested by the elaboration of sex hormones and, prior to this, by the elaboration of enzymes responsible for synthesizing these hormones.

It is possible that, in the future, the electron microscope will reveal some differential characteristics between an undetermined and a determined cell.

It should be noted that differentiation generally closely follows determina-tion. The differentiation of the amphibian nervous system is produced a few hours at most after determination. This determination is produced during gastrulation, and the first differentiation—that of the neural plate—takes place at the end of gastrulation. Similarly, differentiation of the lens, or more precisely the lens vesicle, follows very closely on the induction exercised by the optic cup. In certain cases, differentiation takes longer to become established. In limb morphogenesis of vertebrates, the phase of determination is fairly long. The first determination is induced by the mesenchyme of the limbs at an early stage and it consists of an action on the ectoderm, which is transformed by the inducer into an apical cap (Kieny). It is in this phase that the limb bud appears, but it has as yet no internal differentiation. The determination of the various parts of a limb bud takes place progressively in a proximo-distal direction, i.e. from the base of the limb towards the extremity. The successive stages of this are now well known. They result from the alternating and reciprocal actions of the mesenchyme and the apical cap; they take place step by step, and the whole process is relatively long, lasting around 2 to 3 days in the normal development of the chick embryo.

Whatever its duration, determination is a transient state, generally irreversible, and leading almost inevitably to differentiation. It is because of this ephemeral state that the phenomenon of differentiation has, until now, been so difficult to analyse and understand.

Certain recent investigations carried out by Hadorn and others present improved possibilities for studying this unstable and poorly defined state; the work was carried out in Zurich between 1963 and 1968 (HADORN, 1963, 1964, 1965, 1966, 1967; GARCIA-BELLIDO, 1966; GEHRING, 1966, 1967; NOTHIGER, 1964, NOTHIGER and SCHUBIGER, 1966; SCHUBIGER, 1968; WILDERMUTH, 1968).

Let us recall the principle of Hadorn's experiments. In insect larvae, there are two organisms which are to some extent juxtaposed. One is the larval organism, with its own differentiation; it is almost entirely destined to necrose; there are relatively few larval organs which persist into adult life. At the same time, small islets develop within the larval organism; these are termed the imaginal discs or imaginal primordia, and are as yet still undifferentiated. Almost all the adult organs are formed from these primordia, which are visible and can be identified solely by the position which they occupy in the larva. They are homogenous and their cells are undifferentiated, yet they are often determined at an early stage, as shown by GEIGY (1931) and ABOIM (1945). These imaginal primordia exist throughout larval life without developing, and only differentiate at metamorphosis.

1*

Let us recall here certain classical concepts of insect endocrinology. Two principal hormones are active during larval life. One is the moulting hormone secreted by the prothoracic glands; its chemical nature has been established and it is termed ecdysone; it is also the hormone of metamorphosis, but it only acts in this capacity when another hormone has ceased to exercise its inhibitory function. This other hormone, secreted by the *corpora allata*, is the juvenile hormone which counteracts metamorphosis. What happens in the larva? When both hormones are secreted, the juvenile hormone inhibits metamorphosis and ecdysone only provokes moulting. At the last larval stage, the juvenile hormone ceases to be secreted by the *corpora allata*; the moulting hormone now stimulates not only moulting but also metamorphosis. It is because of this antagonism between the effects of the two hormones that there are several successive larval moults preceding metamorphosis.

Many investigations have shown, by experiments with grafting or ablation of the endocrine glands, that larval life can be prolonged or metamorphosis initiated at will.

After metamorphosis, the *corpora allata* once again begin to secrete juvenile hormone, which then plays a role in growth and physiology of the reproductive organs. But its continued presence in the imago is capable of inhibiting the metamorphosis of a larval organ implanted into the adult organism.

These concepts make it possible to understand Hadorn's research, an account of which follows. This author removes imaginal discs from the larva of *Drosophila melanogaster*, e.g. those of the copulatory apparatus, the antennae, or the wings. He then implants them into the abdomen of an imago. Here, the imaginal primordium multiplies very actively and increases considerably in size, *while still remaining undifferentiated*. It can attain large dimensions, e.g. 2 or 3 mm in length, which is considerable for a *Drosophila* and in comparison with the initial dimensions of an imaginal primordium. If a portion of these grafts is transplanted into the abdomen of another *Drosophila*, they continue to proliferate; they give rise to a second generation of grafts which continue to multiply without differentiating. These primordia will remain in the same undifferentiated but determined state, so long as they continue to be transplanted into the abdomens of adults. However, if a fragment of these imaginal discs is transplanted into the body of a larva, it will undergo metamorphosis at the same time as its host. It then expresses, by its differentiation, its original potentialities. In general, it differentiates in accord with its determination, i.e. according to the destiny assigned to it by its localization in the larva. Figure 1 illustrates the principle of Hadorn's experiment which consists of isolating one portion of the genital disc, e.g. the primordium of the dorsal plates (AA) and retransplanting it several times into imagos.

In this way, what amounts to a long-term culture *in vivo* is achieved, with periodic transfers (sub-cultures) from one adult to another. Each explant is divided into two at each transfer, and one of the explant halves

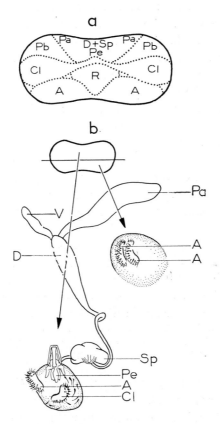

Figure 1 **a** Map of primordia of a male genital disc of *Drosophila melanogaster*. *D*, ductus ejaculatoris, *V*, vasa efferentia, *Sp*, spermatic pump, *Pe* penis, *Pa*, paragonia, *Pb*, peripheral bristles, *Cl*, valves, *A*, anal plates, *R*, rectum.
b Result of a fragmentation experiment (horizontal line). On the left are seen organs and structures obtained after metamorphosis of the anterior portion; on the right, those resulting from metamorphosis of the posterior part (see also figure 4). (after HADORN, 1965).

6 E. WOLFF

is implanted into a larva; here it differentiates, so that its potentialities
can be verified at all times.

Figure 2 schematises HADORN's experiments on the genital armature.
From the left are numbered successive transplantations into the imagos;
from the right, the transplantations into the larvae serving as a test for
each generation.

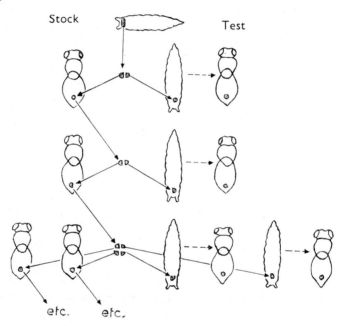

Stock   Test

etc.   etc.

Figure 2 Method used for permanent *in vivo* culture. The stock transplanted into a
series of adults grows continuously but remains undifferentiated (left). Fragments
transplanted into larvae become differentiated after metamorphosis of the latter, serving
as test for each generation of transplants (right). (after HADORN, 1963, 1964).

Figure 3 gives the actual genealogy of cultures carried out in the course
of 55 transfers over two years.

In general, differentiation conforms to the nature of the primordium.
For example, the genital primordium will give rise to different parts of the
genital apparatus. As the primordium is divided at each transfer and one
portion removed, a complete genital apparatus is not always obtained;
this is because a primordium is capable of limited but not total regulation.
It can thus happen that after several transplantations, some genital primordia

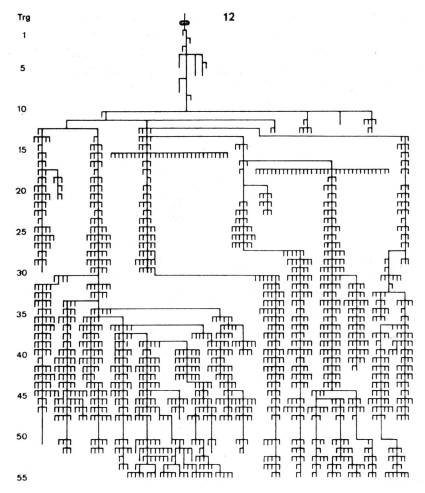

Figure 3 Genealogical tree of genital disc cultures, over 55 generations of transfers (Trg) cultured and tested from October 1962 until September 1964. The short lines represent implants subjected to a differentiation test. The continuous lines indicate continuity relations between successive transfers (after HADORN, 1966).

will produce only genital plates, or only anal plates, a penis, or other parts of the genital armature.

Figure 4 shows an intact genital plate (left), with its presumptive primordia determined, and the parts to which these correspond in the adult (right). If this genital plate is grafted *in toto* into an imago, the various organs

only differentiate when the undifferentiated tissues are transplanted into
a larva. All parts of the apparatus are found, but there may be many
examples of each, e.g. there may be 20 anal plates instead of 2. All differentiations are present, sometimes in an incoherent succession, but they can
all be identified by an experienced observer.

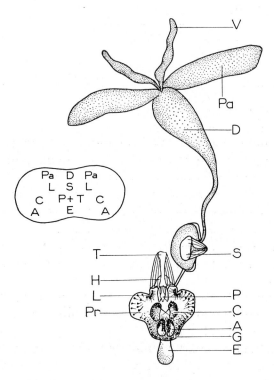

Figure 4 Normal differentiation of a complete genital disc after implantation. *V*, vas
efferens, *Pa*, paragonia, *D*, ductus ejaculatorius, *S*, spermatic pump, *T*, plate-support
(apodime), *H*, hypandrium, *P*, penile apparatus, *L*, lateral plate, *Pr*, peripheral bristles,
C, valves, *A*, anal plate, *G*, genital arch, *E*, terminal intestine (after HADORN and coworkers, 1949, and URSPRUNG, 1959).

In general, the differentiations observed conform to the prospective
nature of the primordium. It is rare to find differentiations which would
not arise from the normally differentiated primordium, and in the course
of the first transfers, abnormal differentiations—i.e. characteristic of
another primordium—do not occur. According to HADORN's terminology,

determination is "autotypic". It is very remarkable that tissues of an imaginal primordium can be maintained in a determined but non-differentiated state for generation after generation. An actual culture *in vivo* of determined but undifferentiated tissues is thus achieved, so that this transitory state of determination can be maintained for years, perhaps indefinitely. In this way, very large amounts of determined material can be obtained; such a result must have great importance for quantitative biochemical investigations.

TRANSDETERMINATION

But things sometimes become complicated. After several generations of transfers, unexpected differentiations may begin to appear; they are aberrant, in that they do not conform to the presumptive fate of the initial primordium; Hadorn terms this occurrence "allotypic" differentiation. Their appearance is fairly constant, but the attendant conditions and factors involved are not fully elucidated. There may be a large percentage of aberrations, e.g. the first formation of antennae in cultures of the genital apparatus may appear in 20% of cultures. They also appear in a definite order. For example, in cultures of genital apparatus, these allotypic differentiations consist at first of antennae, legs, and palps, which are formed at the 8th or 9th generation (figure 5).

This phenomenon is remarkable, as it concerns tissues and organs which can be considered as determined, according to the embryological analysis carried out by various procedures.

The phenomenon is even more curious, since it does not concern homologous organs, as is the case when an antennal primordium gives rise to a leg or vice versa. But the genital apparatus is not the homologue of an appendage. From the 13th generation, wings appear, and lastly, at the 19th generation, formations such as the thorax arise in limited proportions. Apart from instances of aberrant differentiations, the genital plate line generally continues to produce autotypic differentiations through all generations. However, the determination of a certain number of lines becomes definitively modified. This phenomenon is termed "transdetermination" by Hadorn. Transdetermination is thus a common phenomenon, but is still mysterious. It has given rise to diverse and interesting interpretations. Transdetermination is, moreover, reversible, as are certain mutations of *Drosophila*, and a primordial transplant thus modified can revert to its initial determination. For example, an antennal primordium arising from a genital primordium by transdetermination, may revert after a few transplant generations, and once more give rise to genital plates according to its original determination.

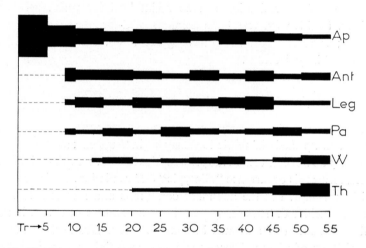

Figure 5 Chronology and relative frequency of differentiation of anal plates (*Ap*), antennae (*Ant*), legs (*Leg*), palps (*Pa*), wings (*W*) and thoraces (*Th*) in 519 test implants derived from a single male genital disc. Distribution from generation 1 (Tr) up to generation 55. The results are combined in groups—5 successive transplant generations to each group (after HADORN, 1965).

Figure 5 shows the genealogy of 55 generations of genital primordial grafts. At the beginning, genital plates only are formed. At the 9th generation, antennae, legs, and then palps appear. Wings appear at the 13th generation, and thoraces at the 19th. At a certain time, transdeterminations are very frequent, and become even more numerous than normal determinations.

Figure 6 shows the result of such transdeterminations. The initial line gives rise to anal plates (figure 6a), which is an autotypic differentiation. From this line, allotypic differentiations have appeared, due to transdetermination. On figures 6b to 6g, derivatives of other appendages or the thorax are seen; one wing, the basal part of a tarsus, the 2nd segment or brush of an antenna, a palp, or a mesothorax, characterized by its large bristles. It can be seen that these elements do not always have a coherent organization, but their differentiations are nonetheless characteristic.

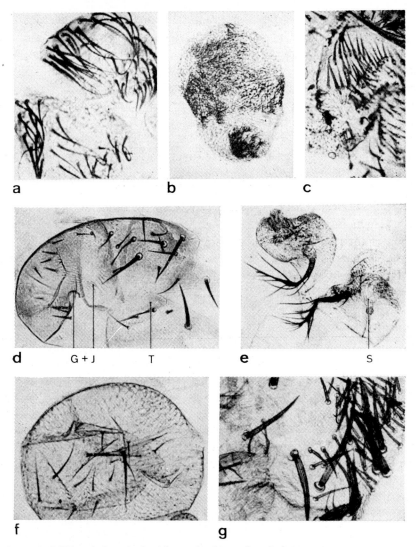

Figure 6 Differentiation obtained in test-implants of anal plates.
a: autotypic anal plates (Tr 41); *b* — *g*: allotypic differentiations; *b*, wing (Tr 20); *c*, basitarsus, with bristles of the transverse discs with "bracts" (Tr 24); *d*, second antennal segment with organ of Johnston (articulation *G* + *J*) and trichome primordium (*T*); *e*, the same test implant as *d* shows the third antennal segment with saccule (*S*) (Tr 33); *f*, palp (Tr 33); *g*, mesothorax with large and small bristles and trichomes (Tr 21).
Enlargement (from original figure): X 290 (a), X 75 (b), X 200 (c, f, g), X 120 (d, e) (after HADORN, 1966).

What exactly is this phenomenon of transdetermination? It might be explained by postulating that determination has not yet been established, or that determination is unstable. But precise experiments have shown that the imaginal primordia are determined at a very early stage; localized lesions of the imaginal primordia completely and definitively suppress certain structures which would otherwise have originated from the primordium.

Figure 1 shows the primordium of the copulatory apparatus. If this primordium is sectioned transversely (figure 1a), the distal part produces anal plates (figure 1b, AA). The remainder gives rise to all other parts of the genital apparatus, excluding anal plates (figure 1b, left). Consequently determination of the various parts is very specific. Similarly, if the anal plate region (figure 1a, AA) is irradiated, e.g. with ultra-violet, only certain parts of the genital apparatus will develop, e.g. the penis and the genital armature may be formed, but neither anal plates nor rectum differentiate.

In another experiment, HADORN mixed fragments of imaginal discs from the same or different organs, taken from individuals of different races, species or sexes. In some instances, several fragments combine to form a whole structure, e.g. genital plates, but within these structures, the areas of different origin can be clearly distinguished, e.g. those of the "Yellow" and "Ebony" races. The different areas are juxtaposed, and do not merge into a unified whole. Thus from the beginning of the experiment, there was virtual segregation, following the determination of the different parts of the primordium.

Nor can transdetermination be explained by the hypothesis of somatic mutation. The differentiation which occurs is consistent with the species genotype, and all potentialities revealed by the phenomenon of transdetermination are present from the start of development in the hereditary constitution of all the cells.

Suppose that a gene C_1 is responsible for a certain differentiation D_1. This differentiation directs the synthesis of proteins and specific substances, passing first through a phase of determination d_1. When transdetermination occurs, the determination d_1 is effaced or masked; it is another gene C_2 which starts another differentiation D_2, corresponding for example to the morphogenesis of antennae or wings, probably after having passed through a phase of determination d_2. How is this modification of determination produced, and to which transformation does it correspond? If it is accepted that a messenger RNA M_1 corresponds to a gene C_1, then a messenger

RNA M_2 must correspond to the gene C_2. At what stage of information transmission is determination produced? How can a first determination be effaced, if it is already inscribed in the chain of information reactions? Is it at the point where DNA is transcribed into messenger RNA, or at the terminal point of the chain, at polyribosome level where the message is translated? We do not know, but this phenomenon represents a major problem in molecular biology. Nor do we know what factors provoke transdetermination, which appears to be a natural development of determination. If these two problems could be resolved, a considerable advance would have been made in understanding the phenomenon of determination.

What is certain, is that although the activation of a gene sets in motion a chain of information transmission, and that this is normally accompanied by the inhibition of all other chains, the total genome (or a part of the genome) is always present and reactivable.

Hadorn stresses the fact that transdetermination is not a gene mutation; it is not due to modification of a gene, but to the intervention of another pre-existing gene, previously repressed. In addition, the frequency of trans-determinations, which can reach 50%, far exceeds the highest percentages observed for spontaneous or experimental mutations in *Drosophila*. This makes it even less probable that transdetermination can be compared to a mutation. Besides this, mutations can be seen to occur in *in vivo* cultures, but they are very different from transdetermination. They correspond to what Hadorn terms "anormotypic" differentiations. For example, there are lines which suddenly acquire giant anal plates, and which for generations continue to produce giant anal plates. There are instances of lines which have totally lost the faculty of differentiating hairs and bristles, whose cuticular plates are completely naked. Again, there are lines which have lost the faculty for differentiating large bristles but not small hairs, so that organs with aberrant pilosity are observed.

Transdetermination is thus not comparable to a mutation. But it must be said that, however strict a determination may be, it can still be labile. Hadorn offers the following explanation: it is possible that the factor responsible for the first determination may become diluted over a very large number of mitoses, to the point where it is no longer sufficiently active to continue functioning. He also believes that this dilution could have the same effect on gene activities as a feed-back phenomenon, and that under these conditions, new genes could become activated. But these are hypotheses which have not so far been demonstrated.

Two very important findings arise from HADORN's research. The first is that we can prolong the state of determination indefinitely, without differentiation taking place. During this time, the imaginal primordium undergoes intense proliferation, passing through about 1500 supplementary mitotic cycles in the course of successive graft generations. The phenomenon of proliferation is thus rendered completely independent of differentiation. Are there any phenomena in the animal world, comparable to these indefinite *in vivo* cultures of tissues which are determined, but whose differentiation can be retarded at will by the experimenter? Are there any analogous phenomena in the biological sphere, either spontaneous or experimental, where determined but undifferentiated tissues persist? Possible examples are the proliferating layers of certain organs, such as the basal strata of cutaneous and mucosal epithelia, which are evidently determined without being differentiated, but which are intimately mingled with differentiated cells. The regeneration cells of many organisms have a certain analogy with the imaginal primordia. In certain species they have some degree of determination, e.g. in amphibia, whose regeneration cells have only a limited capacity for tissue reconstruction. In other groups, such as the triclads (Turbellaria), the regeneration cells retain the capacity to regenerate all structures throughout the life of the individual. These cells are disseminated throughout the body; they behave as dormant cells ready to differentiate under favourable conditions, but, unlike the imaginal discs explanted into imagos, they are not determined.

Then there are the many experiments on transplantation of nuclei in amphibia. When an ovum nucleus is replaced by a somatic nucleus, development may progress, in certain cases, to an adult stage. If somatic nuclei are taken from the blastula, and retransplanted into enucleate ova, a new generation of individuals capable of developing into adults is obtained.

The experiment can be repeated with blastula nuclei taken from this second generation, then from a third, a fourth ... etc. A clone is thus obtained composed of individuals all derived from a single nucleus, and which can be maintained indefinitely in the undifferentiated state. While the tissues at the blastula stage are not determined, the embryos from which they originate are nevertheless determined to give a complete organism. Successive transplantations thus retard the time of differentiation of the organism, as is seen with transplantations of imaginal primordia. Both processes have a common factor, which is that differentiation of determined elements—tissue primordia or nuclei—can be inhibited by their environment: imago lymph in *Drosophila,* pregastrula cytoplasm in the amphibia.

The case of imaginal primordia is, however, much more clear cut, with the two connected but somewhat contradictory phenomena of prolonged determination and transdetermination. While these phenomena still leave many questions unsolved, they have a prime importance for both experimental embryology and genetics. They may provide the key to problems whose solution biologists have been seeking for many years. They offer the possibility for studying a determined tissue from the biochemical aspect. What is the difference, firstly between an undetermined primordium and a determined one, and secondly, between a determined tissue and a differentiated one? Perhaps differences exist between the RNA of one category and another. For example, it might be supposed that determined cells contain the messenger RNA necessary for their differentiation, while the genes corresponding to the undetermined cells have not yet formed messenger RNA. The study of messenger RNA after many series of transplantations, i.e. at a time when transdetermination is frequent, might show differences between certain imaginal primordia of the same origin and same initial determination. The analysis of proteins and enzymes could also be rewarding. The answer to metazoan differentiation, which the specialists in molecular biology have so long sought, might then be found. It is also possible that the study of cell ultrastructure would reveal modifications at the time of transition from the undetermined to the determined state, and from the determined to the differentiated state, when the cells are distinctly separate and in a stable condition.

The phenomenon of transdetermination, though mysterious, is still a promising field, as we have seen. When the factors which determine it are elucidated, when we understand why a gene which is activated and perhaps already transcribed into RNA, becomes effaced or dominated by another, we shall certainly have a better understanding of how information is transmitted from the genes to the cytoplasm in a higher metazoan.

Such are the future perspectives provided by HADORN's noteworthy research.

References

ABOIM, A. N. (1945). Développement embryonnaire et post-embryonnaire des gonades normales et agamétiques de Drosophila melanogaster. *Rev. Suisse Zool.,* **52,** 53–154.

GARCIA-BELLIDO, A. (1966). Pattern reconstruction by dissociated imaginal disk cells of Drosophila melanogaster. *Develop. Biol.,* **14,** 278–306.

GARCIA-BELLIDO, A. (1966). Changes in selective affinity following transdetermination in imaginal disc of Drosophila melanogaster. *Exp. Cell. Res.*, **44**, 382–392.

GEHRING, W. (1966). Webertragung und Änderung der Determinationsqualitäten in Antennenscheiben-Kulturen von Drosophila melanogaster. *J. Embryol. Exp. Morphol.*, **15**, 77–111.

GEHRING, W. (1967). Clonal analysis of determination dynamics in cultures of imaginal disks in Drosophila melanogaster. *Develop. Biol.*, **16**, 438–456.

GEIGY, R. (1931 *a*). Erzeugung rein imaginaler Defekte durch ultraviolette Eibestrahlung bei Drosophila melanogaster. *Arch. Entwicklungsmech. Organ.* (1931), **125**, 406–447.

HADORN, E. (1963). Differenzierungsleistungen wiederholt fragmentierter Teilstücke männlicher Genitalscheiben von Drosophila melanogaster nach Kultur in vivo. *Develop. Biol.* **7**, 617–629.

HADORN, E. (1964). Bedeutungseigene und bedeutungsfremde Entwicklungsleistungen proliferierender Primordien von Drosophila nach Dauerkultur in vivo. *Rev. Suisse. Zool.*, **71**, 99–116.

HADORN, E. (1965). Problems of Determination and Transdetermination. "Genetic Control of differentiation", *Brookhaven Symp. Biol.*, **18**, 148–161.

HADORN, E. (1966). Konstanz, Wechsel und Typus der Determination und Differenzierung in Zellen aus männlichen Genitalanlagen von Drosophila melanogaster nach Dauerkultur in vivo. *Develop. Biol.*, **13**, 424–509.

HADORN, E. (1967). *Dynamics of determination.* "Major Problems in developmental Biology", *Academic Press, New York*, 85–104.

LENDER, Th. (1952). Le rôle inducteur du cerveau dans la régénération des yeux d'une planaire d'eau douce. *Bull. Biol.*, **86**, 140–215.

NOTHIGER, R. (1964). Differenzierungsleistungen in Kombinaten. Hergestellt aus Imaginalscheiben verschiedener Arten, Geschlechter und Körpersegmente von Drosophila. *Arch. Entwicklungsmech. Organ.*, **155**, 269–301.

NOTHIGER, R., and SCHUBIGER, G. (1966). Developmental behaviour of fragments of symmetrical and asymmetrical imaginal discs of Drosophila melanogaster. *J. Embryol. Exp. Morphol.*, **16**, 355–368.

SCHUBIGER, G. (1968). Anlageplan, Determinationszustand und Transdeterminationsleistungen der männlichen Vorderbeinscheibe von Drosophila melanogaster. *Arch. Entwicklungsmech. Organ.*, **160**, 9–40.

WILDERMUTH, H. (1968). Differenzierungsleistungen, Mustergliederung und Transdeterminationsmechanismen in hetero- und homoplastischer Transplantation der Rüsselprimordien von Drosophila. *Arch. Entwicklungsmech. Organ.*, **160**, 41–75.

CHAPTER II

INDUCTIVE MECHANISMS IN KIDNEY ORGANOGENESIS

Etienne Wolff

Collège de France, Paris, and C.N.R.S., Nogent-sur-Marne

THIS CHAPTER and subsequent ones will deal with recent research on induction mechanisms in organogenesis, and interactions between inductive primordia and competent tissues. Much of the research has been conducted in our laboratory. Several organs will be used as examples, and we shall consider first the kidney, whose complex structure and mechanism of formation are today partially elucidated.

Kidney formation in higher vertebrate is in three stages: the pronephros, mesonephros and metanephros. These three are distinct organs, but have the same morphological and physiological significance, succeeding one another during embryonic life. This succession corresponds approximately to the phylogeny of vertebrates, the pronephros, mesonephros and metanephros being characteristic of the adult in very low vertebrates, intermediate, and higher vertebrates respectively. This distinction is not merely a theoretical concept, as might be inferred from an elementary textbook; there are actually three organs, distinguishable by their position and structure. The first two are not always functional in higher groups, even in the embryo, but they appear consistently either as functional organs or vestigial structures. We shall see that certain organs, even though not functional, still play an important role in the genesis of others. This is so for the pronephros.

I GENERAL PROCESSES IN THE FORMATION OF KIDNEYS

The pronephros is formed in the neck region, between the 8th and 12th somite in birds, and for this reason is sometimes called the cephalic kidney.

It is a rudimentary organ, in which nephrostomes can be distinguished; these are funnel-shaped ciliate orifices opening into the main coelomic cavity, extending posteriorly as tubules. These canaliculi of the pronephros

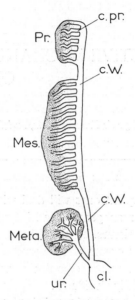

Figure 1 Diagram showing development of successive vertebrate kidneys, particularly in birds.
Pr., pronephros or cephalic kidney; *Mes.*, mesonephros; *Meta.*, metanephros or permanent kidney; *cl.*, cloaca; *c. pr.*, canaliculi of pronephros; *c.W.*, Wolffian duct; *ur.*, ureter.

unite to form the primitive excretory canal, i.e. the Wolffian duct. It is highly significant that, in the absence of the pronephros, there is no Wolffian duct, without which, the mesonephros or metanephros is not formed. This dependence of the two kidneys—mesonephros and metanephros, which function successively in birds—on the vestigial kidney, or pronephros, is

Figure 2 Development of metanephric primordium of an 11-day mouse embryo after 8 days culture.
c, ureteral branches (collecting tubules); *t*, secretory tubules formed from mesenchyme (after GROBSTEIN, 1955).

Figure 3 Histological structure of the metanephric primordium from a 5-day chick embryo, cultured for 5 days on chorio-allantoic membrane. III and IV, ureteral ramifications of 3rd. and 4th order; *ts*, secretory tubules (after BISHOP-CALAME, 1966) ($\times$ 140).

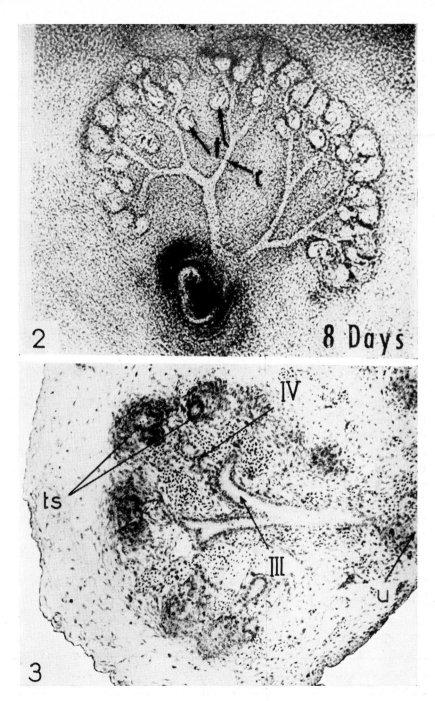

2   8 Days

3

quite remarkable. The Wolffian duct, terminating in a blind ampulla, descends progressively along the trunk somites, and approaches the cloaca. It passes close to a special mesenchyme, situated in the intermediate region between the 12th and 30th somite; this is the mesenchyme of the meso-nephros (figure 1). It is from this contact between the epithelium of the Wolffian duct and the mesonephric mesenchyme that differentiation of the collecting and secretory tubules comes about, by a phenomenon of reciprocal induction. The mesonephros is functional in avian embryos up to the 13th—15th day of incubation. During this time, the Wolffian duct continues its descent and finally anastomoses with the cloaca. At this point, a small outgrowth develops from the Wolffian duct; this is the rudiment of the ureter, the collecting duct of the permanent kidney (figure 1). The ureter develops within a mass of special mesenchyme, the mesenchyme of the metanephros. The metanephros is formed during the period of mesonephric activity, and becomes functional around the 15th day of incubation.

All these mesenchymes which induce the successive kidneys, in collabora-tion with the Wolffian duct and the ureter, are homologous and situated in the same region, which can be called the nephrogenic tract. The genesis of the metanephros provides the clearest example of kidney differentiation. The processes involved in differentiation can be summarized as follows: the metanephric mesenchyme induces the primitive ureter to ramify, forming numerous dichotomized branches of the first, second, third and fourth degree (I to IV) (figures 2, 3 and 6). At the terminal ampullae of the quaternary ramifications, a reciprocal induction phenomenon takes place: the blind endings of these tubules cause the metanephric mesenchyme to form convoluted tubules which subsequently communicate with the quater-nary ramifications; these convoluted tubules give rise to the secretory tubules of the permanent kidney and to the Malpighian glomeruli.

II ANALYSIS OF INDUCTION PHENOMENA DURING DIFFERENTIA-TION OF THE MESONEPHROS

Whilst the mesonephros is a temporary organ in higher vertebrates, it is the definite or permanent kidney of certain lower vertebrates such as the amphibia. Many experiments, including those of WADDINGTON (1938), HOLTFRETER (1944), VAN GEERTRUYDEN (1946) and CAMBAR (1948), have shown that obstruction of the Wolffian duct, i.e. arrest of its passage towards the cloacal region, inhibits formation of the mesonephros in amphibia. Other procedures, such as extirpation of the Wolffian duct, have the same end result: the absence or arrest of mesonephric differentiation. However, HOUILLON (1956) showed that absence of the Wolffian duct did not entirely inhibit formation of some canaliculi. If the descent of the Wolffian duct is impeded by placing an obstacle in its path, a certain number of mesonephric tubules can sometimes be seen to form along the mesenchymal tract which normally gives rise to the mesonephros. It thus seems that, in Amphibia, the Wolffian duct is not absolutely essential for tubule differentiation. This suggests that the mesenchyme in question has already undergone a first determination and can to some extent evolve without induction by the Wolffian duct. Nevertheless, the latter is indispensable for normal differentiation of the organ.

CAMBAR and GIPOULOUX (1956) diverted the Wolffian duct from its normal pathway so that it described a curve a short distance away from the mesodermal tract. Above the diversion, the duct remained in contact with the mesenchyme. More caudally, it deviated from the mesenchyme, but tubules formed nevertheless. At the level of maximum deviation, no mesonephric structures were formed, then tubules began to form once more in a region where the duct approached the mesenchyme but still did not touch it. This proves that the inducer can act at a certain distance. CAMBAR and GIPOULOUX showed by ingenious experiments that the maximum distance at which the inducer was effective, was 100 to 120 μ for *Rana dalmatina* and 130 to 140 μ for the toad, *Bufo bufo*.

Past experiments in birds, such as those of BOYDEN (1924), GRÜNWALD (1937) and WADDINGTON (1938) indicated that if the distal extremity is destroyed or the descent of the Wolffian duct arrested, mesonephric differentiation ceases as in amphibia.

Although these experiments seem to demonstrate that extirpation or destruction of the Wolffian duct inhibits mesonephric differentiation, certain subsequent experiments of GRÜNWALD (1942) gave contradictory results. He found, as did HOUILLON (1956) in amphibia, that a certain number of tubules or tubule-containing masses differentiated despite absence of the Wolffian duct. The problem thus needed re-investigation, and this has been done by BISHOP-CALAME (1962, 1965, 1966) in our laboratory.

We know that the extremity or terminal ampulla of the Wolffian duct is always situated at a very short distance behind the last somite. By placing an obstacle across the organs lateral to the neural tube, behind the last somite, the descent of the Wolffian duct is impeded. In a series of experiments BISHOP-CALAME (1966) implanted a fragment of eggshell membrane

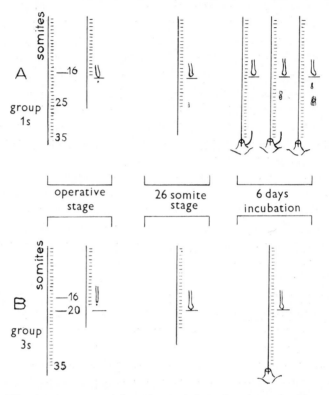

Figure 4 Diagramatic representation of a technique for obstructing descent of the Wolffian duct extremity by means of a mechanical obstacle. A. Group 1s: the obstacle, indicated by a transverse line, is placed at a distance of 1 somite behind the last somite. B. Group 3s: the obstacle is placed at a distance equivalent to 3 somites behind the last formed somite. The black spot indicates the terminal extension of the Wolffian duct; clusters represent mesonephric canaliculi, formed behind the obstacle at 6 days incubation. The U shaped black line growing from the cloaca represents the rudiment of a ureter.

at a distance corresponding to the length of one somite, behind the last differentiated somite (figure 4A). Under these conditions, the Wolffian duct terminates in a large ampulla. Distal to this ampulla, the mesenchyme differentiates into mesonephros. However, despite the arrest of the Wolffian duct, a few clumps of mesonephric tubules are found below this point in

mesenchyme separately. When grafted alone onto the chorio-allantoic membrane, the ureter does not differentiate; it does not ramify and remains a primitive canal, no different in structure from the initial tissue at the time of

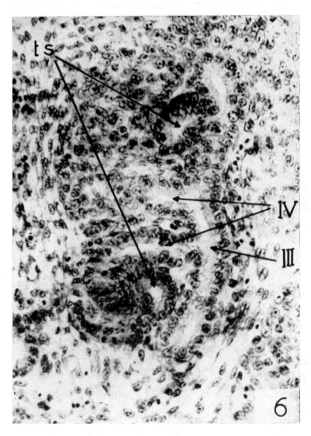

Figure 6   Reassociation of metanephric mesenchyme and ureter, previously dissociated. Development as chorio-allantoic graft. III, IV, 3rd and 4th order ureteral branches; t.s., secretory tubules formed from mesenchyme (after Bishop-Calame) ($\times$ 150).

transplantation. The metanephric mesenchyme, cultured alone on the chorio-allontoic membrane, remains an inactive tissue with no differentiation.

If the two components are re-associated on the same chorio-allantoic membrane, they differentiate normally into metanephros, consisting of excretory tubules originating from the ureteral ramifications, and tubules and glomeruli formed from the mesenchyme (figure 6).

Is the metanephric mesenchyme the only mesenchyme which can respond to ureteral induction? The results of investigating this particular question (BISHOP-CALAME, 1965) have been remarkable. In several instances, the ureter imposes its nephrogenic properties on mesenchymes which have no points in common with the kidney, as is seen with lung mesenchyme.

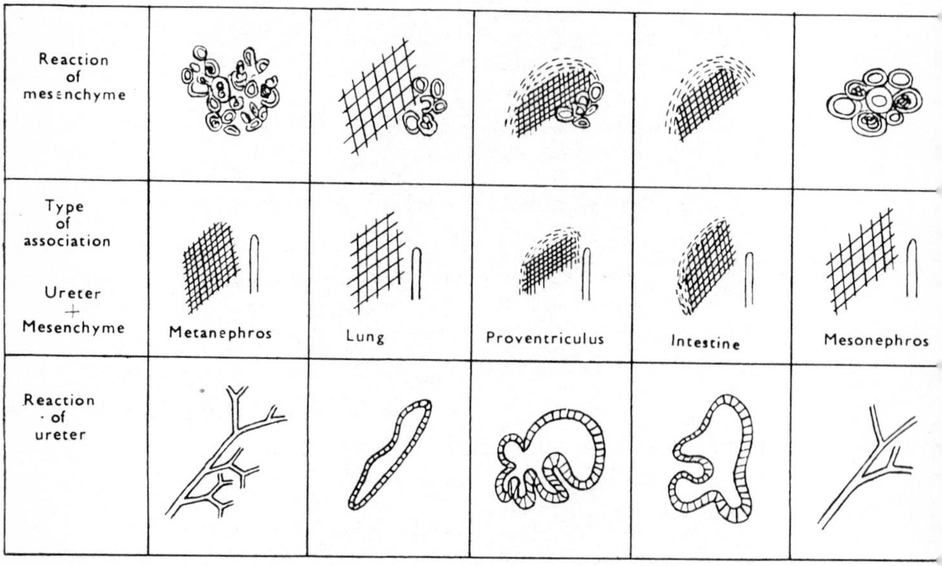

Reaction of mesenchyme					
Type of association Ureter + Mesenchyme	Metanephros	Lung	Proventriculus	Intestine	Mesonephros
Reaction of ureter					

Figure 7 Diagram summarizing the results of associations of ureter with various mesenchymes.

Figure 7 summarises the experiments which have been conducted:

1) Association of metanephric mesenchyme with ureter (i.e. normal conditions).

2) Association of pulmonary mesenchyme with ureter.

3) Association of proventriculus mesenchyme with ureter.

4) Association of intestinal mesenchyme with ureter.

5) Exchange between mesenchymes and excretory ducts of mesonephros and metanephros.

a) *Association between pulmonary mesenchyme and ureter*

The ureter induces dense canaliculi and glomeruli in the pulmonary mesenchyme. Hence it imposes a differentiation consistent with its own nature on a mesenchyme which would not normally give such formations. This shows the ureter's specificity of action. But the ureter itself is influenced by the pulmonary mesenchyme. Instead of remaining as a canal with a single layer of cells, it develops several cell strata—a pseudostratified epithelium. A type of compromise comes about between the inducer and the competent tissue (figure 8). Neither tissue is completely undetermined; each imposes a differentiation on the other in conformity with its own nature.

b) *Association between proventriculus mesenchyme and ureter*

The mesenchyme of the proventriculus forms fairly large urinary tubules with glomeruli; here again, there is renal differentiation, imposed by the ureter on the proventriculus mesenchyme. But in the vicinity of the mesenchyme which it has induced, the ureter itself undergoes some extraordinary transformations. It is totally unlike a ureter, and becomes a canal resembling a proventriculus, with characteristic glands, a stratified epithelium, a muscular zone, and dense connective tissue. The mesenchyme is "nephrotized" by the inducer, but the inducer itself is influenced by the associated mesenchyme, and becomes in effect, "gastricized" (figure 9).

c) *Association between intestinal mesenchyme and ureter*

In this case, there is no reaction of the intestinal mesenchyme, perhaps because it is a very dense tissue, already too advanced in its differentiation. On the other hand, it has a profound effect on the ureter which preserves absolutely nothing of its normal structure; it comes to resemble an intestine, presenting a stratified epithelium with glands and intestine-like folds. The neighbouring mesenchyme is attracted by the ureter, forming a sheath around it like an intestinal epithelium (figure 10).

d) *Association between metanephric mesenchyme and Wolffian duct, and between mesonephric mesenchyme and ureter*

The experiment consists of exchanging ducts and mesenchymes of the metanephros and mesonephros; in this way, an attempt is made to establish whether mesenchymal differentiation is innate, or whether this differentiation is imposed by the canal (Wolffian duct or ureter) associated with it. The two kidneys have a very different structure; they are distinguishable by morphological, histological, biochemical and physiological character-

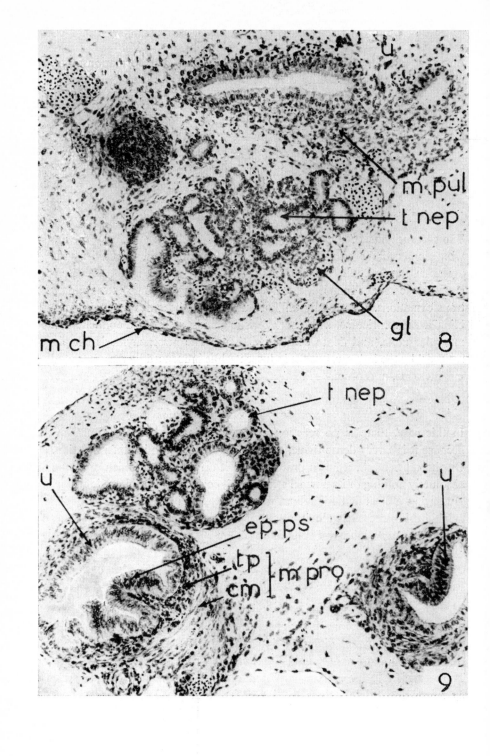

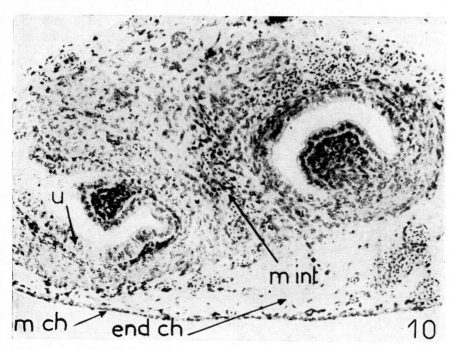

Figure 10   Ureter associated in culture with intestinal rudiment mesenchyme, then transplanted as chorio-allantoic graft for 8 days. Formation of intestinal type villi, with mucosa resembling intestinal structure.
end. ch., chorio-allantoic endoderm; *m. int.*, intestinal mesenchyme; *u.*, transformed ureter (after Bishop-Calame) (× 150).

istics. Their structural differences are clearly apparent on a section passing through both organs at 9 days incubation (figure 11).

1) If a 5-day metanephric mesenchyme is associated with a Wolffian duct taken from embryos of 3 to 3½ days incubation, the result is clear

---

Figure 8   Result of associating ureter with pulmonary mesenchyme (after 18 hours culture and 4 days as chorio-allantoic graft). Formation of an islet of renal tubules with glomeruli.
gl., glomerulus; *m. ch.*, chorio-allantoic membrane; *m. pul.*, pulmonary mesenchyme; *t. nep.*, renal tubules; *u.*, ureter.

Figure 9   Association of ureter with mesenchyme of proventriculus rudiment, after 6 days graft.
c. m., muscular layer; *ep. ps.*, pseudostratified epithelium; *m. pro.*, proventriculus mesenchyme; *t. nep.*, renal tubule; *t. p.*, tunica propria; *u.*, ureter partially transformed (after Bishop-calame).

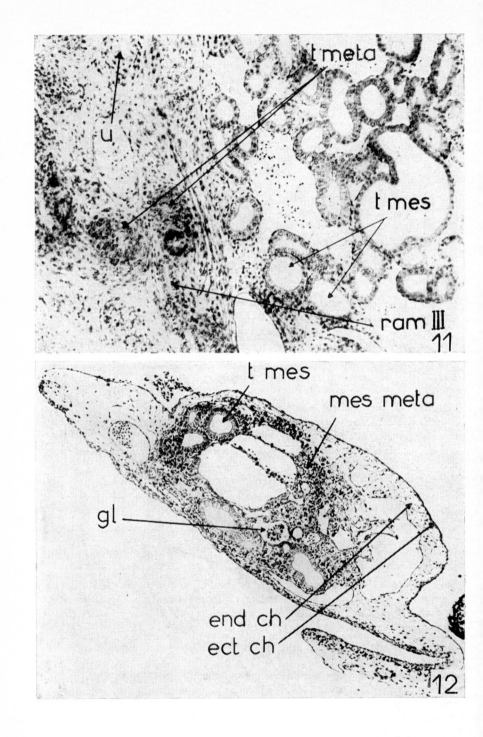

cut. The differentiation established (after 18 hours *in vitro* culture, and 5 days as a chorio-allantoic graft) is of the *mesonephric* type. Large tubules can be seen in the mesenchyme round in section, with large lacunae between them lined by regular cells whose cytoplasm is highly eosinophilic. A secretion is often seen in the lumen of the tubules. Large glomeruli become differentiated. This differentiation is essentially different from metanephric structures. Thus the Wolffian duct imposes its differentiation on the mesenchyme (figure 12).

2) In the reverse association, of mesonephric mesenchyme and ureter, the results obtained hitherto are less well defined, as the experiment could not be conducted up to a sufficiently advanced stage of development. However, the density of the tissues and small calibre of the tubules suggest a metanephric differentiation (figure 7, right hand column). Here again, the inducer canal appears to dictate differentiation of the mesenchyme.

CONCLUSIONS

Some important conclusions can be drawn from these experiments, concerning the properties of inducers, and their relative potency as compared with the associated competent tissues. In certain cases, a compromise is established between the inducer and the competent tissue, through mutual interaction.

In mammals (rodents) the inducer of the metanephros has no strict specificity, since the ureter can be replaced by the neural tube or salivary gland epithelium. Both determine the formation of convoluted tubules in the metanephric mesenchyme (GROBSTEIN).

The avian ureter exerts a powerful inductive action on homologous and heterologous mesenchymes; it imposes its own type of differentiation on renal, pulmonary, and proventriculus mesenchyme, which all produce

---

Figure 11 Histological appearance of a transverse section through a 9-day embryo at gonadal level, showing the different appearance of the mesonephros (right) and the metanephros (left).
ram. III, 3rd order ureteral ramification; *t. mes.*, mesonephric tubules; *t. meta.*, metanephric tubules; *u.*, ureter (after BISHOP-CALAME) ($\times$ 160).

Figure 12 Association of *metanephric* mesenchyme with a Wolffian duct after 4 days graft. Result: differentiation of mesonephric type.
gl., glomerulus; *ect. ch.*, chorionic ectoderm; *end. ch.*, chorioallantoic endomesoderm; *mes. meta.*, metanephric mesoderm; *t. mes.*, mesonephric tubule (after BISHOP-CALAME) ($\times$ 105).

secretory tubules and glomeruli. The ureter in turn is subject to a strong reciprocal influence of the competent tissue; in contact with mesenchyme of lung, proventriculus, and intestine, it tends to assume the epithelial and tubular appearance of these organs. This shows the assimilatory and dominating nature of two primordia where, in the presence of the other, each acts on its partner in certain cases. Results like these demonstrate powerful interactions which are not revealed by experiments associating the normal components of the same organ. They show that the influence of one sometimes dominates the other. We can see that there are strong inducers which determine the type of differentiation, and weak inducers which provoke differentiation but do not determine its actual nature, the latter being consistent with the type of competent tissue. We shall see examples of these processes in the following chapters.

References

BISHOP-CALAME, S. (1965). Nouvelles recherches concernant le rôle du canal de Wolff dans la différenciation du mésonéphros de l'embryon de poulet. *J. Embryol. Exp. Morphol.* **14**, 239–245.

BISHOP-CALAME, S. (1965). Etude d'associations hétérologues de l'uretère et de différents mésenchymes de l'embryon de poulet, par la technique des greffes chorio-allantoïdiennes. *J. Embryol. Exp. Morphol.*, **14**, 247–253.

BISHOP-CALAME, S. (1966). Etude expérimentale de l'organogenèse du système urogénital de l'embryon de poulet. Thèse. *Arch. Anat. Microscop. Morphol. Exp.*, **55**, supplément, 215–309.

BOYDEN, A. E. (1924). An experimental study of the development of the avian cloaca, with special reference to a mechanical factor in the growth of the allantois. *J. Exp. Zool.*, vol. 40, **3**, 437–471.

CALAME, S. (1960). Sur l'existence d'un diverticule du cloaque pouvant donner naissance à l'uretère chez l'embryon de poulet. *C.R. Acad. Sc.*, **250**, 4455–4456.

CALAME, S. (1961). Le rôle des composants épithélial et mésenchymateux du métanéphros, d'après les résultats de la culture *in vitro*. *Arch. Anat. Microscop. Morphol. Exp.*, **50**, 299–308.

CALAME, S. (1962). Contribution expérimentale à l'étude du dévelopement du système urogénital de l'embryon d'oiseau. *Arch. Anat. Histol. Embryol.*, **44**, 43–65.

CAMBAR, R. (1948). Recherches expérimentales sur les facteurs de la morphogenèse du mésonéphros chez les Amphibiens Anoures. *Bull. Biol. France Belg.*, **82**, Fasc. 2–3, 214–285.

CAMBAR, R., and GIPOULOUX, J. D. (1956). Mesure expérimentale de la distance à laquelle l'uretère primaire peut induire la morphogenèse du mésonéphros (Amphibiens Anoures). *C.R. Acad. Sc.*, **242**, 2862–2865.

DAMERON, F. (1961). L'influence de divers mésenchymes sur la différenciation de l'épithélium pulmonaire de l'embryon de poulet en culture *in vitro*. *J. Embryol. Exp. Morphol.*, **9**, 628–633.

VAN GEERTRUYDEN, J. (1946). Recherches expérimentales sur la formation du méso-néphros chez les Amphibiens Anoures. *Arch. Biol.*, **57**, 145–282.

GROBSTEIN, C. (1953 *a*). Inductive epithelio-mesenchymal interaction in cultured organ rudiments of the mouse. *Science*, **118**, 52–55.

GROBSTEIN, C. (1955). Inductive interaction in the development of the mouse metanephros. *J. Exp. Zool.*, **130**, 319–340.

GROBSTEIN, C. (1956). Transfilter induction of tubules in mouse metanephrogenic mesen-chyme. *Exp. Cell. Res.*, **10**, 424–440.

GROBSTEIN, C. (1957). Some transmission characteristics of the tubule-inducing influence on mouse metanephrogenic mesenchyme. *Exp. Cell. Res.*, **13**, 575–587.

GROBSTEIN, C. (1959). Autoradiography of the interzone between tissues in inductive interaction. *J. Exp. Zool.*, **142**, 103–214.

GRÜNWALD, P. (1937). Zur Entwicklungsmechanik des Urogenitalsystems beim Huhn. *Arch. Entwicklungsmech. Organ.*, **136**, 786–813.

GRÜNWALD, P. (1942). Experiments on distribution and activation of the nephrogenic potency in the embryonic mesenchyme. *Physiol. Zool.*, **15**, 396–409.

HOLTFRETER, J. (1944). Experimental studies on the development of the pronephros. *Rev. Can. Biol.*, Vol. 3, **2**, 220–249.

HOUILLON, Ch. (1956). Recherches expérimentales sur la dissociation médullo-corticale dans l'organogenèse des gonades chez le Triton Pleurodeles waltlii Michal. *Bull. Biol. France et Belg.*, **90**, 359–444.

WADDINGTON, Ch. (1938). The nephrogenetic function of a vestigial organ in the chick. *J. Exp. Biol.*, **15**, 371–376.

CHAPTER III

INDUCTION OF DETERMINATION AND INDUCTION OF DIFFERENTIATION DURING DEVELOPMENT OF THE LIVER AND CERTAIN ORGANS OF ENDOMESODERMAL ORIGIN

N. Le Douarin

University of Nantes

DURING THE last fifteen years, much research has been devoted to the phenomenon of induction occurring during organogenesis in higher vertebrates. In primordia of mixed origin especially, where the components are partly epithelial and partly mesenchymal, an interdependence between the two has been demonstrated in a number of instances: the mesenchyme and the epithelium behave successively, with respect to each other, as inductive tissue and effector tissue.

Concerning the organs of endomesodermal origin several researches—notably DAMERON, SIGOT, GOLOSOW and GROBSTEIN—have shown respetively that differentiation of the pulmonary, gastric, and pancreatic epithelium is dependent on an inductive process of mesodermal origin.

I have concentrated on the development of certain endomesodermal derivatives in chick embryo, especially that of the liver; but my studies dealt with much earlier developmental stages than those investigated by the above authors, as the liver is the first endodermal organ to differentiate and become functional in the embryo.

I STEPS OF DEVELOPMENT OF THE PRE-UMBILICAL ENDODERMAL DERIVATIVES

The development of the digestive apparatus in chick embryo begins with the formation of a crescent-shaped endodermal fold, which appears in the anterior part of the embryo after 25 to 30 hours incubation. This fold subsequently takes on the form of a tube, blind at its anterior extremity (figure 1). This first rudiment of the digestive tract constitutes the fore-gut or embryonic pharynx. It is bordered posteriorly by the anterior intestinal portal.

From the start of its formation, the endoderm of the fore-gut ventral surface differs from the other embryonic endodermal regions. Its cells are tall and contain many inclusions, while other endodermal cells, particularly those of the dorsal pharyngeal surface, remain flattened.

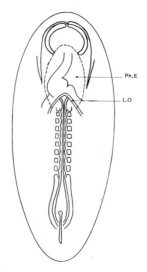

Figure 1   The digestive tract rudiment in a 9-somite chick embryo (ventral view). *Ph. E.*: embryonic pharynx; *L. O.*: anterior intestinal portal.

If this endodermal region is marked by carbon particles in 8 to 10 somite embryos, particles are subsequently found medioventrally in the endodermal organs situated ahead of the umbilicus (LE DOUARIN, 1964). This implies that, at an early stage, the pharyngeal floor contains endodermal cells which take part in the formation of pre-umbilical organs. I wanted to investigate the differentiating capacities of these endodermal cells at an early stage, and my first studies were made on the liver.

1) Presumptive areas of the liver in the embryo at early developmental stages

The first manifestation of hepatic development is the appearance of an endodermal evagination in the anterior intestinal portal, at the 20 to 22 somite stage. This endodermal bud forms epithelial cords which invade the thin mesenchymal layer surrounding the venous sinus (i.e. the *septum transversum*).

The liver is formed from an endomesodermal rudiment, but the study of its organogenesis presents difficulties which do not arise with most other

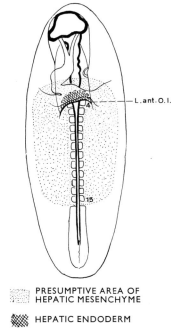

L.ant.O.l.

PRESUMPTIVE AREA OF
HEPATIC MESENCHYME

HEPATIC ENDODERM

Figure 2   Localization of presumptive hepatic endodermal and mesodermal areas in a 15-somite embryo.

organs (lung or intestine, for example). In fact the hepatic mesoderm only forms a distinct rudiment when it is already invaded by cords of hepatocytes of endodermal origin. Before differentiation of the liver, the hepatic mesenchyme is not separate from the splanchnic mesoderm.

In order to study the mechanisms of liver cell differentiation, it was thus necessary to carry out investigations prior to this differentiation.

With this end in view, I determined the localization of the presumptive hepatic area in the 15 to 20 somite embryo. It forms two lateral areas, reaching approximately the level of the 15th somite and joined ventrally in the cardiac fold (figure 2). By various experiments, I also ascertained that at these embryonic stages, the endodermal and mesodermal areas of the liver have a different distribution. The mesodermal region extends over the whole presumptive area, while the endodermal region is narrowly localized in the anterior intestinal portal, where the hepatic rudiments subsequently

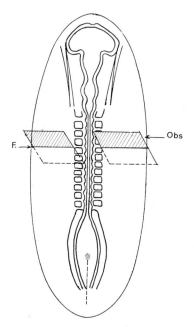

Figure 3 Experimental procedure for isolating the posterior portion of the presumptive hepatic area and preventing colonization of the hepatic mesenchyme by hepatocyte cords of endodermal origin.
Obstacles (*Obs.*) constituted by a rectangular fragment of eggshell membrane are inserted into a transverse slit through the three embryonic layers.

form. From these rudiments, cords of hepatocytes proliferate and invade the mesodermal anlage.

It is possible to avoid complete invasion of the mesoderm and thus obtain it in an isolated state. This is achieved by placing an obstacle, consisting of a rectangular fragment of eggshell membrane, in a transverse slit involving the 3 embryonic layers (figure 3). This mechanical obstacle prevents part of the mesenchyme from being invaded by endodermal cells; the result is that liver tissue only forms ahead of the obstruction, while behind it only the hepatic mesenchyme develops (plate I, figures 1 and 2).

Using this technique, hepatic mesenchyme can be isolated, and its role in endodermal differentiation investigated.

2) Role of homologous mesenchyme in differentiation of the hepatic endoderm

The hepatic endoderm is removed from 20 to 22 somite embryos. The cardiac fold or ventral floor of the fore-gut is treated with trypsin solution, the endoderm becomes detached from the underlying mesenchyme; the region of the hepatic rudiments is then selectively removed (figures 4a and 4b).

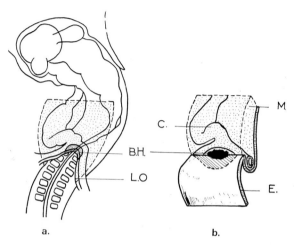

a.   b.

Figure 4 a) *Removal of hepatic endoderm*: 21-somite embryo depicted in ventral aspect. The cardiac fold is removed as indicated by the dotted area.
b) The cardiac fold is treated with trypsin; the endoderm (*E*) is detached from the underlying mesenchyme (*M*), and the hepatic rudiment (*B. H.*) region dissected. *C.*, heart; *L. O.*: anterior intestinal portal.

As with other endodermal rudiments studied by various researchers, the isolated hepatic endoderm cultured *in vitro* or as an intracoelomic graft, does not differentiate and rapidly degenerates. A mesenchymal support is essential for endodermal survival.

Association of hepatic endoderm with homologous mesenchyme was achieved in two ways.

In the first series of experiments, endoderm is associated with mesoderm of the same age. This is done by grafting endoderm into the presumptive area of the hepatic mesenchyme, behind an obstacle (figure 5); in this way, both tissues develop simultaneously in the host embryo. By the 6th day of

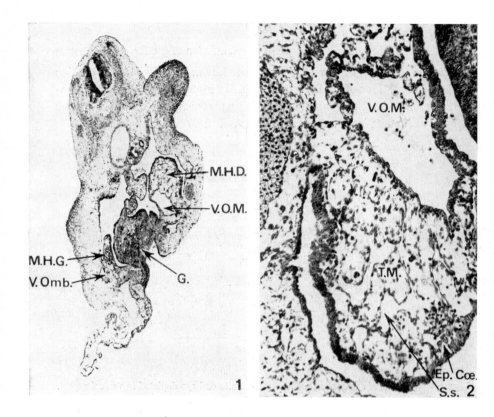

PLATE I

Figure 1 Result of experimental procedure represented in figure 3 of text: transverse section of a 5-day embryo behind the level of the obstacles. Ventral body closure has not taken place behind the obstacles and the gizzard (*G*) remains open ventrally. In the coelomic cavity can be seen two mesenchymal lobes bounded by a coelomic epithelium. The mesenchyme is that of the right and left liver lobes (*M.H.D.* and *M.H.G.*) which develop along the omphalomesenteric vein (*V.O.M.*) and the umbilical vein (*V. Omb*).

Figure 2 Detail of right hepatic lobe mesenchyme. *T.M.*: hepatic mesenchyme devoid of endodermal cords; *S.S.*: blood sinusoids; *Ep. Coel.*: coelomic epithelium.

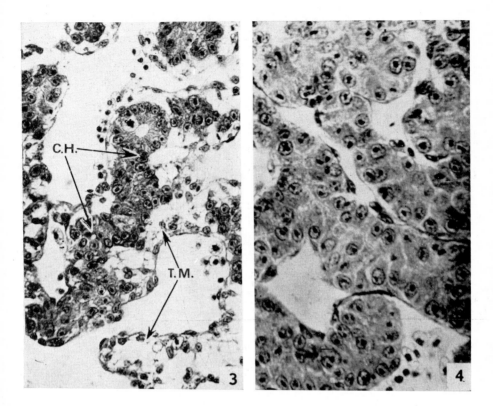

PLATE I

Figure 3 Result of experimental procedure depicted in figure 5 of the text. Transverse section of a 5 day-old host embryo at the level of the hepatic mesenchyme. The hepatic mesenchymal areas (*T.M.*) of the host are colonized by parenchymal cords arising from the grafted endoderm. *C.H.*: cords of hepatocytes.

Figure 4 Same experiment. Section made at 6 days of incubation of the host. The host mesenchyme is completely colonized by endodermal cells arising from the graft. Normal liver is formed. The hepatic mesenchyme forms the endothelium of the blood sinusoids.

incubation, the host hepatic mesenchyme is invaded by cords of hepatocytes arising from the grafted endoderm (plate I, figures 3 and 4). Note also that the mesenchyme has a characteristic hepatic structure even before endoder-

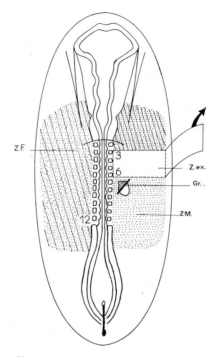

Figure 5 *Association of hepatic endoderm and hepatic mesenchyme in ovo.*
A fragment of the lateral zone is excised (*Z. ex.*) at 4-somite level; that part of the presumptive hepatic area situated behind the level of excision is not colonized by host endoderm. Hepatic mesenchyme alone is formed (*Z. M.*). Normal liver forms on the opposite side and ahead of the excision. Hepatic endodermal rudiments are grafted into the zone constituted solely by hepatic mesenchyme.

mal invasion; the growth of hepatocyte cords is guided by the mesenchymal framework.

The second type of association is carried out between endoderm and mesenchyme of different ages. Endoderm is taken from 20 to 22 somite embryos as before, while 5 day embryos, previously subjected to the insertion of an obstacle, provides the mesenchyme. These two tissues of different ages are associated in *in vitro* culture on the medium of WOLFF and HAFFEN (1952).

After 2 to 3 days in culture, hepatocytes arising from the endodermal rudiment can be seen to invade the mesenchyme. A small liver lobe forms *in vitro*. The periodic acid-Schiff (PAS) reaction shows that the hepatocytes formed accumulate glycogen (plate II, figure 1).

Consequently in liver, as in other endodermal organs studied, the homologous mesenchyme guarantees survival of the endoderm, and is also capable of promoting hepatocyte multiplication and differentiation.

3) Action of heterologous mesenchymes on differentiation of the hepatic endoderm

The hepatic mesenchyme is not the only one permitting development of the hepatic endodermal rudiments. These rudiments were associated with heterologous mesenchymes of the same age, either by grafting *in ovo*, or *in vitro*. The mesenchymes selected were those of the somatopleure and splanchnopleure, from embryos of $2\frac{1}{2}$ to 3 days incubation.

Association with the somatopleure

The endoderm is associated with somatopleure mesenchyme in the embryo *in ovo*, by making a slit in the body wall and introducing the graft into the slit. This can be done either above or below the omphalo-mesenteric artery. Great care must be taken not to let the graft slip through into the coelom; it remains in contact with the mesenchyme of the flank wall where it develops (figure 6a and 6b).

The same association can be carried out *in vitro* by taking a portion of the body wall between the somitic axis and the lateral amniotic fold, in the region between the limb rudiments. The strip of tissue obtained is associated with the endoderm in culture for 12 hours; the explant is then allowed to develop as an intracoelomic graft.

When the association is carried out *in ovo*, a transverse section of the host embryo made 5 days after implantation, shows that the somatopleure provides an entirely suitable environment for endodermal development. Hepatic tissue develops in the internal surface of the body wall, and shows the same degree of evolution as that of the host. If the graft is allowed to develop for a longer period, e.g. until the 16th day of incubation, a small hepatic lobe is found to protrude into the coelomic cavity. This tissue is yellow in colour, and often shows clearly visible biliary canaliculi which may converge and empty into the small gall bladder which is usually present. This liver tissue not only has a biliary function, but also accumulates glycogen, as can be seen on figure 2 of plate II.

Association with the splanchnopleure

The association is carried out *in ovo*. The host embryos are younger than previously, being at the 15 to 20 somite stage with a coelomic cavity as

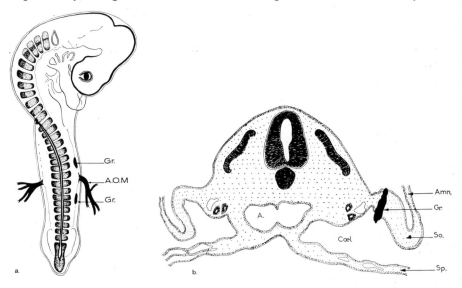

Figure 6   Hepatic endoderm grafted into the somatopleure of a 3-day embryo.
a) The graft is inserted into a slit made either above or below the level of the omphalo-mesenteric artery (*A.O.M.*).

b) Transverse section of the host embryo, showing localization of the graft within the body wall. *A.*, aorta; *Amn.*, amnion; *Coel.*, coelom; *So.*, somatopleure; *Sp.*, splanchnopleure.

yet not highly developed. The graft is introduced into a transverse slit; the position of the slit varies, depending on which part of the digestive tract is intended to receive the graft. The latter comes into contact with the three embryonic layers, developing preferentially in the splanchnic mesoderm. It can develop, for example, in the wall of the small intestine, giving rise to hepatic tissue.

The graft can be made further down the tract, reaching other regions of the intestine—the caecum, or cloacal region. In all cases, fully functional hepatic tissue develops.

Consequently, hepatic endoderm from the anterior intestinal portal is capable of developing not only in specific hepatic mesenchyme, but also in mesenchymes of quite diverse origins.

In the examples described here, the response of the endoderm does not vary, whatever the nature of the host mesenchyme, and ends in the formation of hepatocytes. Thus, at the time of implantation, the hepatic endoderm possesses a pre-existing orientation, i.e. it is already determined.

It should be added that only endoderm from the region of the anterior intestinal portal can form hepatic tissue. Endoderm taken from any other area, even when associated with hepatic mesenchyme, is incapable of being transformed into hepatocytes. Determination of the endoderm is thus shown to be an essential process for final differentiation.

Having established this fact, the next step was to investigate the capacities for differentiation of other endodermal areas present in the ventral floor of the fore-gut.

4) Capacities for differentiation of the pharyngeal endoderm

(LE DOUARIN and BUSSONET, 1966; LE DOUARIN, BUSSONET and CHAUMONT, 1968).
The endoderm is removed from 7 to 28 somites embryos, and associated with somatopleure of $2\frac{1}{2}$ to 3 day embryos.

The morphology of the latero-ventral walls of the embryonic fore-gut becomes considerably modified between these two stages.

In the youngest embryos, the ventral endoderm of the fore-gut shows no marked differentiation, except for a median groove which is to become the future mesobranchial groove and has no prospective significance.

From about the 15 somite stage, the branchial clefts begin to appear, developing in a cephalo-caudal direction. There are four pairs of branchial diverticula in the chick, the first 3 of which are open to the exterior at the base of an endodermal depression; the fourth pair does not perforate, and only exists in the form of pouches.

Towards the 25 to 28 somite stage, a cupola-shaped depression appears ventrally; this represents the first thyroid rudiment.

Subsequently, in the embryo with more than 30 somites, the thyroidal anlage becomes pediculate and tends to lose its connections with the pharyngeal endoderm, while the pulmonary rudiments appear behind the 4th branchial pouches. Two series of experiments were carried out.

In the first series, the posterior a $\frac{2}{3}$ of the pharyngeal endoderm was

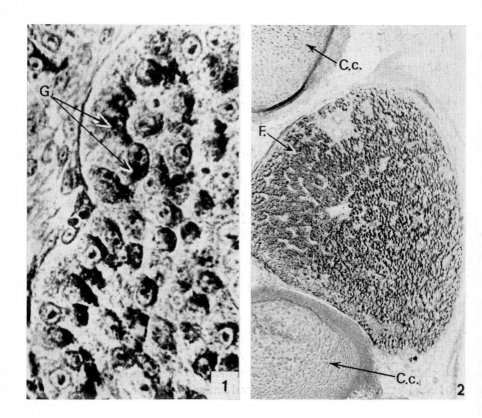

PLATE II

Figure 1 Association *in vitro* of hepatic mesenchyme from a 5-day embryo with hepatic endoderm from a 21-somite embryo. The endoderm proliferates and differentiates of into hepatocyte capable synthesising glycogen (*G.*). P.A.S. stain.

Figure 2 Result of operation depicted in figure 6 of text. The hepatic endoderm grafted into the somatopleure of a 3-days embryo differentiates. A liver lobe (*F.*) rich in glycogen forms in the thickness of the body wall. Section of the host is performed at 17 days incubation. *C.C.*: costal cartilage.

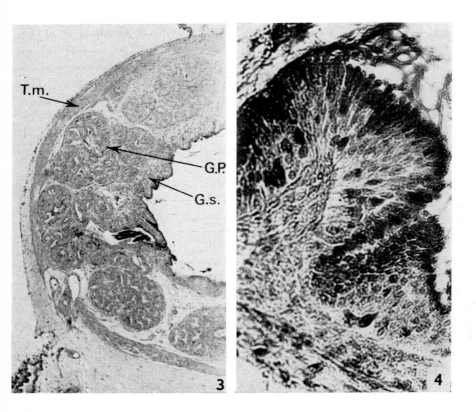

PLATE II

Figure 3 Association of ventral pharyngeal endoderm from an 8-somite embryo with somatopleure of a 3-day embryo. Observation carried out after 14 days graft. A proventriculus differentiates in the host body wall. P.A.S. stain. G.P.: deep glands; *G.s.*: surface glands; *T.m.*: muscular tunic.

Figure 4 Same experiment. The endoderm is from a 15-somite embryo. Differentiation of gizzard epithelium. Abundant mucous secretion.

removed from 7 to 28 somite embryos; this corresponds to the portion situated behind the actual or presumptive branchial region.

After associating the endoderm with somatopleure mesenchyme *in ovo* or in *in vitro* culture followed by intracoelomic grafting, the graft was removed on the 17th day of incubation and treated with PAS after fixation in Gendre's fluid. When the association was carried out *in ovo*, the grafts are found, as before, in the body wall. Histological studies show that in both types of association, development of the following structures can be obtained: *proventriculus, gizzard, small intestine, liver, pancreas*. Table I indicates the differentiations obtained.

Table I   Differentiation of pharyngeal endoderm plus somatopleure mesenchyme

Number of grafts	Differentiations observed					
	P.V.	G.	I.	P.	L.	E. Ind.
Series A: 51	27	11	14	10	28	8
Series B: 10	6	4	2	3	8	3

Series A: grafts *in ovo*. *Series B:* culture *in vitro* followed by intracoelomic grafting. P.V. proventriculus; G. gizzard; I. intestine; P. pancreas; L. liver; E. ind., epithelium remaining locally undifferentiated.

Formations corresponding to the proventriculus were found in 27 out of 50 cases. In some of these, a perfectly formed proventriculus develops in the wall; it possesses the tubular surface glands, the deep alveolus glands, and the characteristic mucosal and muscular layers (plate II, figure 3). Such complete organogenesis is not observed in all cases but there may be predominant development of the surface glands, or possibly of the deep alveolus glands; these structures may equally well differentiate from the endoderm of 7 or 28 somite stage embryos.

Formations corresponding to the gizzard are less frequently observed than those of the proventriculus. The endoderm usually reaches the stage which a normal gizzard would show at 12 to 13 days incubation. The epithelium is tall, stratified, and shows abundant mucous secretions at the surface; in addition, its basal membrane shows indentations which are the first signs of formation of the tubular glands, characteristic of the gizzard at the end of incubation (plate II, figure 4).

The intestinal formations are characteristic and can reach an advanced stage of organogenesis. The connective layer of the mucosa and the muscular layer can be distinguished, as in normal intestine of the same age. The epithelium shows goblet cells whose secretions stain with PAS (plate III, figure 1).

Pancreatic tissue differentiates in some cases; tubules are present, but there are no endocrine islets; it is derived from the ventral pancreatic rudiments which are in the neighbourhood of the hepatic rudiments.

In a second series of experiments, the anterior part of the pharyngeal endoderm is removed from 15 to 28 somite embryos and associated with somatopleure mesenchyme. In this case, the differentiations obtained are those of the thymus, thyroid, oesophageal and pulmonary formations (plate III, figures 2, 3 and 4).

It should be noted that chick embryo somatopleure favours development of endoderm from other species (e.g. quail) as well as that from chick. If quail pharyngeal endoderm is associated with chick somatopleure, it can produce for instance intestinal differentiation, or that of the proventriculus and liver. These various experiments demonstrate that, at an early stage of development, the floor of the fore-gut is heterogeneous and made up of several cell populations which are already determined. The stage of determination is not the same for all rudiments; e.g. determination of the thyroid (which takes place around the 15 somite stage) is later than that of the liver. The exact chronological sequence of these determinations has not yet been established for all endodermal components; however, that of liver is known to take place at the 4 to 6 somite stage in chick embryo.

5) Induction of determination in liver development

By associating endoderm from the anterior intestinal portal with hepatic mesenchyme, it was possible to establish that the endodermal cells destined to form hepatocytes, are determined at the 5 somite stage (LE DOUARIN, 1964).

At earlier stages of development (presomite and first somite stages), the presumptive hepatic area was localized by RAWLES (1936). It coincides with that of the cardiac region, and extends as two lateral areas on either side of the head process and the anterior third of the primitive streak. If the endoderm of these lateral regions is dissociated from the mesoderm of the precardiac area by tripsinization, it is incapable of forming liver tissue when associated with hepatic mesenchyme (figure 7). It thus behaves

4*

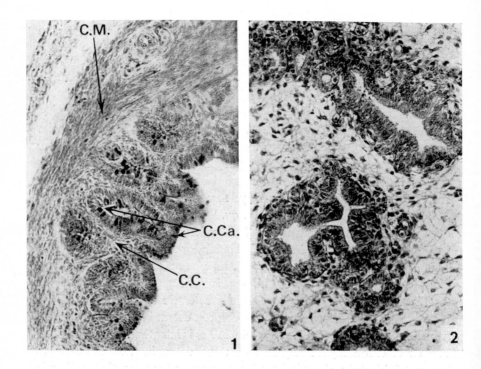

PLATE III

Figure 1 Same experiment as previously (Plate II, figure 3 and 4). Well-organized intestinal formations differentiate in the body wall; *C.M.* and *C.C*: muscular and connective tissue layers of intestinal wall. *C. Ca.*: calciform cells of epithelium.

Figure 2 Same experiment. The grafted endoderm is from an 18-somite embryo. Pulmonary formations arising from differentiation of the grafted endoderm: ramifications of the bronchial epithelium and mesenchymal condensations around the epithelial formations.

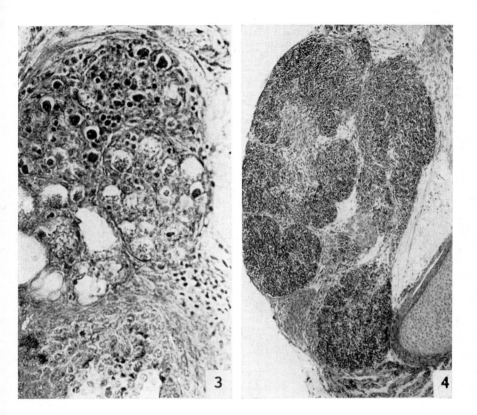

PLATE III

Figure 3 Same experiment. The endoderm is from a 19-somite embryo. Formation of thyroid tissue in the host body wall.

Figure 4 Same experiment. The endoderm is from a 15-somite embryo. Formation of a thymus lobe.

differently from endoderm of the anterior intestinal portal: it is not yet determined.

On the other hand, if this endoderm remains in contact with mesoderm of the cardiac area, and both tissues are then transplanted as a coelomic or chorio-allantoic graft, or if both tissues are associated with hepatic

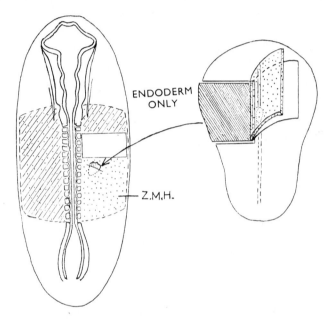

ENDODERM
ONLY

Z.M.H.

Figure 7 *In ovo* association of presumptive hepatic area endoderm, from an embryo at the head process stage, with hepatic mesenchyme of a host embryo. Under these conditions, the endoderm does not differentiate into hepatic cords: it is not determined. *Z. M. H.*: zone of future hepatic mesenchyme formation.

mesenchyme (figure 8), the endoderm differentiates into hepatocytes (plate IV, figure 1). The hepatic endoderm must therefore acquire its determination under the influence of the cardiac area mesoderm. During formation of the anterior intestine, the lateral endodermal areas unite ventrally to form the floor of the foregut (BELLAIRS, 1953, LE DOUARIN, 1964) and the hepatic rudiment becomes localized at an early stage in the anterior intestinal portal. The induction of determination of the hepatic endoderm takes place at the time of its localization in the anterior intestinal portal, at the 4 to 5 somite stage. Although not yet demonstrated for endodermal rudiments

other than liver which are present in the pharyngeal floor, it can be assumed
that their determination, like that of the liver, results from an early induction of mesodermal origin.

Whatever the exact mechanism, the development of these organs takes
place in two stages: an early determination of the epithelial primordium,

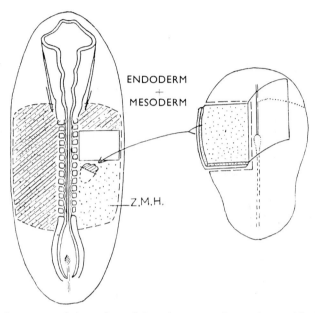

Figure 8 *In ovo* association of cardiohepatic area endomesoderm with the hepatic
mesenchyme of a host embryo.

which conditions the future differentiation of the organ but does not
provide the primordium with any real capacity for autodifferentiation. The
mesoderm is found to be indispensable for definitive endodermal differentiation, even after the induction of determination has taken place.

The second stage in development of the digestive organs is constituted by
the action of the mesoderm on the determined endoderm; this I have
termed *induction of differentiation*, as it is through this action that the organ
finally acquires its permanent form and structure.

The role of the mesoderm in this second stage of development, together
with the respective importance of both inductions—that of determination
and that of differentiation—will now be discussed in the light of recent
results.

II INFLUENCE OF THE NATURE AND DEGREE OF EVOLUTION OF THE MESODERM ON DEVELOPMENT OF THE ALREADY DETERMINED PHARYNGEAL ENDODERM

The experiments previously described, where pharyngeal endoderm from 2 to 3 day old embryos was associated with the still undifferentiated mesenchyme of the somatopleure and splanchnopleure in embryos of the same age, show that in this environment, each determined cellular category can express its potentialities and fulfil its presumptive fate. Thus, the mesenchyme in question does not orientate any of these differentiations, but allows them all to develop. It is *neutral*, since it does not exercise any selectivity, and only provides the framework and nutritive elements necessary for endodermal cell development. On the other hand, the endoderm associated with it exercises a specific morphogenetic action on this mesenchyme. Each endodermal cell population induces the mesenchyme to form the connective-muscular wall or the interstitial tissue appropriate for each organ constituted.

The next question is whether the whole mesoderm of 2 to 3 day embryos, whatever its nature, is capable of collaborating with the endoderm to form digestive organs.

To try and answer this, we carried out the following series of experiments.

1. Influence of mesenchymes of dorsal origin on development of the pharyngeal endoderm

Ventral pharyngeal endoderm is taken from 18 to 25 somite embryos and associated with axial mesoderm (somitic or cephalic) of embryos of the same age, using *in ovo* grafting methods (figure 9). Identical associations have also been made between the endoderm and limb bud mesenchyme, in $3\frac{1}{2}$ day embryos (stage 19 of HAMBURGER and HAMILTON, 1951).

After 12 to 15 days contact, the grafts are examined in the same way as in previous experiments.

The results are identical with these three types of mesenchyme. The pharyngeal endoderm shows little development; it forms a small vesicle bounded by an epithelium of varying thickness, but shows none of the characteristic differentiations obtained in favourable mesodermal environments (plate IV, figure 2).

It thus appears that in the 2 to 3 day embryo, the more dorsal mesenchymes are unfavourable for the development of endodermal derivatives, whichever they may be. They ensure survival of the endoderm, but are incapable of promoting its multiplication or differentiation.

If mesodermal behaviour on contact with endoderm is taken as a criterion, the axial and latero-ventral parts of the mesoderm appear to constitute quite different biochemical environments at an early stage of development. A parallel can be drawn between this, and the fact that differentiation and

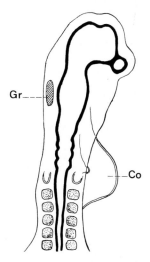

Figure 9 *In ovo* association of ventral pharyngeal endoderm with cephalic mesenchyme of a 20-somite embryo. The endodermal graft (*Gr.*) is introduced into a slit made in the mesenchyme. *Co.*, heart rudiment.

determination of the axial mesodermal regions in vertebrates takes place earlier than that of the lateral zones. At the stage where somitic and cephalic mesoderms are associated with endoderm, they are already orientated towards their own differentiation (STRUDEL, 1963); this could explain why they are no longer competent to respond to endodermal induction, and why they inhibit endodermal development.

2. Influence of splanchnic mesenchymes in process of differentiation on development of the pharyngeal endoderm

Having established these results, the next step was to find out whether, during the development of various endomesodermal organs, the splanchnic mesenchyme specific for each rudiment and already specialized, is still

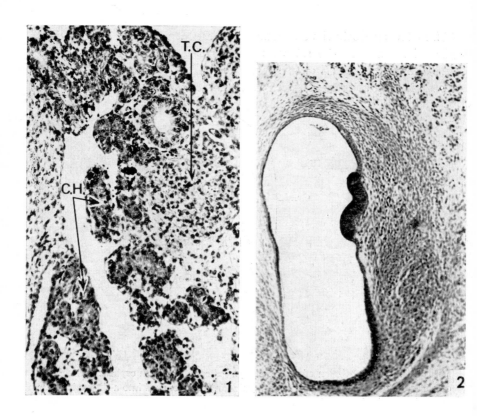

PLATE IV

Figure 1 Result of experiment shown in figure 8 of text. The grafted endoderm has been induced by the cardiac area mesoderm and gives rise to hepatic cords (*C.H.*) which colonize the host hepatic mesenchyme. The cardiac area mesoderm produces masses of cardiac tissue (*T.C.*).

Figure 2 Association of ventral pharyngeal endoderm from a 22-somite embryo with limb bud mesenchyme from a $3\frac{1}{2}$ day embryo. After 12 days graft, a vesicle forms, thick-walled in places, and not showing characteristic differentiation.

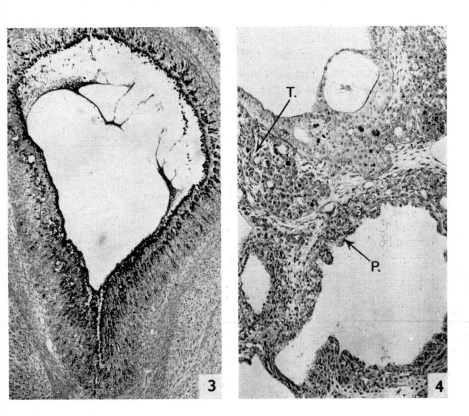

PLATE IV

Figure 3 Association of complete pharyngeal endoderm from a 24-somite embryo with gizzard mesenchyme from a 5-day embryo, 14 days graft. The endoderm differentiates into gizzard epithelium. The other potentialities present in the endoderm are not expressed.

Figure 4 Association of complete pharyngeal endoderm from a 23-somite embryo with pulmonary mesenchyme from a 5-day embryo. Differentiation of pulmonary (*P*) and thyroid (*T*) tissue.

capable of promoting all the differentiations potentially present in the pharyngeal endoderm.

For this investigation, the whole pharyngeal endoderm from 16 to 25 somite embryos is associated with mesenchyme of the gizzard and lung of 5 day embryos. The gizzard and lung mesenchymes are freed from homologous endoderm by trypsin treatment, and associated *in vitro* with ventral pharyngeal endoderm. After 24 hours, the two tissues unite and the explant is allowed to develop as an intracoelomic graft for 14 days. The tissues then develop under good physiological conditions, and the differentiations obtained are clear and easily identified.

It is found that pharyngeal endoderm associated with gizzard mesenchyme differentiates into gizzard epithelium (plate IV, figure 3). Thus the many potential differentiations contained in the pharyngeal endoderm (oesophagus, thymus, thyroid, lung, stomach, intestine, liver, pancreas) cannot be expressed in contact with gizzard mesenchyme. The latter exercises a selective action and thus behaves differently from the undifferentiated somatopleure and splanchnopleure mesenchyme of 2 to 3 day embryos.

There are two possible interpretations of this result:

a) The endodermal potentialities corresponding to the gizzard could be the only one expressed, due to the fact that all the others are inhibited. It might be thought that, although the endodermal cells are already determined, e.g. to constitute the proventriculus, lung, or thyroid, they only divide to a limited extent and finally degenerate if the environment is unfavourable for such development.

b) A contrary explanation might be true, i.e. that the gizzard mesenchyme exercises a transforming influence; in this case, endodermal determination would be a labile phenomenon, and the induction of differentiation would be capable of dominating and annulling the effects of prior induction of determination.

Experiments at present in progress may enable a choice to be made between these two hypotheses.

The association of pulmonary mesenchyme with the pluripotential pharyngeal endoderm gives different results: grafts removed from the host embryo at the 17th day of incubation always show a large proportion of pulmonary tissue, but a few show differentiation of thyroid and hepatic tissue. Thus the pulmonary mesenchyme of 5 day embryos is less rigorously selective with respect to pharyngeal endoderm potentialities than is the gizzard mesenchyme.

These experiments show that during organogenesis, the effector capacities of the mesenchyme are limited and its action on the endoderm becomes more specific. The experiments of SIGOT (1962) on chick embryo stomach, and those of DAMERON (1967) on lung, provide much evidence to suggest that the inductive action of the mesenchyme on the epithelium of these organs at advanced stages of organogenesis is specific, sometimes rigorously so (e.g. for the proventriculus; SIGOT, 1962).

It can be concluded from these findings that, at an early stage of development, the ventral floor of the fore-gut contains endodermal rudiments destined to take part in forming all the pre-umbilical endomesodermal organs. These rudiments are determined at various early stages of development. This determination probably results from an induction of mesodermal origin which at present has only been demonstrated for the liver.

Experiments of heterologous association between pharyngeal endoderm and lateral plate mesenchyme from $2\frac{1}{2}$ to 3 day embryos, show that the determined endoderm possesses morphogenetic properties with respect to the mesoderm. In contact with a suitable mesenchyme, the endoderm exercises a *specific induction* on the latter, which orientates it towards a particular type of differentiation. ALESCIO, CASSINI, and LADU (1963) had already suspected the existence of this inductive power of the epithelium, with repect to mesenchyme, in lung organogenesis. In the absence of mesenchyme, the isolated determined endoderm is incapable of autodifferentiation, even under the favourable physiological conditions represented by intra-coelomic grafting.

During organogenesis, the particular mesenchyme of each rudiment exercises a reciprocal inductive effect on the determined endoderm; this induction is more or less specific, depending on the organ in question, and can be termed induction of differentiation, since its end result is differentiation of endodermal tissue into its permanent form and structure. It should also be noted that at this stage, mesodermal evolution is equally dependent on the presence of endoderm. Many experiments have been conducted where the mesenchymal portion of various endomesodermal organs in process of differentiation has been isolated; it appears that if the mesenchyme is deprived of the epithelial component, it cannot continue to differentiate alone, and degenerates. The various stages of this evolution are summarised in table II. Certain comments on our results are appropriate here:

Table II

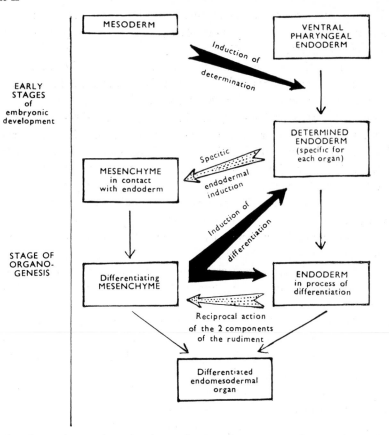

It has been shown that the determined endoderm exercises an inductive effect on the mesoderm, when pharyngeal endoderm is associated with heterologous mesenchyme. However, this requires some qualification. In the case of liver, the experiments previously described on isolation of the hepatic mesenchyme (LE DOUARIN, 1964 a and b) show that even without contact with the determined hepatic endoderm, the splanchnic mesenchyme can form characteristic hepatic mesenchyme; the latter exhibits a true hepatic structure as well as an inductive action towards the undifferentiated endodermal hepatic rudiments. Thus, at least in this instance, the differentiation of mesoderm into hepatic mesenchyme can be autonomous, taking place without endodermal induction. It is still a fact that the hepatic endoderm can induce the somatopleure mesenchyme to form the mesodermal framework of the liver (LE DOUARIN, 1964b; LE DOUARIN and CHAUMONT, 1966). Consequently, although they may not be essential for normal development of the organ, these inductive porperties of the determined endoderm still exist.

Another comment refers to the fact that, from an early stage, the axial mesoderm is unfavourable for the development of these endodermal organs. A possible explanation is that this mesenchyme, which is dense in texture, could mechanically inhibit the proliferation of various glandular epithelia derived from the endoderm. This does not seem to be a valid interpretation for the following reasons: results recently obtained (LE DOUARIN, FERRAND and LE DOUARIN, 1967a and b), on hypophyseal development in chick embryo, show that somitic mesenchyme (from 4 day embryos) can be completely favourable for the development of adenohypophyseal glandular elements. It is therefore more likely that the axial mesenchyme is biochemically rather than mechanically unsuitable as an environment for endodermal development.

Having established these results, our subsequent work dealt primarily with the second stage, i.e. the induction of differentiation in liver development.

In the experiments carried out hitherto, the effects of various mesenchymes on the determined hepatic endoderm have been of two types: favourable and unfavourable. In the first type, the favourable mesenchymes (e.g. somatopleure or lung) permit full morphological and functional differentiation of hepatic tissue and cells; in the second, the unfavourable mesenchymes (cephalic, or somitic) inhibit both proliferation and functional differentiation of the endodermal cells.

Tissue differentiation thus appears to be an all-embracing process, involving closely linked morphological and physiological phenomena.

However, in the experiments which will now be described, we were able to stimulate cell multiplication of determined hepatic endoderm without inducing concomitant biochemical differentiation of the hepatocytes.

This result was achieved by associating hepatic endoderm with mesenchyme of the metanephric rudiment.

III INFLUENCE OF METANEPHRIC MESENCHYME ON DIFFEREN-
TIATION OF THE DETERMINED HEPATIC ENDODERM, AND ON THE
FUNCTIONAL ACTIVITY OF HEPATOCYTES ALREADY DIFFEREN-
TIATED (LE DOUARIN and HOUSSAINT, 1967; LE DOUARIN, 1967)

1. Association of the determined hepatic endoderm with metanephric mesenchyme

The metanephric mesenchyme is taken from 5 to 6 day embryos; the ureteral rudiment is extracted from the renal blastema after trypsin treatment. The hepatic endoderm, prepared as previously, is taken from 21 to 28 somite embryos. The two tissues are associated *in vitro*; after 24 hours culture, they unite to form a single explant which is then cultured as an intracoelomic graft for 10 days.

Histological examination shows that the endoderm has proliferated in contact with the renal mesenchyme, to form cellular cords separated by blood sinusoids. The tissue has the same histological structure as that of embryo liver of the same age (plate V, figure 1). Cytologically, however, the cells formed under these conditions do not possess the large nucleolus characteristic of hepatic cells of the same age. Their nucleolus is distinctly smaller and sometimes fragmented. The PAS reaction shows that the cells are devoid of glycogen; 43 grafts were tested, and all showed a negative PAS reaction.

It thus appears that while metanephric mesenchyme stimulates proliferation of hepatic endodermal cells, it does not provide for complete hepatocyte differentiation. The hepatic cells which differentiate in contact with the renal mesenchyme appear to lack certain enzymic equipment, so that they are unable to synthesise glycogen.

2. Influence of hepatic mesenchyme on hepaiocytes differentiated in contact with the renal mesenchyme

The question then arises, as to whether the hepatocytes formed in the metanephric mesenchyme are irreversibly fixed at the stage of incomplete differentiation reached, or if they can continue to develop given a suitable mesodermal environment.

The problem was investigated as follows: metanephric mesenchyme and determined hepatic endoderm were associated in culture, as previously (1 day *in vitro* and 10 days as an intra-coelomic graft, i.e. 11 days in all). The graft was then removed, and associated *in vitro* with hepatic mesenchyme from 5 to 6 day embryos. The two associated tissues were cultured for 3 days, either *in vitro* or *in vivo* as an intracoelomic graft.

It was found that the endodermal cell cords present in the renal mesenchyme multiplied in contact with the hepatic mesenchyme and invaded it (plate V, figure 2). Some liver tissue formed in the hepatic mesenchyme, and PAS treatment, after fixation with Gendre's fluid at 4°C, showed that the hepatocytes of this tissue are rich in glycogen. In addition, these cells showed highly developed nucleoli characteristic of hepatic cells in embryos of the same age (plate V, figure 3).

This experiment shows that the metanephric mesenchyme stimulates cell proliferation of the determined hepatic endoderm. These cells become organized in a characteristic hepatic pattern, the plan of which is established at the time of determination. However, the renal mesenchyme is incapable permitting functional differentiation of the hepatocytes formed: the latter do not synthesise glycogen.

By this heterologous association, a morphological differentiation is brought about which is not accompanied by the corresponding biochemical differentiation. This indicates that, in liver, the development of histological structure and the acquisition of certain functional capacities arise from different processes. Furthermore, the stage of differentiation attained by the hepatocytes in the renal mesenchyme is not permanently fixed. Placed in contact with hepatic mesenchyme, the pseudo-hepatocytes proliferate and invade the hepatic mesenchyme, whereupon they become capable of synthesising glycogen.

I next wanted to find out whether normal hepatic cells which had differentiated in their own mesenchyme would still be capable of invading the renal mesenchyme if placed in contact with it, and whether, in this environment, they would lose the capacity to synthesise glycogen.

3. Influence of renal mesenchyme on hepatocytes differentiated in contact with hepatic mesenchyme

In this experiment, liver tissue is removed from 4 to 21 day embryos, or from chicks hatched 1 to 2 days previously, and associated in culture with metanephric mesenchyme from 5 to 6 day embryos. When the two tissues have united, the explant is cultured as an intracoelomic graft for 5 days, then fixed in Gendre's fluid. Sections treated with PAS show that the grafts contain two types of hepatic cells; some are full of glycogen, while others on the contrary show a negative reaction to PAS (plate V, figure 4). This

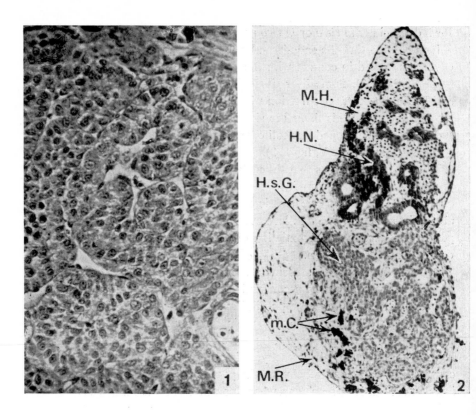

PLATE V

Figure 1 Association of hepatic endoderm from a 25-somite embryo with meta-nephric mesenchyme from a $5\frac{1}{2}$ day embryo. The endoderm has proliferated and given rise to cords of hepatocytes which colonise the mesenchyme. These hepatocytes are devoid of glycogen. P.A.S. stain.

Figure 2 Association of glycogen-free hepatic tissue (obtained previously by associating hepatic endoderm with renal mesenchyme), with hepatic mesenchyme (*M.H.*). The endodermal cells proliferate, invade the hepatic mesenchyme, and synthesise glycogen. The hepatocytes in the renal mesenchyme are devoid of glycogen. *H.N.*, normal hepatocytes containing glycogen, stainable with P.A.S.; *H.s.G.*, glycogen-free hepatocytes in renal mesenchyme; *M.R.*, renal mesenchyme; *m.C.*, carbon marks put on explant at time of grafting.

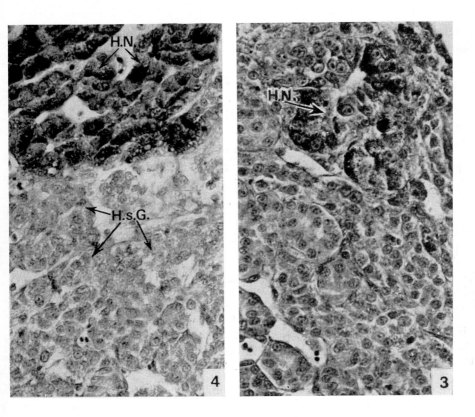

PLATE V

Figure 3 Same experiment showing glycogen-containing hepatocytes, whose nucleus has a large nucleolus (*H.N.*), and glycogen-free hepatocytes present in the renal mesenchyme.

Figure 4 Association of 17-day embryo liver with 6-day embryo renal mesenchyme. The mesenchyme is colonized by cords of hepatocytes (below). The liver contains glycogen stainable with P.A.S.; the hepatocytes which have invaded the renal mesenchyme are devoid of glycogen (*H.s.G.*).

5*

result can be interpreted as follows: hepatic cells which have proliferated in contact with the renal mesenchyme and invaded it, lose their glycogen, while heptocytes which remain in the hepatic mesenchyme retain their capacity to accumulate glycogen.

The renal mesenchyme is thus shown to stimulate the proliferation of hepatocytes, since the latter invade it; it also inhibits glycogen synthesis by these cells. It seems that the functional activity of hepatic parenchyma, at least as regards glycogenesis, is dependent on the surrounding mesenchymal environment. Thus the role of the mesoderm is not confined to bringing about determination and later differentiation of the hepatic endoderm, but extends to the differentiated organ, where it maintains functional activity of the hepatocytes.

CONCLUSIONS

It can be concluded that the development of pre-umbilical endomesodermal derivatives takes place in two main stages: an early determination, followed by a later differentiation of the endoderm. Both processes come about through the inductive influence of the mesoderm. The determined endoderm corresponding to each pre-umbilical organ is localised at an early stage of development in the floor of the fore-gut which seems to be an endodermal region particularly rich in developmental potentialities.

Our experiments also show the reciprocal nature of the inductive influences exercised between the endoderm and mesoderm during organogenesis. The determined endoderm is capable of inducing a heterologous mesenchyme, such as that of the somatopleure, to produce the connective-muscular tunics or connective framework appropriate for each pre-umbilical endomesodermal organ. In addition, in each differentiating rudiment, the endoderm and mesoderm exercise morphogenetic activities on each other, which lead to the permanent formation of the organ.

The potentialities for differentiation of the determined endoderm can be expressed in different mesodermal environments. In the $2\frac{1}{2}$ to 3 day embryo, two quite different mesodermal environments can be distinguished in this respect: the axial mesoderms (cephalic, somitic), which are unfavourable for endodermal evolution, and the mesoderm of the lateral plates, which allows expression of all endodermal potentialities. In the older embryo, certain already specialised splanchnic mesenchymes (such as that of the gizzard or lung in 5 day embryos) limit the capacities for differentiation of the pluripotential pharyngeal endoderm.

Lastly, we were able to obtain the morphological differentiation of hepatic tissue, unaccompanied by its functional differentiation. When the determined hepatic endoderm is associated with metanephric mesenchyme, it proliferates and forms cords of hepatocytes which remain devoid of glycogen detectable by the PAS reaction. In contact with hepatic mesenchyme, these incompletely functional hepatocytes achieve total differentiation and acquire the capacity to synthesise glycogen. Conversely, normal hepatic cells taken from liver, which are fully differentiated, will proliferate in contact with metanephric mesenchyme; they colonise this mesenchyme, and lose their glycogen.

All these experiments show the importance of tissue relations between endoderm and mesoderm. The latter functions not only in the determination and subsequent differentiation of endodermal cells, but also, at least in liver, maintains the functional activity of differentiated cells.

References

ALESCIO, T., CASSINI, A., and LADU, M. (1963). Ricerche sulla riassociazione *in vitro* dell' epitelio e del mesenchima di polmone embrionale di topo dopo dissociazione triptica ed riassociazione con raggi gamma. *Arch. Ital. Anat. Embriol.*, **68**, 1–44.

BELLAIRS, R. (1953). Studies on the development of the foregut in the chick blastoderm -2- The morphogenetic movements. *J. Embryol. Exp. Morphol.*, **1**, 369–385.

DAMERON, F. (1961). Influence de divers mésenchymes sur la différenciation de l'épithélium pulmonaire de l'embryon de poulet en culture *in vitro. J. Embryol. Exp. Morphol.*, **9**, 628–633.

DAMERON, F. (1968). Nature et specificité des interactions épithélio-mésenchymateuses dans l'organogenèse du poumon. *J. Embryol. Exp. Morphol.*, **20**, 151–667.

GOLOSOW, N., and GROBSTEIN, C. (1962). Epithelio-mesenchymal interaction in pancreatic morphogenesis. *Develop. Biol.*, **4**, 242–255.

HAMBURGER, V., and HAMILTON, H. L. (1951). A series of normal stages in the development of the chick embryo. *J. Embryol. Exp. Morphol.*, **88**, 49–92.

LE DOUARIN, N. (1964 *a*). Induction de l'endoderme préhépatique par le mésoderme de l'aire cardiaque chez l'embryon de poulet. *J. Embryol. Exp. Morphol.*, **12**, 651–664.

LE DOUARIN, N. (1964 *b*). Etude expérimentale du développement du tube digestif et du foie chez l'embryon de poulet. *Bull. Biol. Fr. Belg.*, **98**, 543–676.

LE DOUARIN, N., and BUSSONNET, C. (1966). Détermination précoce et rôle inducteur de l'endoderme pharyngien chez l'embryon de poulet. *C. R. Acad. Sc.*, **263**, 1241 –1243.

LE DOUARIN, N., BUSSONNET, C., and CHAUMONT, F. (1967). Etude des capacités de différenciation et du rôle morphogène de l'endoderme pharyngien chez l'embryon d'oiseau. *Ann. Embryol. Morph.*, in press.

LE DOUARIN, N., FERRAND, R., and LE DOUARIN, G. (1967 a). La différenciation de l'ébauche épithéliale de l'hypophyse séparée du plancher encéphalique et placée dans des mésenchymes hétérologues. C. R. Acad. Sc., **264**, 3027–3029.

LE DOUARIN, N., FERRAND, R., and LE DOUARIN, G. (1967 b). Evolution de l'ébauche de l'adénohypophyse isolée du plancher encéphalique aux jeunes stades du développement. C. R. Soc. Biol., in press.

LE DOUARIN, N., and HOUSSAINT, E. (1967). Rôle du mésoderme dans l'induction de la synthèse du glycogène lors de la différenciation de l'endoderme hépatique. C. R. Acad. Sc., **264**, 1872–1874.

SIGOT, M. (1962). Sur le rôle du mésenchyme dans la différenciation des glandes du proventricule chez le poulet. C. R. Acad. Sc., **254**, 2439–2441.

STRUDEL, G. (1963). Autodifférenciation et induction de cartilage à partir de mésenchyme somitique de poulet cultive in vitro. J. Embryol. Exp. Morphol., **11**, 399–412.

WOLFF, Et., and HAFFEN, K. (1952). Sur une méthode de culture d'organes embryonnaires in vitro. Texas Rep. Biol. Med., **10**, 463–472.

CHAPTER IV

MORPHOGENESIS OF THE SKIN
AND THE CUTANEOUS APPENDAGES IN BIRDS

Philippe Sengel

Laboratoire de Zoologie, Faculté des Sciences, Grenoble

INTRODUCTION

THE SKIN, which is one of the characteristic organs in vertebrates, fulfils the important function of protecting the organism against influences of the external environment. In particular, it avoids desiccation or invasion of the deep-lying tissues by water. It is the largest of all the organs.

Like many other organs, it is derived embryologically from the union and superimposition of two categories of cells. Those from the ectodermal layer form the superficial epidermis, while the others come from various parts of the mesoderm and constitute the deep dermis. In adults, both dermis and epidermis consist of several cell layers.

The skin is capable of producing extremely varied integumentary derivatives which play a very important part in the animal's relation to its environment. Some of these structures are essentially dermal in origin, others principally epidermal, but the majority arise from an intimate collaboration between the dermis and the epidermis. Phylogenetically, the archaic vertebrates were protected against injury and dehydration by osseous dermal derivatives; in the ostracoderms, the heavy dermal armour doubtless constituted the principal isolating covering. It was replaced in certain placoderms by small denticulate cosmoid plates, from which all scales of present day fishes, the osteoderms and *gastralia* of amphibia and reptiles, and the teeth of all vertebrates originate. They have also contributed to other skeletal formations such as the dermal bones of the cranium and the scapular girdle.

The dermal scales of present day fishes and the teeth of all vertebrates have a resistant layer of enamel, added by the epidermis.

The dermal derivatives gradually lose their importance as evolution progresses. The small intradermal scales no longer ensure impermeability and the epidermis takes over this function. In fish, it becomes coated with a thin cuticle; in the aquatic vertebrates, numerous epidermal glands differentiate, secreting large amounts of impermeable mucus. With the advent of terrestrial life, the epidermal cells acquire the capacity to produce a highly specialized protein, remarkably resistant to most external agents— namely keratin.

Keratin is present in fish, in the form of small intracytoplasmic granules with no apparent function; in amphibia, it becomes organized as a thin and inconspicuous layer, co-existent with mucus; lastly, in the amniotes, it forms a thick, horny layer which is both supple and resistant. Here it gives rise to various structures, such as horny scales or plates, feathers, hair, spines, horns, claws, hooves, or rhamphotheca. As well as these numerous keratinized derivatives, the epidermis produces glands which secrete a number of substances essential for social life and reproduction in reptiles, birds, and mammals in particular.

Apart from the osteoderm of certain amphibia and reptiles, the bony carapace of turtles and armadillos, and the horns or other head appendages of ruminants, the dermis of tetrapods no longer produces any hard integumental derivatives. Its function is purely nutritive, supplying the epidermis—which is non-vascularized—with the elements necessary for synthesising specific proteins and glandular secretions.

Thus, in the amniotes, the principal visible cutaneous differentiations— the cutaneous appendages—are formed by the epidermis. But what role does the dermis play in the development of these structures? From the point of view of experimental embryology, this question comes into a general category of investigations—that of tissue interactions during ontogenesis. Many such interactions have been described and demonstrated for numerous organs (DE HAAN and URSPRUNG, 1965). The skin lends itself particularly well to experimental investigations of this type, and has been much used by embryologists over the last 12 years. The largest number of results, and the most significant, have been obtained in avian embryos. We now know that, although the epidermis is finally the sole bearer of specific cutaneous differentiations, it can achieve little or nothing without the determining influence of the dermis;

the role of the latter in ontogenesis is in fact far more than purely nutritive.

This account of contemporary knowledge on skin differentiation will be confined to birds. Particular stress will be laid on formation of feathers, the principal epidermal derivative of this class. No mention will be made of skin pigmentation or cutaneous glands, the latter being rare and showing little variation in birds.

I EARLY HISTOGENESIS: FORMATION OF THE SKIN

The ectoderm undergoes differentiation into epidermis well before the sub-ectodermal space is invaded by dermal cells (figure 1). At 20 hours incubation, the ectodermal cells in the cephalic regions adjacent to the neural tube show a tendency to divide into two layers. They become bobbin-shaped, widening towards the exterior and the interior (figure 3). In most of them, the nucleus is deep-lying, against the internal plasma membrane; in others, it is nearer the surface. The first doubtless give rise to the basal layer of the future epidermis; the second, apparently arising from the first, possibly represent the first cells of the periderm. In the lateral and posterior regions, the ectoderm at this stage is still made up of a single layer of cells (figure 2).

The mechanisms of segregation of the basal layer, which is the future generative layer of the epidermis, and the periderm are entirely unknown. As the neural tube closes, the stratification of the ectoderm extends progressively to the presumptive lateral and ventral regions.

At this early stage and during the next 24 hours, the ectoderm is not in direct contact with the mesodermal layer, which preserves its epithelial structure until half way through the 3rd day of incubation. The space separating the two layers is invaded progressively by a fibrous lattice arising from the dermatome and the lateral plates (figure 4 and 5). Mesenchymal cells then begin to migrate from the dermatome to colonize the sub-ectodermal space (figure 6 and 7) which becomes populated progressively by a loose mesenchyme. Similarly, in the lateral zones, somatopleural mesodermal cells approach the ectoderm and make contact with some of its cells. In this way, the dermis is formed. The basal membrane (figure 8 to 10), which underlines the inner plasma membrane of the basal ectodermal cells (KALLMAN, EVANS and WESSELLS, 1967; RUGGERI, 1967), is already formed at a very early stage (at 2 days incubation, and possibly still earlier

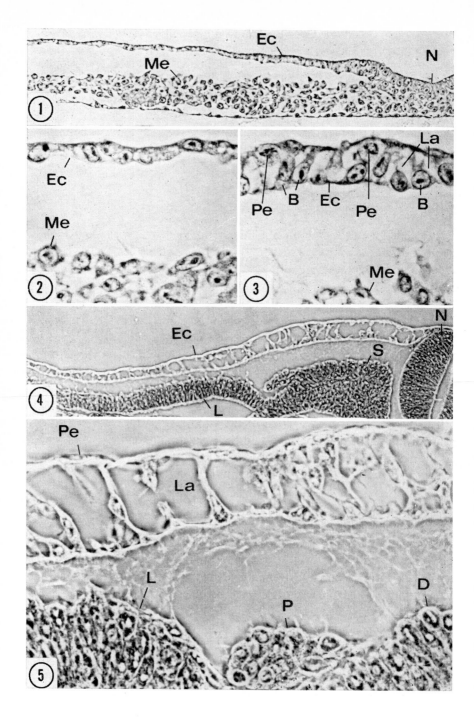

than that), before any close contact is established between ectoderm and mesoderm (SENGEL and RUSAOUËN, 1969). We know nothing of the mechanisms of its formation.

Ectodermal structure remains practically unchanged until the end of 5 days incubation; the peridermal cells are somewhat closer together; intercellular spaces predominate in the basal layer, whose cells are stellate and connected only by fine cytoplasmic filaments.

Up to this time, the only true epithelium separating the internal tissues from the amniotic fluid is constituted by the periderm (McLOUGHLIN, 1961a). The skin as such only begins to differentiate between the 5th and 6th days; the process is not uniform over the whole body surface, but

---

Figure 1 Transverse section through the trunk of a chick embryo at 24 hours incubation (Stage 6 of HAMBURGER and HAMILTON). The ectoderm (*Ec*) is not in contact with the mesoderm (*Me*). Note the difference in thickness between the paramedian ectoderm adjacent to the neutral plate (*N*) and the distant lateral ectoderm, *left*. Phase contrast microscopy ($\times$ 360).

Figure 2 Same embryo as figure 1. Appearance of lateral ectoderm (*Ec*), constituted by a single layer of cells, mean thickness 6 μ. *Me*, mesoderm. Phase contrast microscopy ($\times$ 1,250).

Figure 3 Appearance of cephalic paramedian ectoderm (*Ec*) adjacent to the neural tube of a 24-hour embryo. It is made up of two layers of nuclei, some close to the internal membrane, others, still few (*Pe*), nearer to the superficial membrane. Note the intercellular lacunae (*La*) and the bobbin-shaped cells (*B*); the latter give the ectoderm a greater average thickness (15 μ) than in the lateral regions. *Me*, mesoderm. Phase contrast microscopy ($\times$ 1,250).

Figure 4 Transverse section through a 48-hour chick embryo (stage 12 of HAMBURGER and HAMILTON). The ectoderm (*Ec*) is very thick above the somites (*S*), less so above the lateral plates (*L*), and remains very thin over the neural tube (*N*). It is not in direct contact either with the dermatome or with the somatopleural mesoderm. Phase contrast microscopy ($\times$ 360).

Figure 5 Same embryo as figure 4. The space between the ectoderm and the mesoderm is occupied by a network of criss-crossed fibres. The latter seem to come from the dermatome (*D*) and from the somatopleural layer of the lateral plates (*L*), but not from the pronephric mesomere (*P*). Note the mesenchymal appearance of the ectoderm whose nuclei seem to oscillate between the two cytoplasmic layers, external and deep, separated from each other by large lacunae (*La*). A few nuclei, flattened parallel to the surface, occupy a superficial position and doubtless belong to the peridermal cells (*Pe*) which are still rare. The mean thickness of the paramedian ectoderm at this stage is 26 μ. Phase contrast microscopy ($\times$ 1,375).

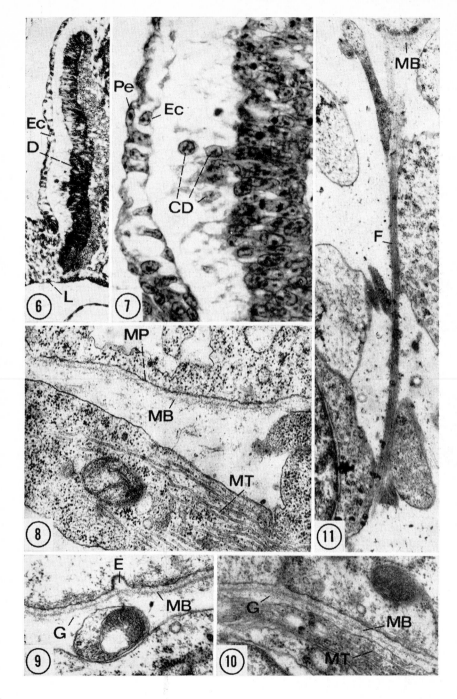

takes place only in certain specialized regions corresponding to the future pterylae—the *feather-forming areas* (WESSELLS, 1965). Outside these zones, skin is formed some days later, at first in the axial regions and thereafter in the limbs.

The feather-forming areas are easily discernible in the whole embryo—either living or fixed—between 5 and 7 days incubation, by an increased tegumentary opacity. The term "crest" as used by HOLMES (1935) to designate these first indications of feather differentiation, does not seem altogether appropriate. They are better described as *areas*, sometimes slightly raised in relation to the neighbouring integument.

Figure 6 Transverse section through a 3-day chick embryo (stage 20 of HAMBURGER and HAMILTON). The space between the dermatome (*D*) and the ectoderm (*Ec*) is beginning to be colonized by a few cells coming from the dermatome. In the lateral regions, the somatopleural mesoderm (*L*) has come into contact with the ectoderm. Hematoxylin-eosin stain (× 280).

Figure 7 Detail of preceding figure showing the first dermal cells (*CD*) migrating out of the dermatome towards the ectoderm (*Ec*). The latter still contains many lacunae. The peridermal cells (*Pe*) form its external epithelial wall (× 1063).

Figure 8 Transverse section of the somatopleure of a 48-hour chick embryo (stage 12 of HAMBURGER and HAMILTON), showing that the basal lamina (*MB*) is already formed at this early stage. It appears as a granular border, still fairly delicate, following the line of the ectodermal plasma membrane (*MP*) at an average distance of 600 Å. In close proximity to the ectoderm, the somatopleural mesodermal cells frequently contain microtubules (*MT*). Uranyl acetate, lead citrate (× 42,000).

Figure 9 Transverse section of dorsal skin from an 8-day chick embryo (stage 33 of HAMBURGER and HAMILTON), showing the basal lamina *MB*) of the epidermis. Its structure has hardly changed since 2 days incubation (cf. figure 8), except for appearing slightly more dense. It is lightly underlined in places by a series of granules (*G*) aligned in parallel with it. At this stage, indentations (*E*) in the deep plasma membrane of the epidermis are frequent; the basal lamina never penetrates into them. Same stain (× 42,000).

Figure 10 Another view of the basal lamina (*MB*) at 8 days incubation, at the junction between two epidermal cells. Note the stippling of granules (*G*) following the line of the basal lamina. Note also the microtubules (*MT*) in the cytoplasm of a dermal cell. Same stain (× 42,000).

Figure 11 Anchor filament (*F*) within the dermis of an 8-day embryo. Constituted by a bundle of parallel fibres, it is attached to the basal lamina (here cut obliquely, *MB*) and terminates at a deep level in a bifurcate extremity. Several dermal cytoplasmic expansions touch the filament. The visible portion of the filament measures about 8 μ. Same stain (× 24,750).

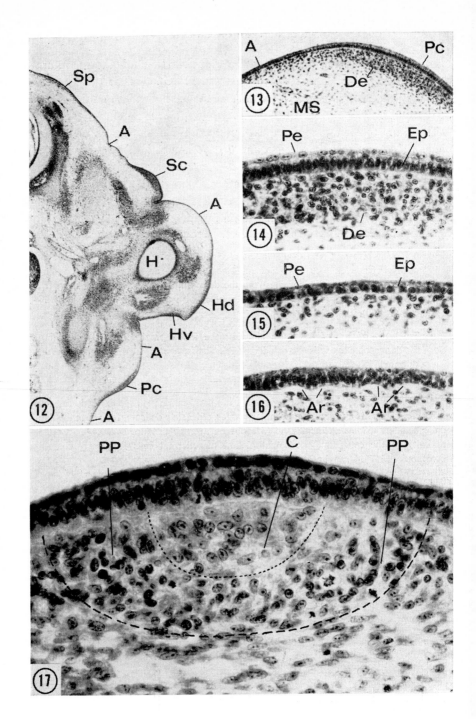

Such areas are well defined after 6 days at the sites of the future pectoral and caudal pterylae. At the beginning of the 7th day, the scapular pteryla is clearly defined by an epaulette-shaped thickening surmounting the base of the humerus. During the 7th day, the ventral areas appear as two slightly raised longitudinal bulges, extending from the umbilicus to the level of the pectoral pterylae. On the other hand, the femoral areas are not especially

Figure 12 Transverse section through a chick embryo at $6^1/_4$ days incubation (stage 29 of HAMBURGER and HAMILTON), showing the localization of the various feather-forming areas visible on this section; the pterylae indicated are: spinal (*Sp*), scapular (*Sc*), dorsal humeral wing (*Hd*), ventral humeral wing (*Hv*), and pectoral (*Pc*). In these areas, the dermis has become individualized through condensation of the sub-epidermal mesenchyme. Between these future pterylae, the future apteria (*A*) are characterized by the absence of dermis: the epidermis—still thin—rests on the loose sub-epidermal mesenchyme. *H*, humerus. Haematoxylin-eosin stain ($\times$ 45).

Figure 13 Detail of figure 12, showing the feather-forming area corresponding to the future pectoral pteryla (*Pc*) and the adjacent apteric zone (future apterium (*A*) situated between the wing and the pectoral pteryla). In the feather-forming area, the dermis (*De*) is distinct from the sub-cutaneous mesenchyme (*MS*); in the apteric zone, the dermis is not yet formed ($\times$ 190).

Figure 14 Detail of pectoral feather-forming area of figure 13. Note the thickened epidermis (*Ep*) with a columnar basal layer and cuboid periderm (*Pe*), and the dense dermis (*De*). Compare figure 15 ($\times$ 560).

Figure 15 Detail of future apterium of figure 13. Note the relatively thin epidermis, whose basal layer (*Ep*) is cuboid, and the periderm (*Pe*) still very thin. The epidermal cells are still separated from each other by numerous lacunae. The dermis is non-existent. Compare figure 14 ($\times$ 560).

Figure 16 Detail of figure 12, showing the feather-forming area corresponding to the future thoracic spinal pteryla. It is characterized by an epidermal basal layer describing arches (*Ar*) whose supporting columns form points of attachment of the epidermis within the dermis. The latter is of relatively low density and not very thick ($\times$ 560).

Figure 17 Transverse section through a feather rudiment of the femoral pteryla, in a chick embryo of $6^1/_4$ days incubation (stage 30 of HAMBURGER and HAMILTON). The epidermal placode of the rudiment possesses basal cells that are taller than those of the surrounding non-feather-forming epidermis. The dermal condensation of the rudiment is made up of two types of cells: at the centre (*C*), a small number of cells with a large light nucleus; at the periphery, and at a deep level (*PP*), a large number of cells with a small dark nucleus, showing numerous mitoses. The dotted line defines the border between these two populations. The line of dashes marks off the dermal feather rudiment from the rest of the dermis. Haematoxylin-eosin stain ($\times$ 880).

marked, and the dorsal skin, similarly, remains relatively translucent until its first feather rudiments appear. The latter constitute a mediodorsal row in the lumbar region, and a pair of paramedian rows in the thoracic region. A fine whitish cord is generally observed along the median region of 6-day embryos; its significance remains obscure. It coincides with the first row of feather rudiments in the lumbar region, but crosses the apteric zone situated between the two first rows of paramedian feather rudiments in the thoracic region. It does not seem to be related to the formation of feather rudiments.

The histology of the feather-forming areas has recently been described by WESSELLS (1965). This author has stressed the mesenchymal modifications which accompany skin differentiation. In the sub-ectodermal mesenchyme of a future apteric zone, the cellular density remains low (1.96 nuclei/ $1000 \mu^3$). The true dermal mesenchyme is not separate from the deep mesenchyme, and is indiscernible from it at 6 to $6\frac{1}{2}$ days incubation (figures 12 to 16). However, in the feather-forming areas (figures 12 to 15), the dermis is individualized and can be distinguished from the underlying mesenchyme by its high cellular density (2.60 nuclei/1000 μ^3). It reaches a thickness of 35 to 40 μ in the dorsal thoracic region. At the same time, the ectoderm undergoes major transformations in the feather-forming areas. The basal layer finally acquires its permanent columnar epithelial character (figures 14, 15 and 17). Its cells are closely aligned one against the other, and elongate perpendicularly to the skin surface. The intercellular spaces become progressively filled. The periderm also thickens and takes on the appearance of a pavement epithelium. Thus the undifferentiated ectoderm becomes transformed into typical embryonic epidermis, whose mean thickness in the dorsal region is about 10 μ.

It is still not known whether formation of the epidermis precedes or follows densification of the dermis in the feather-forming areas. The dense dermis is certainly capable of provoking differentiation of the ectoderm into epidermis (SENGEL, 1958a). This result was obtained by combining 7-day old dermis with 5 day ectoderm, but it may still be true that, in normal development, epidermal differentiation precedes that of the dense dermis.

Apart from the feather-forming areas, the ectoderm remains undifferentiated for some time yet. It only acquires its characteristic epidermal structure at the time when the first feather germs form in the pterylae, or the first scales appear in the tarso-metatarsal region (McLOUGHLIN, 1961a).

II FORMATION OF FEATHER GERMS

The embryonic feathers can first be distinguished macroscopically in the form of small, whitish spots, regularly spaced and distributed over the skin. Histologically, this increased opacity corresponds to the formation of an epidermal placode and an underlying condensation of the dermal cells. The whole constitutes a feather rudiment. Between $6\frac{1}{2}$ and 12 days incubation, as many feather rudiments are formed in the various embryonic feather-forming areas as there will be feathers in the chick pterylae. In the placode, the basal epidermal cells increase in height relative to those of the sur-rounding regions (figure 17); the mean thickness of this layer reaches 14.4 μ (WESSELLS, 1965). At the periphery of the placode, the distal ex-tremities of the cells are slanted towards the centre of the rudiment. On the other hand, the density of basal epidermal and peridermal cells in the placode does not increase: it remains on average 52 nuclei/1000 μ^2 and 20 nuclei/1000 μ^2 respectively (SENGEL and RUSAOUËN, unpublished data). The dermal condensation is shaped like a plano-convex lens, with the convex surface turned inwards. The surface area of the feather rudiment varies from 8000 to 15000 μ^2.

Are both these differentiations—epithelial and mesenchymal—con-comitant, or does one precede the other? This is a very important question, in view of the results of heterochronic combinations of dermis and epidermis (SENGEL, 1958a) which indicate that the dermis acts as the primary inducer of feather differentiation (see later). Contrary to what might have been expected, precise morphological observations on 58 fragments of dorsal skin (light microscopy) have demonstrated clearly that formation of the dermal mass does not precede that of the epidermal placode (SENGEL and RUSAOUËN, 1968). In fact, a comparative count of the longitudinal rows of placodes detectable in the epidermis, and the number of dermal condensa-tions, indicates that epidermal differentiation precedes that of the dermis; it is concluded from such counts that, between the stages 28 and 34 of HAMBURGER and HAMILTON (1951), epidermal differentiation is ahead of dermal differentiation by about 1 longitudinal row, on average (table I) (figures 18 to 24). However, it is still true that under conditions of *in vitro* or *in vivo* (chorio-allantoic membrane) culture, the dense dermis containing the mesenchymal condensations of the feather rudiment can induce the formation of an epidermal placode in epidermis which has not yet differen-tiated, e.g. at 5 days incubation.

As this mesenchymal condensation has such an importance in morpho-

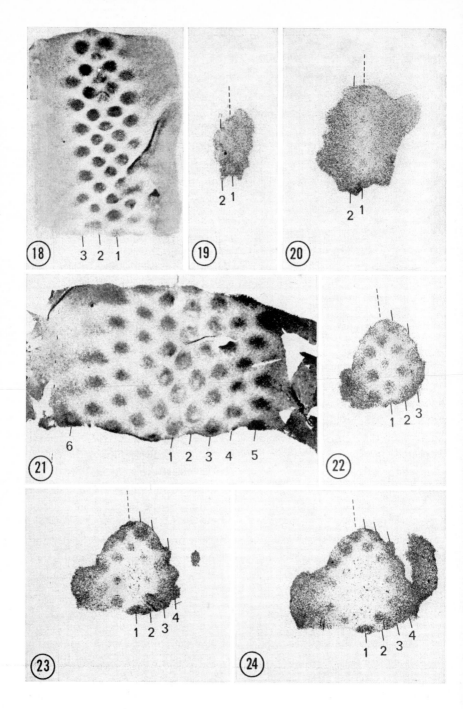

becomes inclined towards the rear of the embryo. In this way, the feather germ arises and is bilaterally symmetrical; this characteristic is underlined at the start of its emergence, by the accumulation of acid mucopolysaccharides at the cranial side of the feather germ base (SENGEL, BESCOL and GUILLAM, 1962). From this time, the feather germ is constituted by an epidermal sheath surrounding a dermal mesenchymal pulp, which is soon invaded by a nutrient blood capillary. Mitotic activity in the epidermis is intense, leading to elongation of the feather germ. In the dermis, only the basal cells multiply to any marked extent; they constitute the future dermal papilla of the feather.

At 10 days incubation, the feather germs of spinal pteryla in chick embryo have attained 0.3 to 0.6 mm in length. At this time, the epidermis is made up of 4 to 5 layers of cells. It now undergoes a new differentiation, leading to the formation of barb ridges, then barbs, barbules and barbicels, in which the specific characters of the future neoptile feather will be expressed. We shall return to this aspect of feather germ differentiation later on (p. 94).

We must first summarize the principal results obtained in experimental analysis of feather germ differentiation. What is known of the mechanisms and morphogenetic factors involved in their formation and growth?

III EXPERIMENTAL INVESTIGATIONS ON THE DIFFERENTIATION OF SKIN, FEATHERS AND SCALES

My own results (SENGEL, 1958a) were obtained mainly from experiments based on the culture method of WOLFF and HAFFEN (1952). The use of a solidified inert substrate, made up of agar and relatively poor nutrient medium, causes skin explants to behave in a particular way.

The explants usually contract rather drastically when put into culture, whatever their age; but the contraction is more intense, the earlier the stage of explantation. Fragments of dorsal skin explanted before the appearance of feather rudiments (*stage 0*: between 5 and 6 days incubation), do not differentiate feather germs when cultured on the medium of WOLFF and HAFFEN*. However, this differentiation is easily obtained by other techniques, e.g. use of a plasma substrate (BELL, 1964) or an organic substrate,

---

* The medium has the following composition:

Agar, 1% concentration in Gey's fluid . . . . 7 parts
Tyrode's solution containing penicillin . . . . 3 parts
Chick embryo extract, 50% in Tyrode's solution . . . . 3 parts

such as a fragment of embryo neural tube (SENGEL, 1958a and 1961a), or by enriching the standard medium of Wolff and Haffen with chick plasma (SENGEL, 1958a) or brain extract (SENGEL, 1961b). These various adjuvants make it possible to obtain feather germs, even from skin explants taken at a stage as early as 4 days incubation. On the standard medium however, or on synthetic media, a very rapid contraction of the epidermis is observed, while on the 2nd day of culture, the dermis tends to disperse at the surface of the medium: the organic unity of the explant is thus destroyed.

More mature dorsal pieces ($6\frac{1}{2}$ to $8\frac{1}{2}$ days incubation) continue their morphogenesis on the standard medium and acquire feather germs. However, the arrangement of the latter in relation to the explant borders varies, depending on whether the skin fragment (taken by cutting along both sides of the mediodorsal line) contains more or less than four rows of feather rudiments at the outset. In the first instance (*stage 1*: $6\frac{1}{2}$ to 7 days), total rearrangement of the explant's dermal elements is observed: the rows of rudiments which were in existence at the time of explantation disappear; new ones are soon formed, the first of which differentiates at a point approximately equidistant from the two longitudinal borders of the explant (SENGEL, 1958b). The fragment thus reorganizes the feather structures within its own borders. In the second instance (*stage 2*: $7\frac{1}{4}$ to $8\frac{1}{2}$ days), the feather rudiments preserve their initial arrangement, and each feather germ arises in the very position of the original rudiments.

By using this particular medium, which is relatively poor nutritionally, the existence of a threshold for feather differentiation is revealed; the explant cultured on this medium *in vitro* cannot cross the threshold without the intervention of a morphogenetic factor. Heterochronic associations of dermis and epidermis have been achieved, where only one of the components has crossed the threshold at the time of explantation; by such combinations, it has been possible to demonstrate the morphogenetic interactions occurring in the skin between 5 and 8 days incubation.

Table II shows the results obtained by culturing epidermal fragments in association with mesenchymal fragments, dermal or otherwise, varying in age and site of origin, prepared by trypsin-induced dissociation of tissues. The main findings are as follows:

1. Histogenesis of the epidermis

The association of stage 1 dorsal dermis with 5-day ectoderm demonstrates the histogenetic action of the dermis. If the 5-day ectoderm, isolated by

Table II   Results of associations of mesenchyme (dermal or otherwise) and epidermis, varying in age and origin, in culture *in vitro*

		Epidermis					
		Dorsal 5 days	Dorsal st. 0	Dorsal st. 1	Dorsal st. 2	Tarso-metatarsal 12 days	Comb 12 days
Dermis	Dorsal st. 0	—	0*	—	feathers	—	—
	Dorsal st. 1	feathers	feathers	feathers	feathers	feathers	feathers
	Dorsal st. 2	—	0	rare and mal-formed feathers	feathers	—	—
	Tarso-metatarsal 11 days	—	—	feathers	feathers	—	—
	Tarso-metatarsal 12 days	—	—	feathers and scales	feathers and scales	scales	—
	Tarso-metatarsal 13 days	—	scales	scales	—	—	—
	Dorsal st. 1 deep face	—	—	—	feathers	—	—
Sub-cutaneous mesenchyme, 6 days		—	—	—	feathers	—	—

* Absence of integumental differentiation.

trypsin digestion, is laid peridermal face down on the dermal fragment, the latter creates a re-arrangement of internal-external polarity, so that the periderm is once again found face upwards at the end of the culture period. At the same time, the flat undifferentiated ectoderm becomes transformed, under the influence of the dermis, into a typical epidermis with a cylindrical basal layer and a pavement or cubic epithelial type periderm. The lability of the internal-external polarity of the 5-day ectoderm might be due to the prior action of trypsin, which could have loosened the arrangement of the two layers of cells. However, this "basal-layer-peridermal" polarity stabilizes between 5 and 6 days in the feather-forming areas, and cannot thereafter be reversed.

2. Formation of the feather germ

If a fragment of stage 1 dorsal dermis is associated with a fragment of stage 0 dorsal epidermis on the standard medium the explant becomes covered by feather germs, while controls (dermis 0 + epidermis 0) do not differentiate. This result demonstrates the inductive role of the dermis in the formation of the epidermal sheath of the feather germ. As from stage 2, the dermis loses its activity on standard medium. The converse association of stage 2 epidermis with stage 0 dermis reveals that the epidermis in turn has an inductive action on the dermis. Under the influence of the epidermis, the dermal cells begin to colonize the epidermal sheath of the feather germ. Thus, even before it has formed mesenchymal condensations, stage 0 dermis is already capable of responding to the morphogenetic action of the epidermis. Moreover, even the deeper dermal layer at stage 0, or the non-dermal subcutaneous mesenchyme react to the epidermal influence by forming normal feather germs. The dermis is thus the primary inducer of feather germ development; having undergone the first dermal stimulus, the induced epidermis in turn becomes the site of a reciprocal morphogenetic action.

3. Orientation of the feather germ

Dorsal dermis and epidermis are associated in culture, and the epidermis is turned through 90° or 180° in relation to the cephalo-caudal axis of the dermis; the results show that the epidermis alone is responsible for the orientation and bilateral symmetry of feather germs. The latter are consistently inclined towards the caudal border of the epidermal fragment, whatever the orientation of the dermal fragment. Other experiments have shown that at a very early stage (2 days incubation) the dorsal ectoderm already contains the factors for this orientation (SENGEL and KIENY, unpublished results).

4. Regional differentiation of the skin

Why do certain skin areas become covered with feathers, while others such as the feet develop scales? What is the tissue responsible for this difference? *In vitro* associations of dermis and epidermis from the dorsal and tarsometatarsal regions demonstrate the role of each skin component in regional differentiation. They show the bipotentiality of chick embryo integument. If stage 1 dorsal dermis is associated with 12-day tarso-metatarsal epidermis, the explant becomes covered with feather germs; however, they differ from normal feather germs in the early keratinization of their epidermis and the exaggerated thickness of their periderm, both of which are scale characteristics. Under the influence of the dorsal dermis, foot epidermis develops anatomically according to the origin of the dermis, but its cytological differentiation remains consistent with its origin. The converse association of 13-day tarso-metatarsal dermis with stage 1 dorsal epidermis gives rise to typical scales. In this case, the keratinization and peridermal thickening of the dorsal epidermis are of the same type as in normal scales. If the tarso-metatarsal dermis associated with dorsal epidermis is not sufficiently differentiated (11 to 12 days incubation) at the time of explantation, a conflict arises, ending either in the formation of feather germs or the concomitant formation of feather germs and scales. These results have been confirmed in analogous associations cultured on the chorio-allantoic membrane (RAWLES, 1963). The dermis thus determines the regional nature of cutaneous differentiation, at least in so far as the macroscopic anatomy of the structures is concerned. The 12-day tarsometatarsal epidermis, however, already contains the factors for scale cytodifferentiation, and these the dorsal dermis cannot counteract.

The determinant role of dermal-epidermal interactions in morphogenesis is further demonstrated by associations where one of the components comes from an embryo bearing a genetic malformation affecting the plumage, such as the "scaleless" mutation (sc). The homozygotes (sc/sc) are characterized by the absence of scales and a deficient plumage; only certain regions of the body develop feathers, and the dorsal skin of the thorax and anterior lumbar region is quite bare. The results of these experiments (SENGEL and ABBOTT, 1963) are given in table III. Explants containing sc epidermis do not differentiate, whether the combination is sc epidermis/normal dermis or sc epidermis/sc dermis. On the other hand, dorsal explants containing normal epidermis form normal feather germs, even if the combination is normal epidermis/sc dermis. With explants of tarso-metatarsal origin, most combinations of normal epidermis and sc dermis form recognisable scales. It is concluded that in the skin of sc embryos, the mutation only affects the epidermis; the latter is incapable of responding to the morphogenetic action of normal or sc dermis, when associated with it in culture. Dermis from sc embryos functions normally, however, and exercises the same differentiating action on normal epidermis as does normal dermis.

The situation is quite different in the skin of normally featherless areas (apteria) in the normal chick embryo. In the integument of the mid-ventral apterium, for example (SENGEL, DHOUAILLY and KIENY, 1969), the dermis remains loose until a very advanced stage of development and has no featherforming capacity, whereas the epidermis is able to respond to the morphogenetic action of dermis obtained from a pteryla and to participate in the formation of normal feather germs.

Table III   Results of associating dermis and epidermis from normal ($+/+$) and scaleless (sc/sc) embryos

DERMIS Dorsal of stage 0 or 1 Tarso-metatarsal of 10 or 11 days		EPIDERMIS Dorsal of stage 0, 1 or 2 Tarso-metatarsal of 10 or 11 days	
		$+/+$	sc/sc
	$+/+$	feathers	0
		scales	0
	sc/sc	feathers	0
		scales	0

The mechanism of differentiation of skin and cutaneous appendages can be summarized as follows:

1st phase

The dermis causes differentiation of ordinary ectoderm into typical epidermis;

2nd phase

Under the influence of a still unidentified factor, the dermis of the dorsal skin forms feather rudiments, while that of the tarso-metatarsal skin forms scale rudiments;

3rd phase

The dermal feather rudiments exercise a brief inductive action on the overlying epidermis, initiating epidermal differentiation. The regional character of this differentiation, i.e. development of feather germs or scales, is determined by the nature of the dermis, i.e. dorsal or tarso-metatarsal respectively;

4th phase

The epidermis in turn induces the dermal cells to colonize the epidermal sheath: the orientation of feather germs is determined by the cephalo-caudal polarity of the epidermis.

5. Role of the nervous system

In this description of skin development, one point remains obscure: what is the factor which, during the second phase, provokes the differentiation of dermal feather rudiments? The question is far from being answered, but a few experiments are worthy of mention. These indicate that the central nervous system of the embryo plays some part in this determination, at least as regards the spinal pteryla. It has been indicated above that, while stage *0* skin does not differentiate on the standard medium based on chick embryo extract, the formation of rudiments followed by feather germs can be brought about by associating a fragment of undifferentiated skin with a fragment of chick embryo neural tube *in vitro*. Under these conditions, the epidermis does not contract; there is no dispersion of the dermis on the medium surface, and integrity of the explant is maintained throughout culture. This morphogenetic action in culture is not connected with neural tube metabolic activity, since the same result is obtained with a fragment of neural tube which has been killed by heat.

Differentiation and growth of feather germs show an even better response if the fragment of associated neural tube is replaced by adult or embryonic chick brain extract. Even when boiled, the brain extract retains its morphogenetic capacity (SENGEL, 1961b). A chemical factor is thus involved, which is capable of initiating feather germ differentiation. Biochemical analysis shows that the factor is present in the supernatant obtained after removing the precipitate formed by boiling. The active substances are insoluble in ether, and are precipitated by cold acetone. They preserve their morphogenetic power when redissolved in Tyrode's solution. Lastly, they are dialysable and resistant to acid or alkaline hydrolysis (SENGEL and FEIGEL-SON, 1963).

Is this factor a specific inducer of feather differentiation, or is it merely nutritive, enabling the skin to cross the "differentiation threshold" *in vitro*? Our knowledge is insufficient at present to answer this question decisively. It is worth noting, however, that in the embryo *in ovo*, excision of part of the neural tube at 2 days incubation consistently leads to non-differentiation of a transverse segment of the spinal pteryla, which remains bare (SENGEL and KIENY, 1963). Thus the absence of a neural tube segment is reflected at skin level by production of an experimental apterium. It should be added that the healing phenomena following excision of the neural tube have no effect on the spinal pteryla (SENGEL and THÉVENET, 1966, THEVENET, 1969). It seems well established that the presence of an intact neural tube is essential for normal differentiation of dorsal feather germs.

6. Specific differentiation of the feather

Experiments have been conducted which demonstrate the role of each skin component in determining the specific form of the neoptile feather; they consisted of xenoplastic associations, where fragments of dorsal

Table IV   Results of xenoplastic associations of feather-forming dermis and epidermis from chick and duck

		DORSAL EPIDERMIS	
		Duck embryo, 9 days	Chick embryo, 7 days
DORSAL DERMIS	Duck embryo, 9 days	*Duck feather:* Well developed rachis, average number of barbs = 18; barbules and spiny barbicels	*Duck feather:* Well developed rachis, average number of barbs = 20; gnarled barbules without barbicels
	Chick embryo, 7 days	*Chick feather:* Rudimentary rachis, average number of barbs = 11; barbules and spiny barbicels	*Chick feather:* Rudimentary rachis, average number of barbs = 12; gnarled barbules without barbicels

dermis and epidermis from 7 to 9 day chick and duck embryos were combined. The associations were explanted onto the chick chorio-allantoic membrane, in preference to *in vitro* culture, so that the explants could reach the stage of neoptile feather development. The results are summarized in table IV (SENGEL and DHOUAILLY, 1966; DHOUAILLY, 1967).

In the spinal pteryla, the neoptile feather (*praepenna*) of the chick is distinguished from that of the duck by its umbelliform appearance, its small number of barbs (11 to 14) and its gnarled barbules, devoid of barbicellar spines. That of the duck has a well-developed rachis, a large number of barbs (14 to 30), and barbules bearing a double row of spiny barbicels (figure 29) (HOSKER, 1936).

Cultures of xenoplastic associations show that the anatomical structure of the neoptile feather is a result of dermal-epidermal collaboration. If duck dermis is combined with chick epidermis, the feather which differentiates exhibits chimerism; it resembles a duck feather in size and shape, but possesses the gnarled barbules characteristic of a chick feather (figures 30 and 31); conversely, the combination of chick dermis with duck epidermis gives feathers of chick type in general appearance, but possessing the spiny barbicels characteristic of duck feathers (figures 32 and 33).

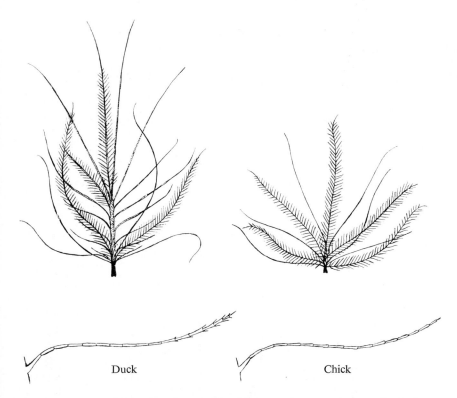

Duck   Chick

Figure 29 Scheme illustrating the specific differences between the neoptile feather (*praepenna*) of duck and chick at birth. *Above*, general morphology of the feather, enlarged about 8 times (for clarity of drawing, barbules have only been shown on a certain number of barbs). *Below*, structure of a barbule, enlarged about 150 times (after DHOUAILLY, 1967).

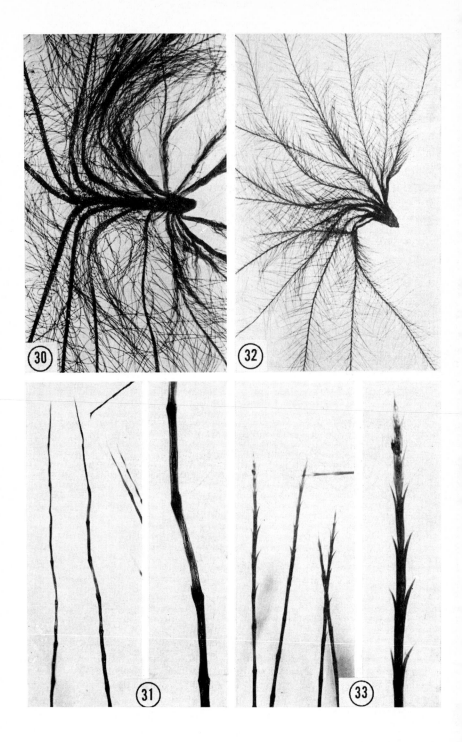

It can be concluded that the morphological organisation of the neoptile feather, i.e. the topographical relationships established between epidermal cells during differentiation, is strictly dependent on the dermal pulp of the feather germ. The dermis determines the specific arrangement of the barb and barbule cells. But the specific character of the cytological differentiation of each barbule cell is inscribed in the epidermis. Recent experiments, still unpublished (DHOUAILLY), show that the factors for this epidermal cytodifferentiation are already present in the 3-day ectoderm.

IV KERATINIZATION. CHEMICAL DIFFERENTIATION OF THE EPIDERMIS

In both embryo and adult, the epidermal cells of the germinative layer continue to proliferate during normal development. Any cell losing contact with the basal membrane loses the capacity to multiply. It thus inevitably dies, and is shed from the organism by superficial desquamation. But before reaching the surface, and during its progressive ascent, it passes through a phase of differentiation—keratinization, which is characterized by complex biosynthetic processes leading to production of the horny layer.

A detailed account cannot be given here of what is currently known on keratin synthesis and the appearance of specific proteins of keratinization during development (cf. MERCER, 1964). A review of this subject has recently been given by BELL (1965). Little was known about keratinization in the chick embryo before the work of MATOLTSY (1958); it has been described in detail by WESSELLS (1961). We shall note simply the main findings. Keratin is characterized principally by its birefringence, its

---

Figures 30 and 31 Chimeric neoptile feather (*praepenna*) resulting from the association of duck dermis with chick epidermis; the general morphology (figure 30) is of duck type with respect to dimensions, number of barbs (22), the existence of a well developed rachis (*horizontal in the figure*) into which are inserted a certain number of cranial and lateral barbs ($\times$ 42). The fine structure of the barbule cells (figure 31) is of chick type (absence of barbicels) ($\times$ 315; $\times$ 800).

Figures 32 and 33 Chimeric neoptile feather (*praepenna*) resulting from the association of chick dermis and duck epidermis; the general morphology (figure 32) is of chick type with respect to dimensions, number of barbs (15), umbelliform structure and absence of a well developed rachis ($\times$ 42). The fine structure of the apical barbule cells (figure 33) is of duck type (each of them bears a pair of barbicellar spines) ($\times$ 315; $\times$ 800).

resistance to trypsin digestion, and by the formation of S–S bonds; it can be detected between 10 and 13 days incubation in the dorsal region of the chick embryo. At this stage, the epidermis is made up of a basal layer, an intermediate layer, a sub-periderm, a secondary periderm, and a superficial primary periderm, in which the first signs of birefringence appear. At 14 days, birefringent granules are present in all the epidermal layers, but become particularly abundant between 15 and 16 days in the primary periderm and the squamous layer—recently developed between the sub-periderm and the intermediate layer. A little before hatching, the peridermal and sub-peridermal cells become completely obliterated by a homogenous, vitreous matrix without visible infrastructure, and are eliminated. Below this the horny layer is formed by progressive flattening of the squamous cells. Birefringent substances are particularly abundant in the latter two layers, while the basal and intermediate layers contain very little. It should be added that, although cornification begins at a relatively late developmental stage, it is possible, by immunochemical methods, to detect a specific antigen of feather-forming skin as early as 6 days incubation (BEN-OR and BELL, 1965). It thus seems that the epidermal cells are destined to become keratinized at a very early stage. It is possible that the appearance of this specific plumage protein at 6 days marks the time of determination of feather tracts; this agrees with histological observations. Between 13 and 15 days, a second specific antigen appears, precisely at the time when keratinization begins.

Experiments of dissociation and re-association of dermis and epidermis show that one of the essential conditions for normal keratinization is the maintenance of an undifferentiated non-keratogenic germinative layer, whose cells retain the ability to multiply. Here again, it is the dermis which contributes the controlling factors necessary for this maintenance (MCLOUGHLIN, 1961a and b; WESSELLS, 1962 and 1964). The isolated epidermis *in vitro* loses the ability to incorporate tritiated thymidine within a few hours. The cell of the basal layer cease to multiply, and begin to keratinize in a disorderly fashion. The epidermis generally rolls up into a cyst-like formation and dies rapidly through total keratinization.

The dermis can exercise its regulatory function through a Millipore filter interposed between the dermis and the epidermis. Moreover, the dermis retains its efficacy even when killed by freezing (DODSON, 1963). However, if killed by heat, it loses these properties and epidermis associated with it degenerates rapidly, becoming keratinized in a drastic manner. The dermis thus seems to exercise its action by producing diffusible substances which it transmits to the epidermis. These substances are destroyed by heat. MCLOUGHLIN (1961a) has shown that epidermal tissue can be maintained and will proliferate if its basal membrane is kept in contact with a small quantity of mucopolysaccharide exudate, obtained by trypsin action on the dermis. The dermis can even be replaced entirely by a reconstituted collagen gel: under these conditions, the epidermis keratinizes more or less normally, maintaining an active basal layer (DODSON, 1963).

Normal keratinization is of course one of the essential conditions for formation of feathers, whose constitution is almost pure keratin. However, factors other than dermal ones play a part in their formation. One of these is the deposition of an intradermal collagen lattice, prior to any keratogenic differentiation. Any disturbance or inhibition of collagen synthesis is reflected in feather differentiation. For example, if hydrocortisone is injected into chick embryos of 5 to 6 days incubation, the formation of plumage may be almost entirely inhibited (MOSCONA and KARNOFSKY, 1960). The various pterylae of the chick embryo show notable differences of sensitivity to hydrocortisone (SENGEL and ZÜST, 1968). The wing, shoulder and tail tracts are never affected. The spinal, breast and thigh tracts are moderately sensitive and cases of total absence of feathers are relatively rare. The head, abdominal and shank tracts are very sensitive and are completely deprived of feathers in about half of the treated embryos. The most severe malformations are obtained only after injections performed at 5 and particularly at 6 days incubation. In the spinal pteryla, the cases of complete featherlessness are obtained with a significant frequency only after treatment at 6 days. Conversely, the absence of the lateral feathers, which corresponds to a less severe malformation, results from injections at 7 and 8 days. These results show that the feather primordia of the spinal pteryla, the differentiation of which spreads out in time from $6\frac{1}{2}$ days to 9 days and in space from the mid-dorsal line to either side, are particularly sensitive to the action of hydrocortisone during the phase preceeding the formation of the epidermal placode and the dermal condensation. Once these structures are established, hydrocortisone has no further effect on the differentiation of the pterylae, even though it may retard the outgrowth and elongation of the feather germs.

Other factors, of hypophyseal origin, may act on the differentiation of plumage (YATVIN, 1966a and b): embryos decapitated at an early stage

7*

continue to develop normally up to 12 days incubation, but their plumage is very deficient. The injection of pituitary extract into decapitated embryos re-establishes normal feather germ differentiation.

CONCLUSIONS

These will be brief and confined to recapitulating the part played by the dermis and epidermis in skin histogenesis and the formation of cutaneous appendages, which result from their collaboration. As far as is known at present, the dermis is the site of the initial morphogenetic stimulus which leads to epidermal outgrowth. It determines the regional nature of the cutaneous appendages, inducing feathers or scales depending on its origin. It transmits to the epidermis the specific information necessary for forming chick or duck feathers, but is incapable of modifying the fine histogenesis of the epidermis, which retains and expresses its own regional and specific characteristics. It is the organizer and regulator of the basal generative layer of the epidermis which, without its continuous influence, degenerates and dies. Lastly, it is the site of a fibrous lattice, still imperfectly defined (collagenous in nature) which probably provides the plumage with its regular arrangement.

Although the mechanism is still obscure, the epidermis appears to contain the factors determining feather orientation. It also relays the initial induction of the dermis by a prolonged morphogenetic action, which results in the elongation of the cutaneous appendages. Through its capacity to synthesise keratin, it evidently provides the construction material for all hard cutaneous products. For this horny substance to be arranged in specific formations, with an ordered structure, it depends on the dermis. But at 3 days of incubation, it already possesses the information necessary for typical cytodifferentiation of its constituent elements.

Numerous problems remain to be solved. Among the most important is the question of determination of the feather tracts, i.e. that of the division between naked zones (apteria) and feathered areas (pterylae). Some preliminary work has recently been done to answer it (SENGEL and KIENY, 1967a and b; SENGEL and MAUGER, 1967). If it is true that the dermis imposes the regional nature of epidermal differentiation, from where is this property of the dermis derived? How and at what stage are the dermatome and the lateral somatopleural plates from which it arises, determined to produce the dorsal feathers, the wing remiges, the tail rectrices, the tarso-metatarsal scales, or the plantar pads? Lastly, which molecules produce, relay, carry, receive and interpret the multiple and complex messages which can be experimentally detected between the rudiments of an organ?

References

BELL, E. (1964). The induction of differentiation and the response to the inducer. *Cancer Res.*, **24**, 28–34.

BELL, E. (1965). The Skin. In *"Organogenesis"* (DeHaan R.L. and Ursprung H., eds.). Holt, Rinehart and Winston, New York, Chicago, San Francisco, Toronto, London, 361–370.

BEN-OR, S., and BELL, E. (1965). Skin antigens in the chick embryo in relation to other developmental events. *Develop. Biol.*, **11**, 184–201.

DEHAAN, R. L., and URSPRUNG, H. (1965). *Organogenesis*. Holt, Rinehart and Winston, New York, Chicago, San Francisco, Toronto, London.

DHOUAILLY, D. (1967). Analyse des facteurs de la différenciation spécifique de la plume néoptile chez le canard et le poulet. *J. Embryol. Exp. Morphol.*, **18**, 389–400.

DODSON, J. W. (1963). On the nature of tissue interactions in embryonic skin. *Exptl. Cell Res.*, **31**, 233–235.

HAMBURGER, V., and HAMILTON, H. L. (1951). A series of normal stages in the development of the chick embryo. *J. Morphol.*, **88**, 49–92.

HOLMES, A. (1935). The pattern and symmetry of adult plumage units in relation to the order and locus of origin of the embryonic feather papillae. *Am. J. Anat.*, **56**, 513–535.

HOSKER, A. (1936). Studies in the epidermal structures of birds. *Philos. Trans. Roy. Soc. London*, **226** B, 143–188.

KALLMAN, F., EVANS, J., and WESSELLS, N. K. (1967). Anchor filament bundles in embryonic feather germs and skin. *J. Cell Biol.*, **32**, 236–240.

McLOUGHLIN, C. B. (1961 *a*). The importance of mesenchymal factors in the differentiation of chick epidermis. I. The differentiation in culture of the isolated epidermis of the embryonic chick and its response to excess vitamin A. *J. Embryol. Exp. Morphol.*, **9**, 370–384.

McLOUGHLIN, C. B. (1961 *b*). The importance of mesenchymal factors in the differentiation of chick epidermis. II. Modification of epidermal differentiation by contact with different types of mesenchyme. *J. Embryol. Exp. Morphol.*, **9**, 385–409.

MATOLTSY, A. (1958). Keratinization of embryonic skin. *J. Invest. Dermatol.*, **31**, 343–346.

MERCER, E. H. (1964). Protein synthesis and epidermal differentiation. In *"The Epidermis"* (Montagna W. and Lobitz W.C., eds.), Academic Press, New York, London, 161–178.

MOSCONA, M. H., and KARNOFSKY, D. A. (1960). Cortisone induced modifications in the development of the chick embryo. *Endocrinology*, **66**, 533–549.

RAWLES, M. E. (1963). Tissue interactions in scale and feather development as studied in dermal-epidermal recombinations. *J. Embryol. Exp. Morphol.*, **11**, 765–789.

RUGGERI, A. (1967). Ricerche ultrastrutturali sull'ectoderma dell'embrione di pollo. *Z. Zellforsch. Mikroskop. Anat.*, **77**, 361–376.

SENGEL, P. (1958 *a*). Recherches expérimentales sur la différenciation des germes plumaires et du pigment de la peau de l'embryon de poulet en culture *in vitro*. *Ann. Sc. Nat. Zool.*, **11**, 430–514.

SENGEL, P. (1958 b). La différenciation de la peau et des germes plumaires de l'embryon de poulet en culture in vitro. Ann. Biol., 34, 29–52.

SENGEL, P. (1961 a). Action morphogène du système nerveux et de divers extraits de cerveau sur la peau d'embryon de poulet cultivée in vitro. Colloq. Intern. Centre Nat. Rech. Sci., 101, 95–116.

SENGEL, P. (1961 b). Action morphogène de divers extraits de cerveau sur la peau d'embryon de poulet cultivée in vitro. Arch. Anat. Hist. Embryol. norm. exp., 44, 217–239.

SENGEL, P., and ABBOTT, U. K. (1963). In vitro studies with the scaleless mutant : Interactions during feather and scale differentiation. J. Heredity, 54, 254–262.

SENGEL, P., BESCOL-LIVERSAC, J., and GUILLAM, C. (1962). Les mucopolysaccharides— sulfates au cours de la morphogenèse des germes plumaires de l'embryon de poulet. Develop. Biol., 4, 274–288.

SENGEL, P., and DHOUAILLY, D. (1966). Différenciation en greffe chorioallantoïdienne de chimères interspécifiques de peau embryonnaire de poulet et de canard. C.R. Acad. Sci. Paris, 263, 601–604.

SENGEL, P., DHOUAILLY, D., and KIENY, M. (1969). Aptitude des constituants cutanés de l'aptérie médio-ventrale du poulet à former des plumes. Develop. Biol., 19, 436–446.

SENGEL, P., and FEIGELSON, M. (1963). Sur les propriétés biochimiques d'un facteur morphogène agissant sur la différenciation des germes plumaires. C.R. Acad. Sci. Paris, 257, 4024–4027.

SENGEL, P., and KIENY, M. (1963). Sur le rôle des organes axiaux dans la différenciation de la ptéryle spinale de l'embryon de poulet. C.R. Acad. Sci. Paris, 256, 774–777.

SENGEL, P., and KIENY, M. (1967 a). Production d'une ptéryle supplémentaire chez l'embryon de poulet. I. Etude morphologique. Arch. Anat. Microscop. Morphol. Exp., 56, 11–30.

SENGEL, P., and KIENY, M. (1967 b). Production d'une ptéryle supplémentaire chez l'embryon de poulet. II. Analyse expérimentale. Develop. Biol., 16, 532–563.

SENGEL, P., and MAUGER, A. (1967). La métamérie de la ptéryle spinale, étudiée chez l'embryon de poulet à l'aide d'irradiations localisées aux rayons X. C.R. Acad. Sci. Paris, 256, 919–922.

SENGEL, P., and RUSAOUËN, M. (1968). Aspects histologiques de la différenciation précoce des ébauches plumaires chez le poulet. C.R. Acad. Sci. Paris, 266, 795–797.

SENGEL, P., and RUSAOUËN, M. (1969). Modifications ultrastructurales au cours de l'histogenèse de la peau chez l'embryon de poulet. Arch. Anat. Microsc. Morphol. Exp., 58, 77–96.

SENGEL, P., and THÉVENET, A. (1966). Sur les modalités de la cicatrisation de l'ectoderme dorsal en la présence et en l'absence du tube neural chez l'embryon de poulet. C.R. Acad. Sci. Paris, 263, 278–280.

SENGEL, P., and ZÜST, B. (1968). Malformations du plumage obtenues par l'injection d'hydrocortisone à l'embryon de poulet. C.R. Acad. Sci. Paris, 267, 1304–1307.

STUART, E. S., and MOSCONA, A. A. (1967). Embryonic morphogenesis: role of fibrous lattice in the development of feathers and feather patterns. Science, 157, 947–948.

THÉVENET, A. (1969). Sur les modalités de la cicatrisation de l'ectoderme dorsal chez l'embryon de poulet au cours de 3ᵉ jour d'incubation. *Ann. Embryol. Morphog.*, **2**, 71–85.

WEISS, P. (1958). Cell Contact. *Intern. Rev. Cytol.*, **7**, 1–30.

WESSELLS, N. K. (1961). An analysis of chick epidermal differentiation *in situ* and *in vitro* in chemically defined media. *Develop. Biol.*, **3**, 355–389.

WESSELLS, N. K. (1962). Tissue interaction during skin histodifferentiation. *Develop. Biol.*, **4**, 87–107.

WESSELLS, N. K. (1964). Substrate and nutrient effects upon epidermal basal cell orientation and proliferation. *Proc. Nat. Acad. Sci. U.S.*, **52**, 252–258.

WESSELLS, N. K. (1965). Morphology and proliferation during early feather development. *Develop. Biol.*, **12**, 131–153.

WESSELLS, N. K., and EVANS, J. (1968). The ultrastructure of orientated cells and extra-cellular materials between developing feathers. *Develop. Biol.*, **18**, 42–61.

WOLFF, E., and HAFFEN, K. (1952). Sur une méthode de culture d'organes embryonnaires *in vitro*. *Tex. Rep. Biol. Med.*, **10**, 463–472.

YATVIN, M. B. (1966 *a*). Polysome morphology: Evidence for endocrine control during chick embryogenesis. *Science*, **151**, 1001–1003.

YATVIN, M. B. (1966 *b*). Hypophyseal control of genetic expression during chick feather and skin differentiation. *Science*, **153**, 184–185.

CHAPTER V

MORPHOGENESIS OF THE NEUROGRANIUM

J. Benoit and J. Schowing

Laboratoire d'Embryologie Expérimentale, Collège de France and C.N.R.S.,
Nogent-sur-Marne

THE TERM neurocranium designates that portion of the skeleton which encloses the brain and sense organs. This chapter consists of two parts, the first dealing with formation of the otic cartilage, and the second with the development of certain parts of the skeleton enveloping the brain.

PART ONE
DEVELOPMENT OF THE AUDITORY CARTILAGE IN CHICK EMBRYO

The successive steps of the appearance of cartilage around the membranous labyrinth of the internal ear will be reviewed first.

The auditory epithelial rudiment is formed from the ectoderm, under the inductive influence of the parachordal cephalic mesoderm, part of the primary inducer. This was recognized by WADDINGTON (1937) and LEVI-MONTALCINI (1946).

But a second induction, arising from the hind-brain, takes over from the previous one and is necessary for complete development of the epithelial ear (WADDINGTON, 1937). We have established the rudimentary appearance of the ear when the hind-brain is suppressed at an early stage (BENOIT, 1960).

Once the membranous labyrinth is formed, a cartilaginous capsule develops around it. The first observations concerning development of this capsule are noted in passing by researchers using other material (REAGAN, 1915 and 1917; YNTEMA, 1944). We have investigated the problem in detail.

105

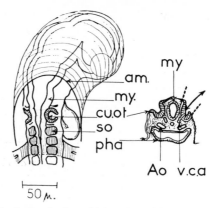

Figure 1 Excision of otic cupula, in a chick embryo with 19 pairs of somites.
am., amnion; *Ao.*, dorsal aortic artery; *cu. ot.*, otic cupula; *my.*, myelencephalon; *pha.*,
pharynx; *so.*, somite; *v.c.a.*, anterior cardinal vein.

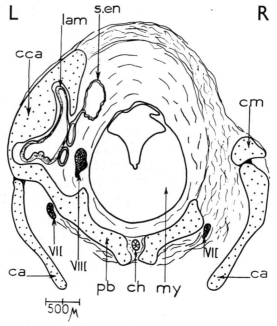

Figure 2 Transverse section of the chondrocranium in chick embryo after excision
of the right otic cupula.
ca., quadrate; *cca.*, otic capsule, canalicular part; *ch.*, notochord; *cm.*, metotic cartilage;
lam., membranous labyrinth; *my.*, myelencephalon; *pb.*, basal plate; *s. en.*, endolymphatic
sac; *VII.*, facial nerve; *VIII.*, acoustic nerve.

1. Suppression of the auditory epithelium

We used young chick embryos (about 48 hours incubation) possessing 15 to 21 pairs of somites (stages 12 to 14 of HAMBURGER and HAMILTON); whatever the technique—surgical excision of the otic cupula (figure 1) (BENOIT, 1955), localized X-irradiation (BENOIT, 1957b), or diathermo-coagulation (BENOIT, 1963)—the results were identical. In the absence of otic epithelium, in no case does the mesenchyme develop into cartilage (figure 2, operated side on right; normal side, left, serves as control). Mesenchymal differentiation thus depends on the inductive action of the membranous ear. The direction of this 3rd induction, where the epithelium (ectodermal derivative) acts on the mesenchyme (of mesodermal origin), is thus reversed with respect to the first induction, where the mesoderm exerts its effect on the ectoderm. Numerous comparable findings have been observed in the course of ontogenesis.

2. Specificity of the inducing organ

Inductive organ specificity could usefully be studied, as it is possible to replace the otic epithelial rudiment by other organs.

In the first series of experiments, the normal inducer was replaced by a fragment of medulla or notochord, taken from embryos of the same age (BENOIT, 1956). The result was positive in both cases, i.e. cartilage developed in presence of medulla or notochord. Where medulla was substituted (figure 3), supernumary isolated cartilage developed. The notochord (figure 4) became surrounded by cartilage, mingled on all sides with the neighbouring parts of the chondrocranium.

In the second series of experiments, the otic epithelial rudiment was replaced by a lens or lens fragment taken from a 3 or 4 day old donor, or by a particle of carbon-labelled paraffin (BENOIT, 1957a). Contrary to the preceding instances, the results were negative in all cases, and the mesenchyme remained undifferentiated in contact with the implants (figures 5 and 6). It is significant to compare figures 3 and 5 on the one hand, and 4 and 6 on the other.

In conclusion, the auditory epithelium is not the sole inducer of ear cartilage, since it shares this capacity with at least two organs—the medulla and the notochord—grafted heterotopically.

However, as cartilage is absent following implantation of a lens or particle of paraffin, the inducer cannot be totally specific. There must be partial specificity, and here a statistical study would be of value.

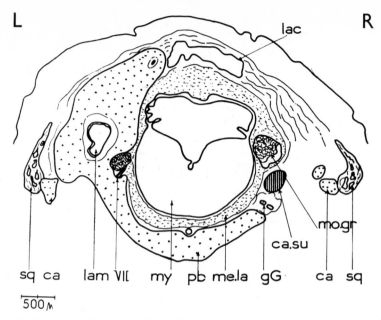

Figure 3 Graft of a fragment of medulla, after excision of right otic rudiment. *ca.*, quadrate; *ca. su.*, supernumary cartilage; *gG.*, Gasserian ganglion; *lac.*, lacuna; *la.m.*, membranous labyrinth; *me. la.*, loose meningeal mesenchyme; *mo.gr.*, grafted medulla; *my.*, myelencephalon; *pb.*, basal plate; *sq.*, squamosal; *VII.*, facial nerve.

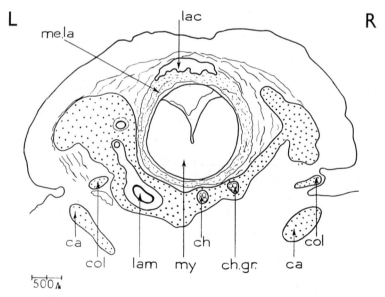

Figure 4 Graft of a fragment of notochord after excision of the right otic rudiment. *ca.*, quadrate; *ch.*, notochord; *ch.gr.*, grafted notochord; *col.*, columella; *lac.*, lacuna; *lam.*, membranous labyrinth; *me.la.*, loose meningeal mesenchyme; *my.*, myelencephalon.

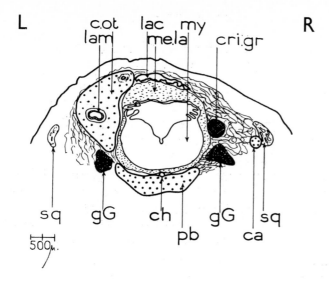

Figure 5   Graft of a lens after excision of the right otic rudiment.
ca., quadrate; *ch.*, notochord; *c. ot.*, otic cartilage; *cri. gr.*, grafted lens; *g.G.*, Gasserian ganglion; *lac.*, lacuna; *lam.*, membranous labyrinth; *me. la.*, loose meningeal mesenchyme; *my.*, myelencephalon; *pb.*, basal plate; *sq.*, squamosal.

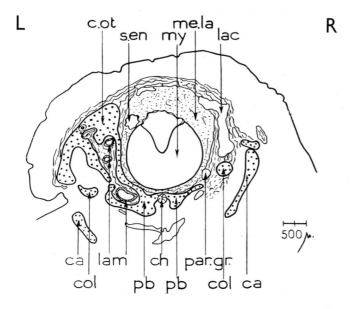

Figure 6   Implantation of a particle of paraffin after excision of right otic rudiment.
ca., quadrate; *ch.*, notochord; *col.*, columella; *c.ot.*, otic cartilage; *lac.*, lacuna; *lam.*, membranous labyrinth; *me.la.*, loose meningeal mesenchyme; *my.*, myelencephalon; *par. gr.*, implanted paraffin; *pb.*, basal plate; *S.en.*, endolymphatic sac.

3. Competence of the mesenchymal reactive tissue

In this series of experiments, the normal inducer was used throughout and was associated with various mesenchymes. The first observations deal with the consequences of incomplete otic rudiment excision. It happened that an otic epithelial fragment was displaced fortuitously downwards, against the rhombencephalon, or towards the surface into the dermis. In these two extreme positions, the normal inducer did not induce cartilage. Only the intermediate mesenchyme, between the dermis and the meninges, is capable of responding to otic induction—in other words, it is competent (BENOIT, 1960). The term "competence", employed by WADDINGTON (1937) characterizes a transitory state of the ectoderm with respect to chorda-mesodermal induction in amphibia. In the case of otic mesenchyme, competence may be connected with a particular stage of maturation, but this has not so far been verified.

Mesenchyme thus appears to be competent or incompetent, depending on its origin. There is in fact some indication that certain meningeal elements are mesectodermal in origin, while the otic mesenchyme is derived from mesentoderm (RAVEN, 1936, SENO and NIEUWKOOP, 1958). However, there is as yet no experimental proof of this.

Observations comparable to those concerning displacements of the normal inducer have been made with medullary implantation. Figure 3 shows a fragment of medulla placed in a meningeal area. Here, cartilage appeared, not in this deep zone, but just outside it in the inter-mediate otic zone.

Other experiments with *in vivo* and *in vitro* associations have shown that the somitic mesenchyme is also incompetent with respect to the otic inducer (BENOIT, 1960).

Thus, while the specificity of the inducer is not absolute, mesenchymal competence appears to be restricted exclusively to an area between the meninges and the dermis.

4. Chronology of induction

Positive experimental results have shown that the auditory epithelium exerts its inductive action through the agency of a diffusible substance (BENOIT, 1960). Because of the difficulties involved in obtaining an otocyst extract, we decided to use the vitelline membrane method (Et. and Em. WOLFF) for studying the duration of induction of otic cartilage.

a) *Duration of inductive action*

In this experiment, a strip of vitelline membrane from a non-incubated hen's egg was interposed between 3.5 day old otocysts cultured on the medium of WOLFF and HAFFEN (1951) and mesenchymal fragments of the same age assembled in a plastic ring. After 1, 2 or 3 days, the mesenchyme was separated from the inducer, and culture extended for a few days. The results of these experiments are given in the table I.

Table I

Structure	Mesenchyme	Precartilage			Cartilage		Totals
Stages	0	1	2	3	4	5	
Association 24 hrs oto + mes.	1	6	9	5			21
Association 48 hrs		3	6	3	4		16
Association 72 hrs		2	7	3	3		15

If the various developmental stages are numbered 0–5 for reference purposes, it can clearly be seen that mesenchyme requires at least 48 hrs induction before it can differentiate into cartilage (stage 4). The $3\frac{1}{2}$ day old mesenchymal controls cultured alone remain as undifferentiated mesenchyme or evolve only as far as precartilage 1—stages which differ very little from each other. On the other hand, $5\frac{1}{2}$ day old mesenchyme cultured alone can develop into cartilage (stage 5). These results are illustrated by histograms and microphotographs.

It seems, therefore, that the otic mesenchyme must undergo 2 days of epithelial inductive action in order to reach the stage of determination at around $5\frac{1}{2}$ days. Such an estimation of the length of the inductive period *in vitro* can only be approximate, but must be of about the right order. To sum up, a period of about 2 days must elapse for the diffusible inducer substance to bring the mesenchyme up to the stage of determination; this determination is characterized by the capacity of the mesenchyme to evolve into cartilage when cultured alone.

b) *Duration of the inductive capacity of the epithelium*

It has been shown that the otic mesenchyme begins responding to the inductive influence of the epithelium during the 3rd day. The next question was to find out whether the inductive capacity of the auditory labyrinth persists beyond the end of the inductive period (estimated at about 2 days).

We substituted a somewhat older rudiment for the normal one in 48 hours old embryos.

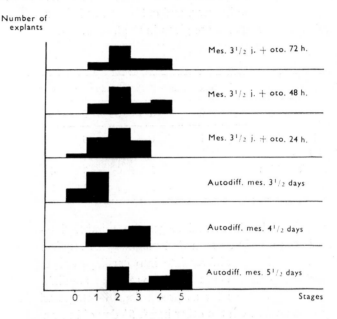

Figure 7 Histograms showing the differentiation of $3\frac{1}{2}$ day old mesenchyme, induced for 72, 48 or 24 hours (above) and auto-differentiation of isolated mesenchyme of various ages (below).

Stages: *0*, mesenchyme; *1, 2, 3*: precartilage (stage 1 differs very little from stage *0*); *4, 5*: cartilage.

Note the presence of cartilage with $3\frac{1}{2}$ day old explants induced for 48 and 72 hours. Controls of the same age remain at the stage of precartilage *0* not very far advanced (stage 1), while mesenchyme of $5\frac{1}{2}$ days undergoes autodifferentiation into cartilage.

When the grafted epithelium is aged 6, 7 or 8 days, it is capable of inducing a cartilaginous capsule (figure 9).

After 9 days, the auditory epithelium is inactive (figure 10). As 8 day epithelium is still inductive, and as the duration of induction is about 2 days, inductive capacity can be taken to last for around 10 days, i.e. a good deal longer than the effective period.

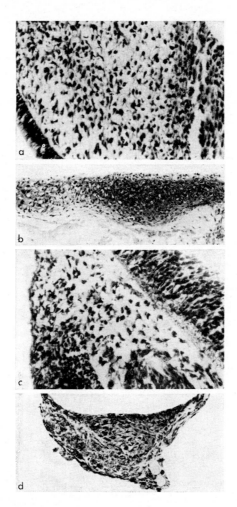

Figure 8 a) mesenchyme of $5\frac{1}{2}$ days ($\times$ 450); b) autodifferentiation of $5\frac{1}{2}$ day old mesenchyme into cartilage ($\times$ 180); c) mesenchyme of $3\frac{1}{2}$ days ($\times$ 450); d) differentiation of a cartilaginous portion (above and in the middle) from a mesenchymal explant of $3\frac{1}{2}$ days induced for 72 hours then isolated.

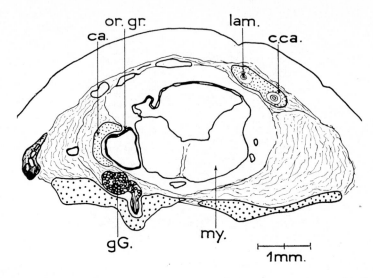

Figure 9 Graft of auditory epithelium, 6 day old. Transverse section passing through the anterior otic region.
ca., induced cartilage; *c.ca.*, otic cartilaginous capsule; canalicular part. *g.G.*, Gasserian ganglion; *lam.*, membranous labyrinth; *my.*, myelencephalon; *or. gr.*, grafted ear.

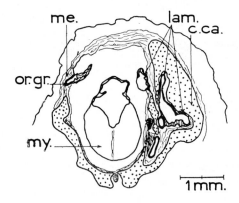

Figure 10 Graft of auditory epithelium, 10 day old.
c.ca., otic cartilaginous capsule; *lam.*, membranous labyrinth; *me.*, mesenchyme; *my.*, myelencephalon; *or. gr.*, grafted ear.

CONCLUSIONS

To sum up, the otic epithelial inducer does not have an absolute specificity but shares its inductive capacity with selected embryonic organs. Mesenchymal competence in turn, is limited to a restricted area, localized between the meninges and the integument. This "qualitative" aspect of induction is still awaiting biochemical confirmation.

But whatever the relative importance of these processes—nature of the activation and role of the mesenchyme—by far the most difficult problems arise with respect to the latter, which concerns the processes involved in the response to induction.

The "quantitative" aspect of the problem has been expressed in terms of a requisite duration of induction. This still obscure notion perhaps implies a certain rate of reaction per cell unit and for the whole tissue.

The solution to some of these outstanding problems should help to provide a further measure of clarification to the principles of specificity, competence and determination.

PART TWO

INFLUENCE OF THE EMBRYONIC BRAIN ON DEVELOPMENT OF BONES OF THE NEUROCRANIUM

The results obtained by STRUDEL (1955) and BENOIT (1960) emphasise the important role played by the neural tube and notochord in the genesis of cartilage. The next question is whether the embryonic brain (which in the early stages is only a simple neural tube surrounded by mesenchyme) possesses the capacity to induce the formation of cranial bones, in the same way as the medulla induces the formation of vertebral arches. This question is all the more interesting, as the cranial bones do not always have the same origin.

In the normal cranium (figure 11), certain bones are preceded by a cartilaginous rudiment. This is true of the basisphenoid, which forms part of the cranial floor, and of the occipital complex, itself made up of the basioccipital, the exoccipital and the supraoccipital, bordering the skull posteriorly.

Other bones make their appearance directly in the dermis, without being preceded by a cartilaginous framework. These are called membrane bones, and include the frontal, parietal and squamosal bones, which constitute the skull roof. The cranial floor consists essentially of the parasphenoid,

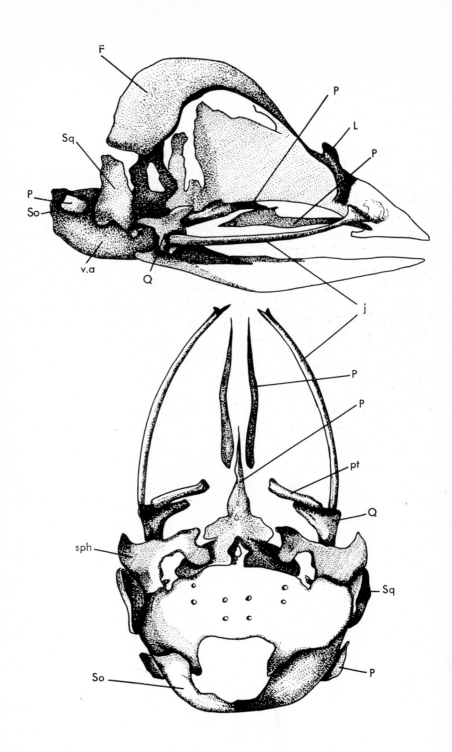

situated in front of the basisphenoid and characterized by an anterior projection or rostrum which is inserted between the palatine bones.

In what way might the embryonic brain be considered to influence the development of these bones?

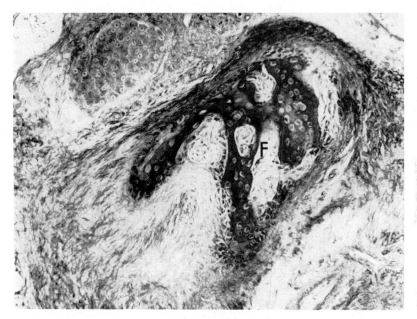

Figure 12 Membrane bone obtained in chorio-allantoic graft from a cephalic mesenchyme of more than 60 hours incubation. (× 160)

Preliminary experiments have shown that the bones of the neurocranium, particularly those of the skull roof, originate from strictly localized cells in the cephalic mesenchyme.

If these presumptive areas are isolated at different stages, and cultured as chorio-allantoic grafts, it is found that explants older than 60 hrs incubation always differentiate into membrane bones (figure 12), while those under 48 hrs never differentiate.

Figure 11 Cranium of a normal embryo.

a) side view; b) dorsal view.

F., frontal; j., jugal arch; L., lacrimal; P., parietal; Pa., palatine; Ps., parasphenoid; pt., pterygoid; Q., quadrate; So., supraoccipital; sph., sphenolateral plate; Sq., squamosal; v.a., auditory vesicle.

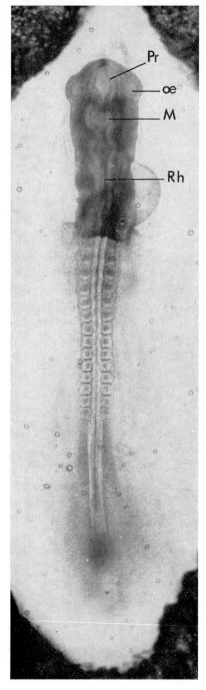

Figure 13   15 somite chick embryo, showing brain rudiments.
Pr., prosencephalon; *M.*, mesencephalon; *Rh.*, rhombencephalon; *oe.*, eye.

This indicates that at some time between 48 and 60 hours incubation, the cephalic mesenchyme must receive an induction which determines its osseous differentiation. If, under these conditions, we remove the embryonic brain before 48 hours incubation, will the cephalic mesenchyme still be capable of differentiating into cranial bones?

EXPERIMENTS ON EXCISION OF VARIOUS BRAIN AREAS

Microsurgery was used for partial or total elimination of the embryonic brain at very early stages. Chick embryos about 45 hours old were used, corresponding to the 15 somite stage; at this stage of development, the embryonic brain consists of three primary vesicles: prosencephalon, mesencephalon and rhombencephalon (figure 13). One, two or all three of these rudiments were excised in the various experiments, some of which also included extirpation of the anterior neural tube.

In the first experimental series, we excised successively: the prosencephalon, prosencephalon plus mesencephalon, then the whole brain.

These experiments were complemented by others where the brain rudiments were excised in the reverse order, i.e.: rhombencephalon, then rhombencephalon plus mesencephalon.

1. Excisions of prosencephalon, prosencephalon plus mesencephalon, and whole brain

These operations generally result in more or less total fusion of the optic rudiments. The embryos are either synophthalmic, i.e. the eyes, though fused with one another, preserve a certain individuality, or cyclops, i.e. the optic rudiments fuse completely to form a single perfectly constituted eye. Synophthalmic embryos can sometimes possess a superior beak, but cyclops never develop in this way. The appearance of these various monstrosities has been described (SCHOWING, 1964, 1965).

The cranial malformations resulting from these operations are more severe, the larger the excised area. Thus excision of the prosencephalon alone leads to reduction of the frontal bones; these disappear completely if both prosencephalon and mesencephalon are excised. In both cases, the other bones of the skull roof remain intact (figure 14). The cranial floor is not affected: only the parasphenoid may be modified if the frontal rudiment is excised with the prosencephalon. The parasphenoid then loses its rostrum

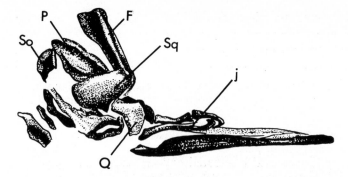

Figure 14 Cranium of a 14 day old chick embryo deprived of prosencephalon and face.
F., frontal; *j.*, jugal arch.; *P.*, parietal; *So.*, supraoccipital; *Sq.*, squamosal; *Q.*, quadrate.

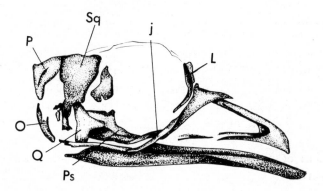

Figure 15 Cranium of a 14 day old chick embryo deprived of prosencephalon and mesencephalon.
j., jugal arch; *L.*, lacrimal; *O.*, occipital arch; *P.*, parietal; *Ps.*, parasphenoid; *Q.*, quadrate; *Sq.*, squamosal.

and this modification is accompanied by a considerable reduction of the palatines.

This modification of the anterior cranial floor depends on the presence or absence of the superior beak. Figure 15 shows the cranium of an embryo deprived of prosencephalon and mesencephalon, but possessing the face. It can be seen that the cranial floor is comparable to that of a normal embryo. On the other hand, the skull roof is characterized by the absence of frontal bones, while the squamosal and parietal bones are intact.

Neurocranial modifications reach a peak when the entire encephalon is removed. In this case, all the bones constituting the skull roof apart from the squamosal, disappear. This is accompanied by disappearance of the supraoccipitals if the anterior neural tube is excised with the brain (figure 16). The exoccipitals, the basioccipital and the basisphenoid are then reduced; they too disappear if the notochord is excised with the neural tissue.

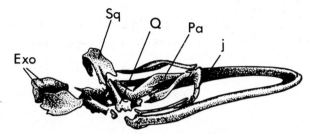

Figure 16 Cranium of a 14 day old chick embryo deprived of whole brain and face. *j.*, jugal arch; *Pa.*, palatine; *Q.*, quadrate; *Sq.*, squamosal. *Exo.*, exoccipital.

2. Excision of rhombencephalon, and rhombencephalon plus mesencephalon

Embryos subjected to these operations are characterized by a shorter superior beak than normal embryos, and by a depression in the dorsal part of the head corresponding to the level of the operation.

If the rhombencephalon is excised alone, the first result is a reduction of the parietal bones (figure 17). The squamosal and frontal bones are not affected. The occipitals and basisphenoid are reduced. The supraoccipitals

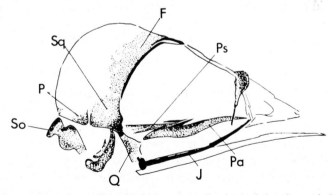

Figure 17 Cranium of a 14 day old chick embryo deprived of rhombencephalon. *F.*, frontal; *j.*, jugal arch; *P.*, parietal; *Pa.*, palatine; *Ps.*, parasphenoid; *Q.*, quadrate; *So.*, supraoccipital; *Sq.*, squamosal.

disappear if the anterior neural tube is excised with the rhombencephalon; the whole occipital complex and basisphenoid disappear if the notochord is also excised.

Disappearance of the parietals comes about following simultaneous excision of the rhombencephalon and mesencephalon (figure 18). It is accompanied by reduction of the squamosals, while the frontals are unaffected. In this case, the occipital and basisphenoid modifications are of the same type as in the preceding experiment.

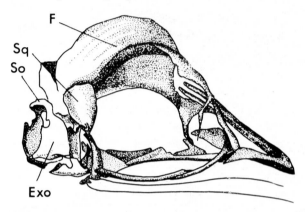

Figure 18 Cranium of a 14 day old chick embryo deprived of mesencephalon and rhombencephalon.
Exo., exoccipital; *F.*, frontal; *So.*, supraoccipital; *Sq.*, squamosal.

It should be noted that disappearance of the parietals is connected with simultaneous excision of the rhombencephalon and mesencephalon, just as disappearance of the frontal bones is connected with simultaneous excision of the prosencephalon and mesencephalon.

In order to try and assess the importance of the mesencephalon in skull development, we carried out excision of the mesencephalon alone. This operation has little repercussion on cranial development; in some cases, the frontal bones carry traces of the operation in their posterior portion, which seems to be telescoped with the anterior portion of the parietals. Thus the mesencephalon does not appear to have a predominant individual role, but rather acts in an auxiliary manner, complementing the influence of the prosencephalon and rhombencephalon. The frontal and parietal bones are thus under the influence of the three primary brain areas, as schematized in figure 19.

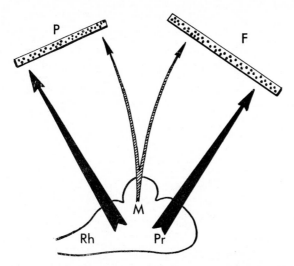

Figure 19 Diagram showing the influences of brain areas on bones of the cranial vault. The frontal bone (*F*) is induced by both actions of the prosencephalon (*Pr*) and the mesencephalon (*M*).
The parietal (*P*) is induced by both actions of the mesencephalon (*M*) and the rhombencephalon (*Rh*).

INVESTIGATIONS ON THE SPECIFICITY OF THE OSTEOGENIC INDUCER

The work of STRUDEL (1955), GROBSTEIN and HOLTZER (1955), BENOIT (1956), LASH, HOLTZER and HOLTZER (1957) shows that the neural tube and notochord are the specific inducers of chick vertebrae. Can it be considered that the osteogenic inducer is also specific? Each primary brain vesicle exerts its action on the bones in its immediate vicinity; is there a neural area other than the brain, capable of determining the appearance of bones in the embryonic head? What happens if one brain area is replaced by another?

We conducted two series of experiments. The first consisted of replacing the entire brain of an embryo by a fragment of neural tube, taken from between the 10th and 20th pair of somites of a donor embryo. The second consisted of excising the whole brain of an embryo, then replacing it after turning it through 180°. The second type of experiment was accompanied by a control: here the embryonic brain was replaced in a normal alignment, some minutes after excision.

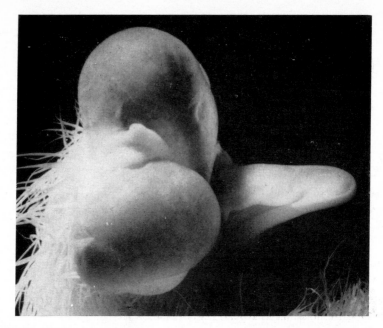

Figure 20 Chick embryo, 14 days, whose brain has been replaced by a fragment of neural tube.
Note the defect in neural tube closure.

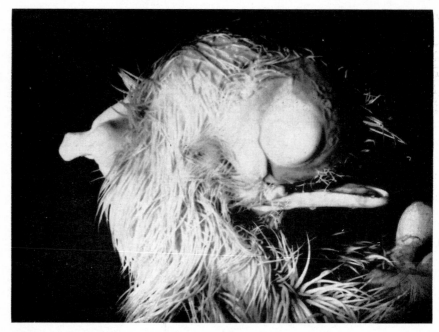

Figure 21 14 day old chick embryo whose brain has been reversed. Note the development of the upper beak, in the occipital region.

1. Substitution of a fragment of neural tube for the brain

These embryos have no face. Their eyes are individualized and are separated by the fragment of neural tube, which is well developed and sometimes shows traces of *spina bifida* (figure 20). The skull has no roof, and only the supraoccipitals and squamosals are present. The cranial floor is modified in the same way as after facial excision; the course of events is just as if the whole brain had been removed.

2. Reversal of brain position

While the control embryos present no cranial malformations, the experimental embryos are peculiar in possessing a rudiment of superior beak in the occipital region of the head (figure 21). The position of the eyes is normal; they are separated in this case by the rhombencephalon. The whole is covered by a normal epidermis. The inferior beak is well developed.

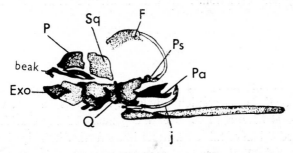

Figure 22   Cranium of a 14 day old chick embryo, after reversal of brain.
Exo., exoccipital; *F.*, frontal; *j.*, jugal arch; *P.*, parietal; *Pa.*, palatine; *Ps.*, parasphenoid; *Q.*, quadrate; *Sq.*, squamosal.

The skull roof in these embryos is greatly reduced (figure 22). It is composed of the squamosals, reduced in their dorsal portion, the frontal bones, reduced to two plates on each side of the mesencephalon, and the parietals which cover the prosencephalon. It thus seems as if the rhombencephalon were incapable of inducing frontal bones at its level, the latter only appearing in the mesencephalic region. Similarly, the parietals are not induced by the prosencephalon. If the prosencephalon is substituted for the rhombencephalon of the same embryo, after removal of the mesencephalon, the cranium which results is identical to that of an embryo deprived of its whole brain. The frontals and parietals seen in this experimental series thus owe their presence to that of the mesencephalon.

CONCLUSIONS

Replacement of the embryonic brain by a fragment of neural tube does not favour development of the roof of the skull. It is thereby deduced that the osteogenic inducer is specific and that axial nervous tissue cannot replace brain nervous tissue.

Experiments in which the brain is reversed, or the prosencephalon substituted for the rhombencephalon of the same embryo, give results which complicate the problem still further. They show that there is not one cerebral inducer of the cranial bones, but several, corresponding in localization to the primary brain vesicles. It seems that the rhombencephalon cannot induce the formation of the frontal bones, which only develop in the immediate vicinity of the mesencephalon. Similarly, the parietals only differentiate if the mesencephalon is nearby. Removal of the mesencephalon leads to disappearance of the parietals, as the prosencephalon is incapable of inducing their formation. These conclusions are summarized in a scheme complementary to the one in figure 19 (figure 23).

Each encephalic inducer acts specifically on one or more determined osseous rudiments. If we also take into account the actions of the notochord and neural tube on the cranial floor and occipital complex, we obtain a general scheme indicating the various phenomena of induction leading to formation of the neurocranium (figure 24). On this scheme, we see that the squamosal bone appears to be independent of any outside influence. The disputed origin of this bone necessitates further investigation.

These experimental results demonstrate the complexity of induction phenomena. The inducers are not arrowly localized; a relatively large area has to be excised to bring about the disappearance of a particular bony area. For example, disappearance of the whole occipital complex is only obtained by ablation of the rhombencephalon, the anterior neural tube, and the notochord—an enormous area relative to the small size of the embryo at the stage of operation.

In cranial development, the contents induce the container; in this way, the brain surrounds itself with a means of protection, in which it finally becomes imprisoned. The skull does not actually hinder brain growth, but as has been shown by HUBER (1957), it limits the direction of expansion; this is shown by a rearrangement of the cerebral hemispheres, which come to occupy a more posterior position.

The complexity of cranial structure is thus demonstrated, as well as the great malleability of its component parts.

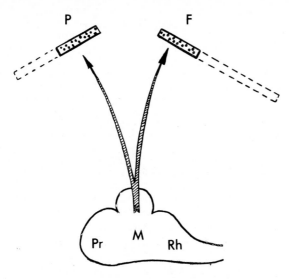

Figure 23 Diagram showing the influences of brain areas on bones of the cranial vault when the brain has been reversed through 180°. The frontal (*F*) is under the single influence of the mesencephalon (*M*). The rhombencephalon (*Rh*) has no action on it. The parietal (*P*) is under the single influence of the mesencephalon (*M*), the prosencephalon (*Pr*) having no action on it.

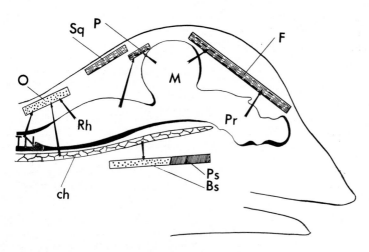

Figure 24 General diagram showing the various inductive actions of the brain and notochrod on the bones of the neurocranium.

References

Part One

BENOIT, J. A. A. (1955). De l'excision de l'otocyste chez l'embryon de poulet et ses conséquences sur la morphogenèse de la capsule otique cartilageneuse. *Compt. Rend. Soc. Biol.*, **149**, 998–1000.

BENOIT, J. A. A. (1956). Chondrogenèse otique après excision de l'otocyste et implantation de moelle et de chorde chez l'embryon de poulet. *Compt. Rend. Soc. Biol.*, **150**, 240–242.

BENOIT, J. A. A. (1957 *a*). Absence de chondrogenèse otique après remplacement de l'otocyste par le cristallin ou un grain de paraffine. *Compt. Rend. Soc. Biol.*, **151**, 1298–1300.

BENOIT, J. A. A. (1957 *b*). Irradiation localisée de l'otocyste chez les embryons de poulet et de truite. *Bull. Soc. Zool. Fr.*, **82**, *238–243*.

BENOIT, J. A. A. (1960). Etude expérimentale des facteurs de l'induction du cartilage otique chez les embryons de poulet et de truite. *Ann. Sci. Nat. Zool.*, 12ᵉ Série **2**, 323–385.

BENOIT, J. A. A. (1963). Chronologie de l'induction du cartilage otique chez l'embryon de poulet. *Arch. Anat. Micro.*, **52**, n° 4, 573–590.

HAMBURGER, V., and HAMILTON, H. L. (1951). A series of normal stages in the development of the chick embryo. *J. Morphol.*, **88**, 49–92.

LEVI-MONTALCINI, R. (1946). Ricerche sperimentali sulla determinazione del placode otico nell' embrione di pollo. *Rend. Accad. Nazl. Lincei*, ser, 8, 1, 443–448.

RAVEN, C. P. (1936). Zur Entwicklung der Ganglienleiste. V. Über Differenzierung des Rumpfganglienleisten-Materials. *Arch. Entwicklungsmech. Organ*, **134**, 122–146.

REAGAN, F. P. (1915). A genetic interpretation of the stapes, based on a study of avian embryos in which the development of the cartilaginous otic capsule has been experimentally inhibited. *Proc. Am. Assoc. Anat.*, **9**, 114–115.

REAGAN, F. P. (1917). The role of auditory sensory epithelium in the formation of the stapedial plate. *J. Exp. Zool.*, **23**, 85–108.

SENO, T., and NIEUWKOOP, P. D. (1958). The autonomous and dependent differentiations of the neural crest in Amphibians. *Koninkl. Ned. Akad. Wetenschap., Proc., Ser. C*, **61**, 489–498.

WADDINGTON, C. H. (1937). The determination of the auditory placode in the chick. *J. Exp. Biol.*, **14**, 232–239.

WADDINGTON, C. H. (1954). *Principles of Embryology*, London, G. Allen & Unwin Ltd.

WOLFF, E., HAFFEN, K. (1951). Sur la culture *in vitro* des glandes génitales des embryons d'oiseau: obtention de la différenciation sexuelle normale et de l'intersexualité expérimentale de gonades explantées. *C. R. Acad. Sci.*, **233**, 439–441.

WOLFF, E., HAFFEN, K. (1952). Sur une méthode de culture d'organes embryonnaires *in vitro*. *Texas Rep. Biol. Med.*, **10**, 463–472.

WOLFF, E., WOLFF, Em. (1960). Mise en évidence de substances favorables à la prolifération des cellules cancéreuses dans le rein embryonnaire de poulet. *C.R. Acad. Sci.*, **250**, 4076–4077.

Part Two

BENOIT, J. A. A. (1956). Chondrogenèse otique après excision de l'otocyste et implantation de moelle ou de chorde chez l'embryon de Poulet. *Compt. Rend. Soc. Biol.*, **150**, 2, 240–242.

BENOIT, J. A. A. (1960). Etude expérimentale des facteurs de l'induction du cartilage otique chez les embryons de Poulet et de Truite. *Ann. Sc. Nat. Zool.*, **12**, II, 323–385.

GROBSTEIN, C., and HOLTZER, H. (1955). "In vitro" studies of cartilage induction in mouse somites mesoderm. *J. Exp. Zool.*, **128**, 333–357.

HUBER, W. (1957). Analyse experimentale des facteurs topogénétiques qui régissent la formation de l'encéphale et de la tête chez l'embryon de poulet. *Arch. Anat. Microscop. Morphol. Exp.*, **46**, 325–405.

LASH, J., HOLTZER, S. and HOLTZER, H. (1957). An experimental analysis of the development of the spinal column. Aspects of cartilage induction. *Exp. Cell. Res.*, **13**, 292–303.

SCHOWING, J. (1964). Modalités d'obtention expèrimentale de monstres cyclopes par microchirurgie chez l'embryon de Poulet. *C.R. Acad. Sci., Paris*, **259**, 2020–2023.

SCHOWING, J. (1965). Obtention expérimentale de cyclopes parfaits par microchirurgie chez l'embryon de Poulet. Etude histologique. *J. Embryol. Exp. Morphol.*, **14**, 255–263.

STRUDEL, G. (1955). L'action morphogène du tube nerveux et de la chorde sur la différenciation des vertèbres et des muscles vertébraux chez l'embryon de poulet. *Arch. Anat. Microscop. Morphol. Exp.*, **44**, 209–235.

CHAPTER VI

INDUCTION PHENOMENA
IN LUNG ORGANOGENESIS IN CHICK EMBRYO

F. Dameron

Institut d'Embryologie expérimentale du Collège de France et du C.N.R.S.,
Nogent-sur-Marne

I INTRODUCTION

TWO IMPORTANT events take place during the initial stages of lung organogenesis in chick embryo.

a) The first of these occurs at a very early stage, and consists of an evagination of the pharyngeal endoderm into the neighbouring mesenchyme; this takes place at about 52 hours incubation. The two narrow pouches thus formed are the lung rudiments, and consist of a mesodermal sac enveloping an endodermal tubule or future bronchus.

b) The second step takes place at the start of the 5th day of incubation; the first endodermal ramifications now appear (plate I, figures 4 and 5), and these subsequently give rise to the whole bronchial tree which will later fulfil respiratory functions.

We wanted to find out how the lung becomes organized from its two components, epithelial and mesenchymal. What factors determine the differentiation of each component? Are there inductive interactions between the two tissues, as has been found for other organs of dual origin?

To try and answer these questions, we studied morphogenetic processes in 5 day old lung rudiments.

II MATERIAL AND METHODS

White Leghorn chick embryos were used.

We used the organotypic culture method of WOLFF and HAFFEN (1952), enriching the standard medium with serum (Et. WOLFF and Em. WOLFF,

9*   131

1952). Explants were cultured for 4 to 6 days on a fragment of hen's egg vitelline membrane spread out on the culture medium.

In certain cases, drawings were made using a camera lucida, in order to follow explant development during culture.

In some experiments, the explants were cultured for a longer period using the *in ovo* graft technique, so as to reach a more advanced stage of development. In this case, epithelium and mesenchyme were cultured together *in vitro* for 18 hours, then introduced into the coelomic cavity of a 3 day old embryo, or grafted onto the chorio-allantoic membrane of a 7 day embryo.

The bronchus was separated from its mesenchymal envelope by trypsin treatment, using a technique derived from that of Moscona (1952).

At the end of the experiment, most explants were prepared for histological study; they were fixed in Bouin's fluid, then stained with hemalum and Gabe. Some were stained *in toto* using alcoholic carmine hydrochloride.

III DEVELOPMENT OF THE LUNG IN "IN VITRO" CULTURE

Lung rudiments were removed and explanted between 114 and 120 hours incubation, i.e. just at the start of bronchial differentiation. At this time, the rudiments of the two first secondary bronchi, or entobronchi, can be distinguished; they arise as two small dilatations, about the middle of the primary bronchus (plate I, figure 4).

The morphological development of these explants *in vitro* is shown on figure 1. The mesenchyme, which appears homogenous when taken from the embryo, becomes reorganised into two layers during culture; one part condenses along the bronchus, the rest disperses towards the periphery. The mesobronchus grows and ramifies. The secondary bronchi, already present in rudimentary form, develop. New buds appear, especially between the 2nd and 4th days of culture. But the form and spatial distribution of the projections are modified, as growth is principally in a single plane.

Histological study (plate I, figure 6) shows that the epithelium has proliferated intensely, and has formed numerous ramifications. It has differentiated into columnar or pseudostratified epithelium, with tall closely packed cells.

Although morphogenesis is somewhat slower than in normal development, there is still very clear differentiation of the lung rudiment under conditions of *in vitro* culture.

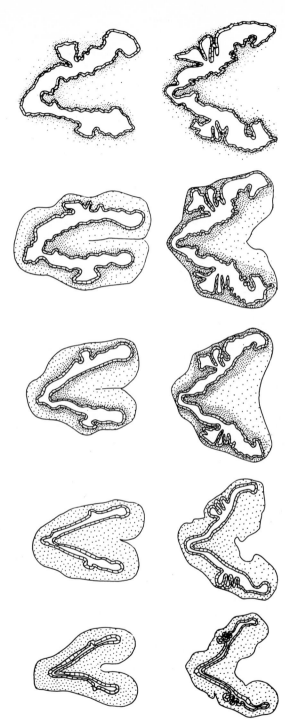

Figure 1 Morphological development of lung rudiments explanted at 114 and 120 hours incubation, during 4 days culture. Drawings made using camera lucida, at time of explantation, then after 24, 48, 72 and 96 hours culture. Note condensation of the mesenchyme around the epithelium, the growth and ramification of the bronchi.

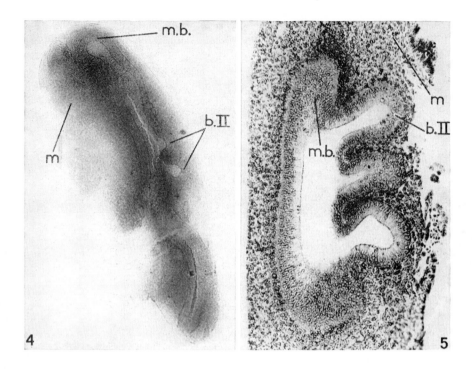

PLATE 1

Figure 4 Five day old lung rudiment stained *in toto* with alcoholic carmine HCl. Note the two first secondary bronchi (entobronchi) towards the middle of the primary bronchus (mesobronchus) (× 88).

Figure 5 Histological appearance of a six day old lung rudiment. Longitudinal section, showing the rudiments of the three first secondary bronchi (entobronchi). The mesobronchus is sectioned at its two extremities (× 240).

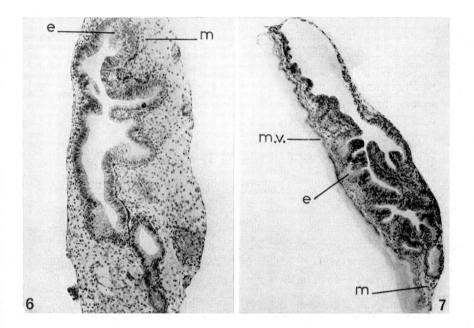

PLATE I

Figure 6 Histological appearance after 5 days culture of a lung rudiment, explanted at 114 hours incubation. Longitudinal section. Differentiation and ramification of the bronchus ($\times$ 160).

Figure 7 Histological appearance after 5 days culture of an association of lung epithelium and mesenchyme. Differentiation and ramification of the bronchial epithelium ($\times$ 120). *b. II.*, secondary bronchus; *e.*, bronchial epithelium; *m.*, pulmonary mesenchyme; *m.b.*, mesobronchus; *m.v.*, vitelline membrane.

IV DEMONSTRATION OF INTERACTIONS BETWEEN LUNG EPITHELIUM AND MESENCHYME

1. In chick

We wanted to find out whether the epithelial and mesenchymal components were able to differentiate independently of each other.

RUDNICK (1933) showed that if the mesodermal envelope is almost wholly removed from 4 and 5 day old lung rudiments, they are unable to develop any further when grafted onto a chorio-allantoic membrane: the epithelial rudiment does not ramify.

We repeated these experiments *in vitro*, using a technique by which the two pulmonary components could be kept completely separate.

a) *Development of the bronchial epithelium in the absence of lung mesenchyme*

73 bronchi were cultured as isolated preparations; all became disorganised, with dedifferentiation and necrosis of the epithelium.

Even when several epithelial tubules were cultured together, they were unable to differentiate in the absence of mesenchyme.

b) *Development of lung mesenchyme in the absence of bronchial epithelium*

Fragments of lung mesenchyme were associated (11 associations) on culture media in the absence of bronchial epithelium. The mesenchyme gradually spread out on the vitelline membrane, and after 5 days of culture, was completely dispersed.

c) *Influence of lung mesenchyme on morphogenesis of the bronchus*

If the two components are reassociated, morphogenetic processes are reestablished: out of a total of 191 explants, 180 developed. The morphological development (figure 2) of these associations is comparable to that of an intact lung rudiment *in vitro*. The mesenchymal fragments associated with the bronchus fuse in the first 48 hours of culture; part of the mesenchyme forms a sheath around the bronchus, impeding epithelial dispersion. The bronchus grows, widens, and begins to bud after the 2nd day of culture.

Histological study (plate I, figure 7) shows that the epithelium has proliferated intensely and has formed numerous ramifications. It has

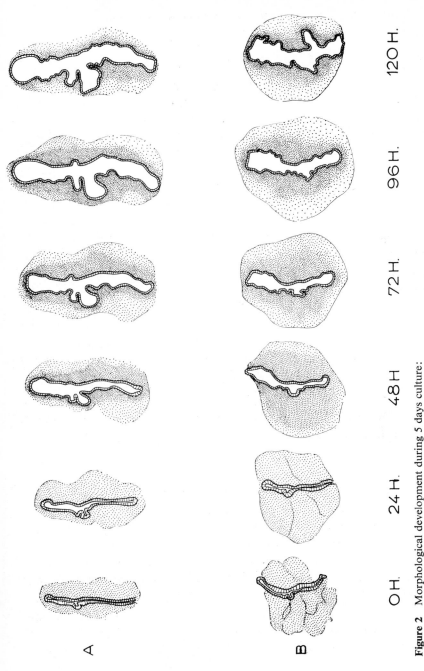

Figure 2 Morphological development during 5 days culture:
A—a normal lung;   B—an association of lung mesenchyme and epithelium.
Drawings made using camera lucida, at time of explantation, then after 24, 48, 72, 96 and 120 hours culture. In both cases, condensation of the mesenchyme around the bronchial epithelium as well as growth and ramification of the bronchus can be observed.

differentiated into pseudostratified epithelium in the primary bronchus, and cuboidal epithelium in the newly formed secondary bronchi.

Thus lung morphogenesis can only come about when both components are united; interactions take place between the epithelium and the mesenchyme which are essential for lung growth and differentiation.

2. In mice

Similar interactions have been demonstrated in mouse embryo lung by ALESCIO and CASSINI (1962). Using trypsin, they isolate the bronchial epithelium of 11 day old embryos, including a portion of tracheal epithelium; the explant is placed on a culture medium and surrounded with fragments of pulmonary mesenchyme. The authors observe that explant morphogenesis progresses in accord with normal lung development; however, they also note the formation of buds arising from the tracheal epithelium, which does not take place under normal conditions. It was found possible to reproduce this phenomenon in 50% of cases, by establishing contact between the tracheal epithelium and the bronchial mesenchyme (plate II, figure 8).

These results demonstrate the existence of epithelio-mesenchymal interactions during development of the lung rudiment: they also indicate that adjacent and apparently homogenous mesenchymal regions, such as the tracheal and bronchial mesenchymes, may not have the same inductive activities.

V NATURE OF EPITHELIO-MESENCHYMAL INTERACTIONS DURING LUNG ORGANOGENESIS

Our next question concerned the nature of epithelio-mesenchymal interactions taking place in the lung rudiment: is tissue contact between the epithelium and the mesenchyme essential for bronchial morphogenesis? To determine this we cultured the two reactive tissues together, but kept them apart by a dialysing membrane.

1. Development of the bronchus separated from the lung mesenchyme by a vitelline membrane

We used hen's egg vitelline membrane, following the technique of WOLFF (1960). The procedure is as follows: (figure 3): the mesenchyme is deposited directly onto the culture medium then covered with a fragment of vitelline

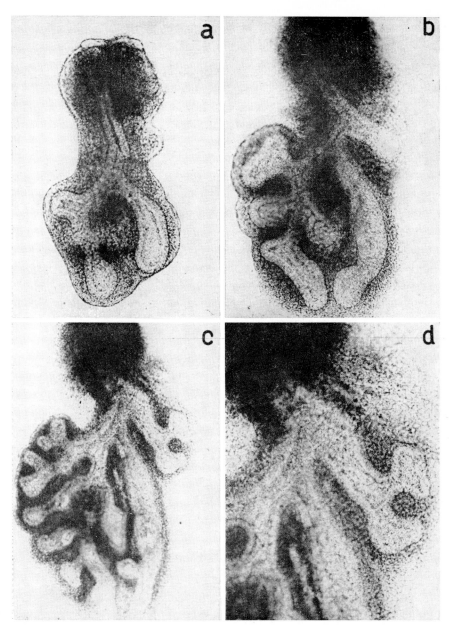

PLATE II

Figure 8   Plate taken from *J. Exp. Zool.*, 1962, **150**, 83–94.

membrane. The bronchus is laid on top of the membrane, just above the mesenchyme.

21 bronchi were cultured under these conditions.

—13 of them retained their tubular structure (see plate III, figure 9); the epithelium was healthy and columnar, and had formed digitations or folds.

—the 8 other bronchi became spread out on the vitelline membrane (see plate III, figure 10); however, the epithelium was organised into

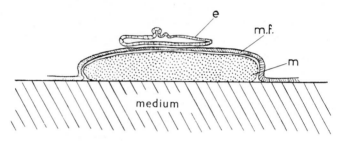

Figure 3 Scheme showing the technique of culture, with interposition of a membrane filter. The mesenchyme, deposited on the culture medium, is covered with the membrane. The epithelium is placed on the membrane, just above the mesenchyme.
e., bronchial epithelium; *m.*, lung mesenchyme; *m.f.*, membrane filter.

columnar form, and had produced a certain number of folds, indicating a fair degree of epithelial proliferation. This level of organisation and proliferation was never observed in bronchi cultured alone.

To sum up, the bronchus separated from the lung mesenchyme by a vitelline membrane does undergo some degree of morphogenesis; there is, however, less differentiation than that seen when the two tissues are in direct contact.

2. Conclusions

In conclusion, direct contact between the lung epithelium and mesenchyme is not essential for bronchial morphogenesis. The latter takes place under the influence of an inductive substance synthesised by the mesenchyme. This substance diffuses towards the epithelium, initiating its differentiation.

The mesenchyme normally provides some physical support, and this plays quite an important part in maintaining the tubular organisation of the bronchus. It also facilitates the development of epithelial ramifications, by providing them with a supporting tissue framework.

VI SPECIFICITY OF EPITHELIO-MESENCHYMAL INTERACTIONS: DEVELOPMENT OF THE BRONCHUS IN CONTACT WITH HETEROLOGOUS MESENCHYMES

Having established the morphogenetic activity of the pulmonary mesenchyme in bronchial differentiation, we wanted to find out whether this differentiation could also be induced by other tissues of mesodermal origin (DAMERON, 1961 and 1966).

If the bronchus is placed in contact with a heterologous mesenchyme, will it develop according to its innate potentialities, or will its morphogenesis be modified depending on the nature of the associated mesenchyme?

We tested the influence of various mesenchymes, of widely differing origin and type:

1) mesenchymes of the same embryological origin as the lung mesenchyme, such as those of the digestive tract (proventriculus, gizzard, intestine);

2) specialised mesenchymes of various types, such as those of the skin, metanephros, mesonephros, head and allantois;

3) a very primitive mesenchyme, the somitic mesenchyme;

4) a homologous xenoplastic mesenchyme, mouse lung mesenchyme.

The associations were carried out either *in vitro*, and cultured for 5 or 6 days, or as a graft *in ovo* following a brief 18 hour culture *in vitro*. The second procedure enables explants to reach a more advanced developmental stage.

1. Influence of the lung mesenchyme on morphogenesis of the bronchus grafted "in ovo"

We know the way in which the bronchus develops in association with its own mesenchyme *in vitro*.

Figure 11 (plate III) shows what happens to a similar association grafted *in ovo* after a brief period *in vitro* culture: the graft vascularises rapidly, and soon attains a large size. The bronchus ramifies profusely in the loose mesenchyme; mesobronchus, secondary bronchi and parabronchi, and air sacs are recognisable. Growth is very similar to that of a lung developing under normal conditions, but the morphological aspect is atypical.

2. Influence of digestive tract mesenchymes, having the same embryological origin as the lung mesenchyme

Proventriculus, gizzard, intestine.

Interactions are rapidly established between the bronchial epithelium and the associated mesenchyme.

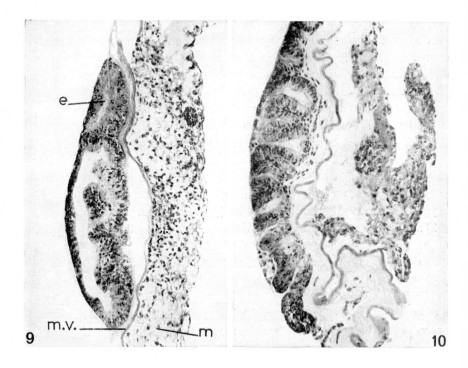

PLATE III

Figures 9 and **10** Interposition of a vitelline membrane between the lung epithelium and mesenchyme. Histological appearance after 5 days culture.

Figure 9 The bronchial epithelium has differentiated, particularly on the mesenchymal side, and has proliferated forming folds (× 225).

Figure 10 The tubular structure of the bronchus is no longer recognisable but the epithelium has differentiated and formed numerous folds (× 250).

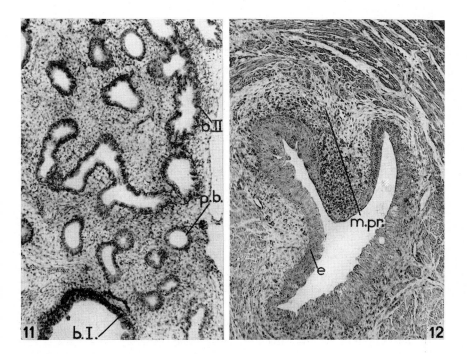

PLATE III

Figure 11 Bronchus associated with pulmonary mesenchyme. Histological appearance after 18 hours *in vitro* culture followed by 6 days *in ovo*. Intense morphogenesis (× 105).

Figure 12 Bronchus associated with proventriculus mesenchyme. Histological appearance after 18 hours *in vitro* culture and 6 days as a graft. The bronchus is pluristratified; it is surroundet by muscular layers which have differentiated in the proventriculus mesenchyme (× 164).

b. I., primary bronchus; *b. II.*, secondary bronchus; *e.*, bronchial epithelium; *m.*, pulmonary mesenchyme; *m.pr.*, proventriculus mesenchyme; *m.v.*, vitelline membrane; *p.b.*, parabronchus.

In contact with proventriculus mesenchyme, the bronchus becomes stratified. It develops folds or villi, but does not form true ramifications. The mesenchyme (plate III, figure 12) gives rise to muscular structures around the bronchus which can impede ramification.

Bronchial development in gizzard or intestinal mesenchyme is fairly similar. Surrounded by a muscular sheath, the bronchus does not ramify, but forms intestinal-like folds; it is made up of stratified epithelium.

To sum up, bronchial morphology appears to be modified under the influence of these mesenchymes; it takes on the appearance of a digestive tract, both as a graft *in ovo* and in culture, development being more pronounced *in ovo*.

3. Influence of specialized mesenchymes from other organs

a) *Dermal mesenchyme*

In presence of dermis, all 28 bronchi cultured differentiated. There was intense proliferation of the columnar epithelium, and numerous ramifications were formed (plate IV, figure 13). Morphogenesis was marked.

In 6 explants cultured *in vitro*, a vitelline membrane was interposed between the dermis and the bronchial epithelium. 2 explants remained structurally intact, and 4 partially lost their integrity. However, the epithelium differentiated and proliferated in all cases (see plate IV, figure 14). The dermis therefore acts on the bronchial epithelium via the medium of a diffusible morphogenetic substance.

b) *Metanephric mesenchyme*

When associated with metanephric mesenchyme, bronchi cultured *in vitro* differentiated in 17 out of 23 instances, and in 7 out of 12 cases *in ovo*. The bronchial epithelium thinned and became cuboidal; it proliferated well in culture. But the most interesting changes were obtained *in ovo*: the bronchus forms a simple tubule, with one or two layers of cells; it exercises a reciprocal induction on the mesenchyme, which differentiates secretory tubules and glomeruli (plate IV, figure 15). These results confirm those of GROBSTEIN (1953a, 1953b, 1955); the salivary epithelium and neural tube are equally capable of inducing differentiation of the metanephric mesenchyme. BISHOP-CALAME (1966) obtains the converse effect: the ureter, developing in pulmonary mesenchyme, induces the latter to form renal tubules.

We interposed a vitelline membrane between the metanephric mesenchyme and the bronchial epithelium. Out of 21 explants, 12 preserved their structure while the 9 others became spread out. However, the epithelium remained healthy in all cases; the cells were cuboidal. There was proliferation, and formation of folds (plate IV, figure 16). The metanephric mesenchyme is thus capable of influencing the bronchus at a distance.

c) *Other mesenchymes tested*

The mesonephric, cephalic, and allantoic mesenchymes, and a primitive mesenchyme—the somitic—have no morphogenetic activity on the bronchial epithelium; in contact with these mesenchymes, the bronchus consistently developed into a thin-walled vesicle (plate V, figure 17).

d) *Conclusions*

The bronchus responds to the induction of a few heterologous specialised mesenchymes: the dermal and metanephric mesenchyme enable it to differentiate, acting via the medium of a diffusible morphogenetic substance. Alternatively, other mesenchymes tested—particularly the mesonephric—are unfavourable for bronchial development.

4. Homologous, xenoplastic mesenchyme: mouse lung mesenchyme

Lastly, we wanted to find out whether the chick lung rudiment was capable of developing in a xenoplastic mesenchyme, such as mouse lung mesenchyme.

Explant survival is limited, as mouse tissues tend to necrose rapidly. However 12 out of 17 explants developed, as did 4 out of 5 grafts. In all instances, the bronchus differentiated into pseudostratified epithelium and ramified. It developed numerous buds, particularly *in ovo* (plate V, figures 18 and 19), the appearance being typically pulmonary. Budding was either monopodic or dichotomous (it is interesting to recall that ramification normally proceeds monopodically in chicks and dichotomously in mice).

The affinities and collaboration between mouse lung mesenchyme and chick bronchus show that, in a chimera, tissue homologies are more important than zoological differences.

5. Conclusions

Interactions which do not exist under normal conditions become established between the bronchial epithelium and various heterologous mesenchymes associated with it.

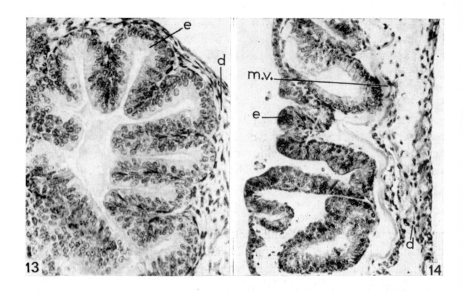

PLATE IV

Figure 13 Bronchus associated with dermis. Histological appearance after 5 days culture. Differentiation and ramification of the bronchial epithelium (× 420).

Figure 14 Bronchus associated with dermis, with a vitelline membrane between the two tissues. Histological appearance after 5 days culture. The dermis acts at a distance on the bronchial epithelium which has differentiated and ramified (× 245).

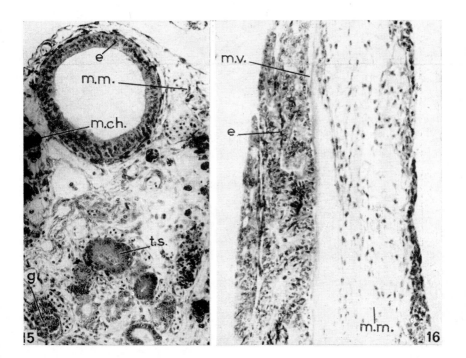

PLATE IV

Figure 15 Bronchus associated with metanephric mesenchyme. Histological appearance after 18 hours culture and 5 days as a graft. The bronchus is a simple tube, of a columnar to pseudostratified epithelium. Note the differentiation of secretory tubules and glomeruli in the metanephric mesenchyme (× 252).

Figure 16 Vitelline membrane interposed between the two tissues: the metanephric mesenchyme acts at a distance on the bronchial epithelium which has differentiated and proliferated (× 300).

d., dermis; *e.*, bronchial epithelium; *g.*, glomerulus; *m.ch.*, carbon marker; *m.m.*, metanephric mesenchyme; *m.v.*, vitelline membrane; *t.s.*, secretory tubules.

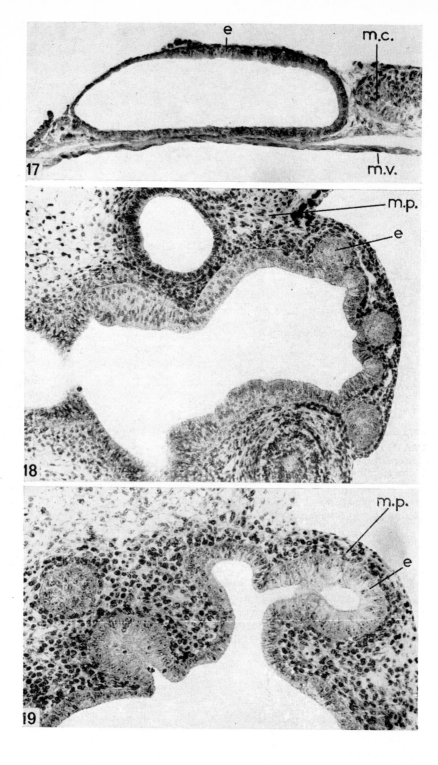

PLATE V

Figure 17 Bronchus associated with cephalic mesenchyme. Histological appearance after 5 days culture. Swelling of bronchus ($\times$ 256).

Figures 18–19 Bronchus associated with mouse lung mesenchyme.

Figure 18 Histological appearance after 18 hours culture and 5 days as a graft. The chick bronchial epithelium is pluristratified. It has formed numerous buds ($\times$ 200).

Figure 19 Histological appearance after 18 hours culture and 5 days as a graft. Detail showing, on right, dichotomous budding, and on left, a monopodic bud. The buds have a typical pulmonary appearance ($\times$ 256).
e., bronchial epithelium; *m.c.*, cephalic mesenchyme; *m.p.*, lung mesenchyme; *m.v.*, vitelline membrane.

In contact with this epithelium, most mesenchymes differentiate character-istically: they are already determined at the time of explantation. This is so for, e.g., the digestive tract and metanephric mesenchymes.

The bronchus cannot develop without mesenchymal induction, and behaves in various ways, depending on the circumstances.

a) Certain mesenchymes, the cephalic, mesonephric, allantoic and somitic, do not allow the bronchus to develop; it swells into a thin-walled vesicle or regresses.

b) Other mesenchymes, with the same embryological origin as the lung mesenchyme (proventriculus, gizzard, intestine), and others of very different type (dermis, metanephros) allow the rudiment to develop but modify its structural organisation. These mesenchymes can act at a distance, via the medium of a diffusible morphogenetic substance.

c) Lastly, the bronchus can only differentiate along typical pulmonary lines in contact with chick or mouse lung mesenchyme. The mode of budding and cell differentiation are characteristic, but the morphogenetic aspect of explants is disturbed by tissue treatments and developmental conditions.

VI CONCLUSIONS

Like many other embryonic rudiments, lung morphogenesis comes about through inductive interactions between the epithelium and its corresponding mesenchyme.

These interactions can be exercised at a distance by a diffusible morphogen-etic substance elaborated by the mesenchyme, whose nature is still unknown.

Characteristic differentiation of the bronchus comes about specifically under the influence of the lung mesenchyme.

The bronchus can still develop in contact with certain heterologous mesenchymes, but the latter modify its structural organisation.

References

ALESCIO, T., and CASSINI, A. (1962). Induction "in vitro" of tracheal buds by pulmonary mesenchyme grafted on tracheal epithelium. *J. Exp. Zool.*, **150**, 83–94.

CALAME-BISHOP, S. (1966). Etude expérimentale de l'organogenèse du système uro-génital de l'embryon de poulet. *Arch. Anat. Microscop. Morphol. Exp.*, **55**, 215–309.

DAMERON, F. (1961). L'influence de divers mésenchymes sur la différenciation de l'épithé-lium pulmonaire de l'embryon de poulet en culture *in vitro*. *J. Embryol. Exp. Morpholog.*, **9**, 628–633.

DAMERON, F. (1966). Etude de la morphogenèse de la bronche de l'embryon de poulet associée à différents mésenchymes en culture *in vitro* C. R. Acad. Sci., **262**, 1642–1645.

GROBSTEIN, C. (1953). Epitheliomesenchymal specificity in the morphogenesis of mouse submandibular rudiments *in vitro*. J. Exp. Zool., **124**, 383–414.

GROBSTEIN, C. (1953). Morphogenetic interaction between embryonic mouse tissues separated by a membrane filter. *Nature* (London), **172**, 869–870.

GROBSTEIN, C. (1955). Inductive interaction in the development of the mouse metanephros. J. Exp. Zool., **130**, 319–340.

MOSCONA, A. A. (1952). Cell suspensions from organ rudiments of chick embryo. *Exp. Cell. Res.*, **3**, 535–539.

RUDNICK, D. (1933). Developmental capacities of the chick lung in chorioallantoic grafts. J. Exp. Zool., **66**, 125–153.

WOLFF, Et. (1960). Sur une nouvelle modalité de la culture organotypique. *C. R. Acad. Sci.*, Paris, **250**, 3881–3882.

WOLFF, Et., and HAFFEN, K. (1952). Sur une méthode de culture d'organes embryonnaires *in vitro*. *Tex. Rep. Biol. Med.*, **10**, 463–472.

WOLFF, Et., and WOLFF, Em. (1952). Le déterminisme de la différenciation sexuelle de la syrinx de canard cultivée *in vitro*. *Bull. Biol. de la France et de la Belgique*. **86**, 325–350.

CHAPTER VII

STUDY OF STOMACH MORPHOGENESIS IN CHICK EMBRYO

M. Sigot

Laboratoire d'Embryologie expérimentale Collège de France and C.N.R.S.,
Nogent-sur-Marne

THE STOMACH of birds consists of two parts: an anterior, glandular part—the proventriculus, or succenturiate ventriculus, and a caudal muscular part—the gizzard. The two parts differ physiologically and morphologically. The glands of the proventriculus secrete digestive enzymes, while the gizzard, which is primarily a grinding organ, has no digestive secretions; its muscular activity replaces mastication.

At 5 days incubation, the avian stomach resembles the pulmonary rudiment in structure; it is tubular, with walls made up of two types of tissue (figure 1, plate I)—columnar epithelium on the inside, and mesenchyme on the outside. The proventriculus glands begin to form on the 6th day of incubation, starting as an invagination of the epithelium into the surrounding mesenchyme; in this way the organ acquires its characteristic morphology. At the same stage, the gizzard undergoes little in the way of morphological changes, apart from a certain degree of epithelial thickening (SJÖGREN, 1941 and HIBBARD, 1942).

At 7 days incubation—a stage of active gland formation—the proventriculus and gizzard differ greatly in their glycogen content and mucus secretion. The epithelium of the proventriculus contains little or no glycogen and secretes very little mucus. Gizzard epithelium, on the contrary, is rich in glycogen and secretes large quantities of mucus (figure 2, plate II). Glycogen is detected by Hotchkiss-MacManus or P.A.S. staining, after fixation in Rossmann's fluid (SIGOT, 1963).

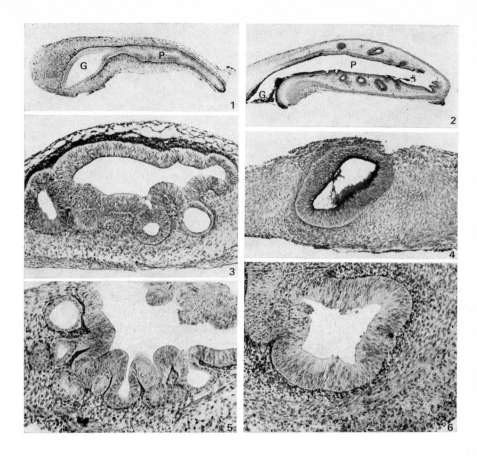

PLATE I

Figure 1 Stomach, 5 days incubation. Longitudinal section. Left—gizzard, right—proventriculus. Stain: Groat's haematoxylin, eosin (× 52).

Figure 2 Stomach, 7 days incubation. Longitudinal section. Left—beginning of gizzard, right—proventriculus. Stain: P.A.S. (× 37).

Figure 3 Proventriculus, 5 days incubation, cultured *in vitro*. Stain: P.A.S. (× 205).

Figure 4 Gizzard, 5 days incubation, cultured *in vitro*. Stain: P.A.S. (× 205).

Figure 5 Association of 5 day proventriculus epithelium and 5 day proventriculus mesenchyme. Stain: Groat's haematoxylin, eosin (× 290).

Figure 6 Association of 5 day proventriculus epithelium and 5 day gizzard mesenchyme. Stain: Groat's haematoxylin, eosin (× 290).
P, proventriculus; *G*, gizzard.

What are the mechanisms and inductive processes which produce invagination of the proventriculus glands? In order to investigate these phenomena, we used the *in vitro* culture technique of WOLFF and HAFFEN (1952).

I EXPERIMENTAL STUDY OF STOMACH MORPHOGENESIS

1. Development of proventriculus and gizzard in culture

The organs were explanted at 5 days incubation; at this stage, the proventriculus has as yet undergone no invagination. Development in culture is found to proceed more slowly than *in ovo*, and differentiation does not reach such an advanced stage. It is, however, sufficient to analyse the inductive mechanisms. After 6 days culture, the explants were comparable to the same organs developed *in vivo* at 7 days incubation (figures 3 and 4, plate I).

2. Study of epithelio-mesenchymal relations during stomach morphogenesis

We wanted to study possible epithelio-mesenchymal influences occurring during stomach morphogenesis. We used the technique of MOSCONA (1952) for dissociation of tissues by trypsin digestion. In this way, we were able to isolate the epithelial tube and associate it, in culture, with various mesenchymes (SIGOT, 1962).

a) *Homologous associations*

We first cultured epithelium and mesenchyme of the 5 day proventriculus, in association. The explants developed in exactly the same way as the undissociated proventriculus in culture (figure 5, plate I).

b) *Heterologous associations*

Gizzard mesenchyme (5 days incubation) was associated with 5 day proventriculus epithelium. The results were quite different (figure 6, plate I); no glands were formed, and the epithelial structure was modified, becoming thicker, with taller and more closely packed cells than normally seen in the proventriculus. The nuclei occupied a more centrifugal position. Thus the epithelium came to resemble gizzard epithelium.

c) *Epithelium cultured in absence of mesenchyme*

We cultured the epithelium of 5 day proventriculus alone; in this instance, the explant degenerated, probably through lack of support.

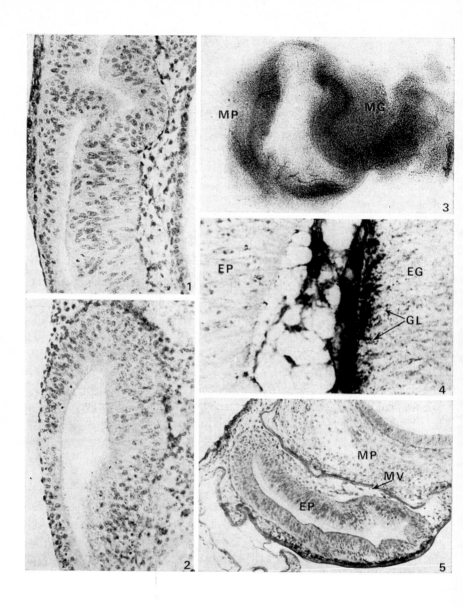

PLATE II

Figure 1 Association of 2 proventriculus epithelia (5 days old). Stain: Groat's haematoxylin, eosin (× 450).

Figure 2 Association of 5 day proventriculus epithelium with 8½ day mesonephros. Stain: Groat's haematoxylin, eosin (× 450).

Figure 3 Mixed association. Left—proventriculus mesenchyme, right—gizzard mesenchyme. Stained *in toto* with carmine (× 112).

Figure 4 Detail of a mixed association. Left *M* epithelium in contact with proventriculus mesenchyme, right *M* epithelium in contact with gizzard mesenchyme. Stain: P.A.S. (× 1125).

Figure 5 Association of epithelium and mesenchyme of 5 day proventriculus, separated by a vitelline membrane. Stain: P.A.S. (× 240).
EG., proventriculus epithelium in contact with gizzard mesenchyme; *EP.*, proventriculus epithelium; *GL.*, glycogen; *MG.*, gizzard mesenchyme; *MP.*, proventriculus mesenchyme; *MV.*, vitelline membrane.

We then carried out two types of association, intended to provide the epithelium with adequate support:

1) *Association of 2 proventriculus epithelial tubes, at 5 days incubation*
The epithelium became transformed into gizzard-type epithelium (figure 1, plate II);

2) *Association of 5 day proventriculus epithelium with 8½ day mesonephros*
The same phenomenon is observed as before, i.e. the epithelium became transformed into gizzard-type epithelium (figure 2, plate II).

These experiments show the vital role played by the mesenchyme in the process of glandular epithelial invagination. It is also found that proventriculus epithelium when left to develop in isolation, or associated with gizzard mesenchyme or with a neutral organ such as the mesonephros, differentiates into gizzard-type epithelium. This structure probably represents the autodifferentiated form of stomach epithelium.

d) *Mixed association*

Further verification of the preceding experiments was obtained by carrying out a mixed association, using 5 day proventriculus mesenchyme +5 day proventriculus epithelium +5 day gizzard mesenchyme. The epithelium differentiates into mixed tissue—proventriculus on the side of the proventriculus mesenchyme, and gizzard on the side of the gizzard mesenchyme (figures 3 and 4, plate II).

How can induction in this instance be explained?

According to generally accepted opinion, induction is due to a diffusible substance originating in the mesenchyme. However, the result of mixed association suggests certain modifications of this explanation; as the action of the mesenchyme only becomes manifest where it is in contact with the epithelium, it looks as if the inductive substance either diffuses over a very short distance, or is inhibited by another substance diffusing from the other mesenchyme. It is also possible that direct contact between the inductive tissue and the reactive tissue is necessary (SIGOT, 1963).

e) *Association with interposition of vitelline membrane*

We associated 5 day proventriculus epithelium with the corresponding mesenchyme, separating the two tissues by a vitelline membrane (WOLFF, 1961). The epithelium developed in the same way as when cultured alone or associated with mesonephros or gizzard mesenchyme (figure 5, plate II).

It appears that, if a substance has crossed the membrane, it has not been sufficient to initiate normal differentiation of the proventriculus epithelium; direct contact between the two tissues appears to be necessary.

II ROLE OF GLYCOGEN

We attempted to find out what might correspond to the difference in glycogen levels between the proventriculus and the gizzard. Here are the main points arising from our observations.

1) There is a season during the year—on average from mid-June to mid-October—which is particularly unfavourable for fertilisation and normal embryonic development. *In vitro* development is likewise poor during this period, and explants of proventriculus cultured *in vitro* show little or no glandular development. Now, if the glucose level of the culture medium is increased, good glandular development is obtained. Histological examination reveals normal glycogen levels in these explants, i.e. the proventriculus epithelium contains very little or none.

If the same experiment is repeated at a different time of the year, increasing the glucose content of the medium by the same amount as before, no difference in glandular development is observed. This development is good, but it is now found that the proventriculus epithelium has accumulated glycogen.

2) After carrying out micro-respirometric measurements, we found that at 7 days, the respiratory rate of the proventriculus is twice as great as that of the gizzard.

These findings, together with the concomitant low level or absence of glycogen in the proventriculus, and the large amounts present in the gizzard, suggest the following: the proventriculus, actively engaged in differentiation, uses all the glucose at its disposal, whereas the gizzard, which develops to only a small extent, stores glucose as glycogen. If the proventriculus has more glucose available than necessary, it can also store the excess in the same way as the gizzard; this is what happens when the proventriculus is cultured in a glucose-enriched medium during a season favourable to development.

III CONCLUSIONS

The experiments just described demonstrate the inductive properties of the proventriculus mesenchyme. What substance or substances are responsible for these phenomena? This is still not known.

We were unable to show induction through a simple diffusion across a porous membrane, in the case of the proventriculus, though many other workers have done so for other organs. Our results appear to indicate that contact between the two tissues is necessary. However, it is possible that some substance, diffusing from the mesenchyme to the epithelium, may stimulate the latter to become irreversibly competent. Direct contact between the mesenchyme and the epithelium may then be necessary for glandular formation.

There is a definite disparity between the morphological differentiation (structural characteristics, nucleo-cytoplasmic relations, etc.) and the physiological differentiation of a tissue. Inductive substances must, in themselves, orientate the tissue in a certain direction—that of normal differentiation; however, at this stage of morphogenesis—a relatively advanced one in digestive tract development—it is possible that subsequent contact between the inductive and competent tissues is necessary to ensure complete differentiation of the epithelio-mesenchymal complex. Such a contact involves both the physical and chemical properties of the tissues.

References

HIBBARD, H. (1942). *J. Morphol.*, **70**, 121.

SIGOT, M. (1962). *C.R. Acad. Sc.*, **254**, 2439.

SIGOT, M. (1963). *C.R. Acad. Sc.*, **256**, 4970.

SIGOT, M. (1963). 88e Congrès des Sociétés Savantes, II, 619.

SJÖGREN, S. J. (1941). *Morphol. Jahrb.*, **86**, 382.

WOLFF, Et. (1961). *Develop. Biol.*, **3**, 767.

WOLFF, Et., and HAFFEN, K. (1952). *Texas Rept. Biol. Med.*, **10**, 463.

CHAPTER VIII

DEVELOPMENT OF LUNG AND STOMACH EPITHELIAL RUDIMENTS IN CONTACT WITH SURFACES CONDITIONED BY MESENCHYMAL CULTURES

L. Marin

Laboratoire d'Embryologie expérimentale du Collège de France et du Centre National de la Recherche Scientifique, Nogent-sur-Marne

---

As WE have just seen, the stomach, like the lung, has a dual origin. In both cases, differentiation of the rudiment comes about through interactions established between the two components, epithelial and mesenchymal.

In this chapter, a set of investigations will be described which were conducted partly in collaboration with DAMERON, and partly with SIGOT. By using a specific culture technique, we were able to obtain the differentiation of pulmonary and gastric epithelia, in the absence of those mesenchymes which are normally responsible for their induction.

CULTURE METHOD

The starting point of our method is as follows: when living cells are cultured for a period of time in contact with a solid support, and subsequently detached, they leave behind a certain quantity of organic material (WEISS, 1961; ROSENBERG, 1960; MARIN, 1962, 1965). If the cultured tissue were an inducer, as are the mesenchymes of lung and stomach, we wondered whether the material remaining on the support could also be inductive and hence allow the differentiation of epithelial rudiments placed in contact with it.

The outline of the culture method used to study this question will be described. Certain modifications had to be made to adapt the method for culturing each type of rudiment studied. These will be indicated as the corresponding results are given.

In all cases, culture consisted of at least two stages: the first, or *primary culture*, comprised the collection of material formed by the inductive mesenchyme; the second, or *experimental culture*, was designed to test the effect of this material on the competent epithelium.

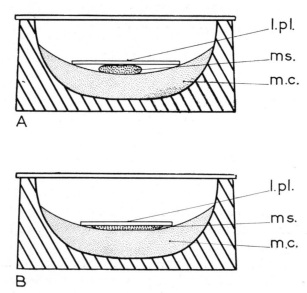

Figure 1   Diagram of primary culture
A at the beginning of the culture
B after a few days of culture
mc, culture medium; *ms*, inductive mesenchyme; *l.pl.*, plexiglass coverslip.

Primary culture

The mesenchymal fragments taken from the rudiments are distributed over the surface of nutrient agar media, prepared according to the technique of WOLFF and HAFFEN (1952). Each explant is covered with plexiglass (figure 1A) and incubated for a few days at 38°C. The mesenchyme very quickly spreads out to form a thin sheet which adheres to the plexiglass coverslips (figure 1B).

After a few days (4 to 7, depending on the type of mesenchyme), the coverslips are removed and immersed in Tyrode's solution. The contours of the adhering mesenchymal sheets are engraved with the point of a fine scalpel, after which the tissues are detached. The plexiglass coverslips, now free of cultures, are kept in Tyrode's solution until required for the experimental culture.

Experimental culture

For this second stage, the rudiments are dissociated by trypsin digestion, using the techniques already described in chapters VI and VII. The epithelial tubes, now without mesenchyme, are placed on the surface of fresh culture media; a coverslip from the primary culture is laid on top of each explant, arranged so that the explant comes in contact with the zone which originally bore the inductive mesenchyme.

These preparations are incubated for varying periods, depending on the type of rudiment. The degree of epithelial differentiation is assessed either by following its morphological development during culture (drawings made using the camera lucida), or histologically after fixation and staining.

RESULTS

1. Culture of lung epithelium

The mesenchyme intended for primary culture is taken from the lungs of 5 day old embryos, and maintained for 4 days in culture, in contact with plexiglass. The reactive epithelium used for experimental culture is also taken from the lungs of 5 day old embryos.

Bronchial development is observed daily by camera lucida drawings.

A) *Culture of bronchi in direct contact with the medium*

In a preliminary series of experiments, we cultured isolated bronchi, depositing them directly onto the culture medium and covering them with plexiglass coverslips from primary cultures. Control bronchi, also free of mesenchyme, were similarly placed on culture media and covered with plexiglass coverslips—which in this case had not previously borne a mesenchymal culture.

Cultured under these conditions, the bronchi spread out rapidly in a histiotypic culture and become disorganised. However, despite progressive structural obliteration, three types of development can be obtained: the bronchi may either regress completely in a very short space of time, or may retain a recognizable structure for 24 to 48 hours, or, lastly, they may attain

11*

some degree of differentiation; under these conditions, they elongate and the dilatations at the time of explantation become accentuated.

Table I shows the number of bronchi in each of these categories, both for those cultured in contact with plates previously exposed to mesenchymal cultures, and those cultured in contact with fresh coverslips.

Table I

	Total	Regressed	Undifferen-tiated	Differen-tiated
Bronchi cultured in contact with mesenchyme-conditioned plates	32	2	12	18
Control bronchi	31	20	8	3

The first result shows that when epithelial rudiments are cultured in contact with coverslips that have previously carried pulmonary mesenchyme, a large number differentiate (18 out of 32). On the other hand, when cultured in contact with fresh coverslips, the majority of bronchi regress (20 out of 31).

B) *Culture of bronchi associated with a supporting tissue*

The rapid transformation of bronchi into dedifferentiated cellular sheets when placed in direct contact with the medium makes very transient any sign of differentiation. This transformation makes histological examination equally impossible.

Our next move was to try to preserve the organized structure of the bronchi as far as possible. Instead of culturing them alone, we associated them with a supporting tissue, the cephalic mesenchyme, which is known to exert no inductive influence on the bronchi.

The explants were taken from 5 day old embryos; the fragments were cut as large and as thin as possible, then laid on the culture media. Bronchi free of pulmonary mesenchyme were then placed on these explants (figure 2), and the preparation was covered:

1) either by plexiglass coverslips from a primary culture of pulmonary mesenchyme;

2) or by clean coverslips;

3) or, lastly, by coverslips from a primary culture of non-inductive tissue, the metanephros.

Under these conditions, the bronchi remain well-organised for some

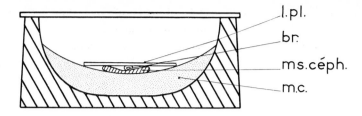

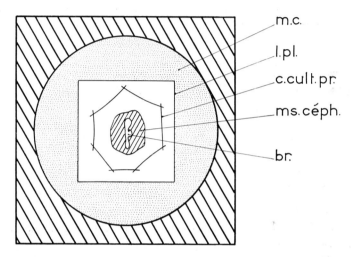

Figure 2   Diagram of secondary culture of bronchus.
mc., culture medium; *ms.*, *céph.*, cephalic mesenchyme; *br.*, bronchus; *l.pl.*, plexiglass coverslip; *c.cult. pr.*, contours of primary culture.

days, although the supporting cephalic mesenchyme spreads out in contact with the coverslips.

As in the previous series of experiments, three types of development can be observed:

a) the bronchi may regress: dilatations present at the time of explantation disappear, the walls become thinner, and the bronchus becomes distended and swollen. Figure 3 shows an example of this type of development.

b) Alternatively, the general appearance of the bronchus may be maintained during culture (figure 4).

c) Lastly, the bronchi may differentiate: they elongate, and dilatations

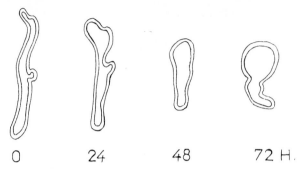

Figure 3 Example of bronchus regressing, after 24, 48 and 72 hours culture (drawings made by camera lucida).

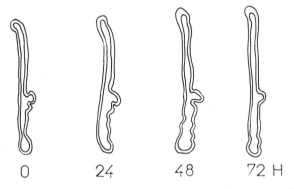

Figure 4 Example of bronchus maintaining its structure; drawings made by camera lucida, after 24, 48 and 72 hours culture.

present at the time of explantation grow and increase in complexity; fresh dilatations sometimes appear. Figure 5 shows two examples of this type of development.

Table II shows the results obtained in this series.

Table II

Nature of primary culture carried by plates	Appearance of bronchi after culture					
	Total	Regressed		Undifferentiated		Differentiated
Lung mesenchyme	76	5	6.6%	18	24%	52	69.4%
Mesonephros	42	8	22.2%	15	41.7%	13	36.1%
No primary culture	36	15	35%	17	40.5%	10	24.8%

Like the preceding one, this table shows that the percentage differentiation is high when bronchi are cultured in contact with coverslips from a primary culture of lung mesenchyme, but low in contact either with clean coverslips or coverslips from primary cultures of mesonephros. Conversely, there is a high frequency of regression in the last two cases, and only a small percentage in the first.

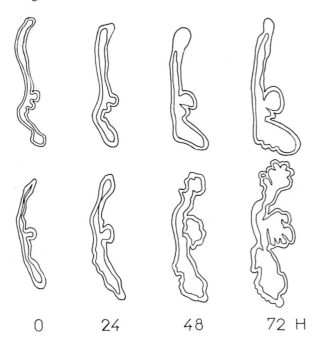

0   24   48   72 H

Figure 5   Examples of bronchi differentiating in culture. Drawings made by camera lucida after 24, 48 and 72 hours culture.

Histological examination of cultures detached from their supporting tissue confirms these results: sections of bronchi cultured in contact with plates from primary cultures of pulmonary mesenchyme show a thickened epithelium, with folds (plate I, figure A). On the contrary, bronchi cultured in contact with clean coverslips show a very thin and flattened epithelium (plate II, figure B).

The sum total of these results, both morphological and histological, shows that it is possible to obtain bronchial differentiation in the absence of pulmonary mesenchyme.

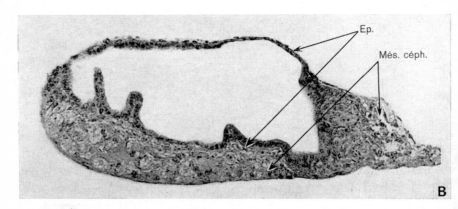

PLATE I

A Longitudinal section of a bronchus cultured in contact with a coverslip that has originally carried lung mesenchyme. Note the thickened epithelium and fold formation.

B Longitudinal section of a bronchus cultured in contact with a clean coverslip. The epithelium is very flattened.

ep.: lung epithelium; *més. céph.*: cephalic mesenchyme.

I CULTURE OF PROVENTRICULUS EPITHELIUM

A) Differentiation of proventriculus epithelium in the absence of mesenchyme

Our first question was whether the gizzard and proventriculus mesenchymes, when cultured, could leave behind a material capable of influencing epithelial differentiation (MARIN and SIGOT, 1963).

Accordingly, we took fragments of proventriculus mesenchyme from 5 day old embryos and cultured them in contact with plexiglass coverslips. At the same time, and under the same conditions, we cultured gizzard mesenchyme of the same age. After one week of culture, the cellular sheets formed were detached from the plexiglass supports as in the previous series of experiments.

For the experimental culture, we used 5 day old epithelial proventriculus tubes free of mesenchyme.

These were divided into three groups:

1) the first was cultured in contact with coverslips which had previously carried proventriculus mesenchyme;

2) the second was cultured in contact with coverslips that had carried gizzard mesenchyme;

3) the third was cultured in contact with clean coverslips.

These cultures were left to develop for about a week; they were then detached from the supporting coverslips, placed on fresh media, and cultured for about 24 hours, without being covered by coverslips. The explants were then fixed and stained by the Hotchkiss-MacManus technique.

Those explants cultured in contact with coverslips from primary cultures of proventriculus mesenchyme showed little thickening of the epithelium; the latter contained almost no glycogen and did not secrete mucus (plate II, A). There is a great similarity between this picture and that of epithelium cultured with proventriculus mesenchyme, despite the rarity of glandular folds.

In the two other groups of explants, the epithelium became thick, contained glycogen, and secreted abundant mucus (plate II, B, C). In this case also, epithelium cultured in contact with clean coverslips or coverslips that had previously carried gizzard mesenchyme, was comparable in appearance to epithelium cultured alone or associated with gizzard mesenchyme.

It can thus be said that proventriculus mesenchyme, like lung mesenchyme, leaves a material behind on its support, which is capable of influencing the competent epithelium.

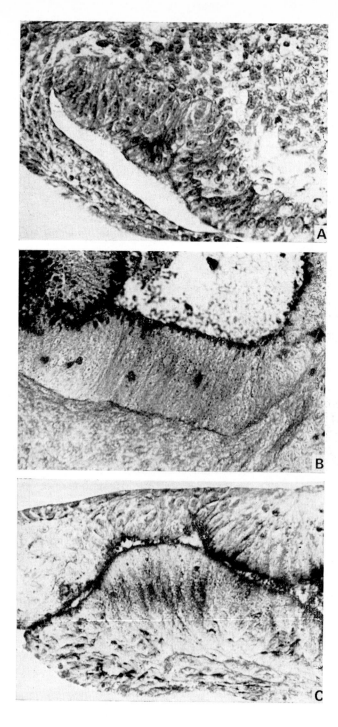

PLATE II

A   Proventriculus epithelium cultured in contact with a coverslip that has carried proventriculus mesenchyme. The epithelium is thin and contains no glycogen.

B   Proventriculus epithelium after culture in contact with a coverslip that has previously carried gizzard mesenchyme. The epithelium is thick, rich in glycogen, and has secreted abundant mucus.

C   Proventriculus epithelium after culture in contact with a clean plate. It has the same appearance as B.

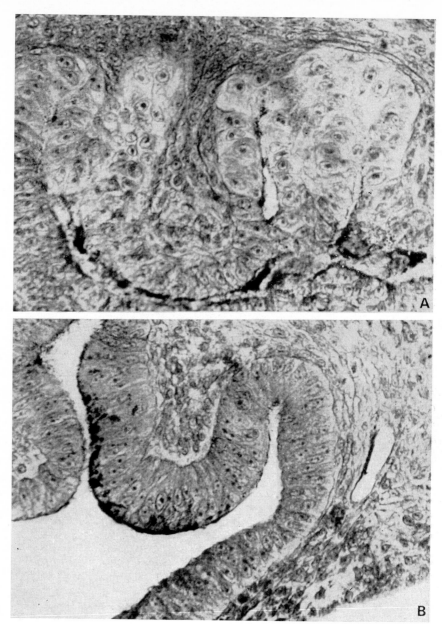

PLATE III

A Proventriculus mesenchyme reassociated with homologous mesenchyme, after being cultured in contact with a clean coverslip. Differentiation has been resumed; the epithelium has become thinner, and has formed glandular folds.

B Proventriculus epithelium reassociated with homologous mesenchyme after being in contact with the material formed by the gizzard mesenchyme. Differentiation is not resumed; the epithelium remains thick and rich in glycogen.

B) Role of gizzard mesenchyme

As we have just seen, proventriculus epithelium cultured alone or in contact with clean coverslips, develops in the same way as when associated with gizzard mesenchyme. It may then be asked whether the latter plays a part in differentiation (MARIN and SIGOT, 1965).

To try to solve this question, we used the method previously described: epithelial tubes, freed from mesenchyme, were cultured in contact with coverslips that had originally carried gizzard mesenchyme. At the same time, control epithelial tubes were cultured in contact with clean coverslips. After one week of culture, *all explants were detached* from the coverslips, and *all were reassociated with proventriculus mesenchyme* for a few days.

Plate III shows the histological appearance of such explants. It can be seen that when the epithelium has been in contact with a clean coverslip, before being reassociated with proventriculus mesenchyme, it is capable of resuming normal differentiation. It becomes thinner, forms numerous folds and contains very little glycogen (plate III, A).

On the other hand, when epithelium has been in contact with a coverslip that has previously carried gizzard mesenchyme, and is then reassociated with proventriculus mesenchyme, the result is very different; the epithelium no longer differentiates in response to proventriculus mesenchyme induction: it forms no glandular folds, and remains thick and rich in glycogen (plate III, B).

The material left behind on the supporting coverslips by the gizzard mesenchyme has therefore left its mark: the proventriculus epithelium even when reassociated with its own mesenchyme, can no longer resume normal differentiation.

In conclusion, our culture method has made it possible to obtain the differentiation of two types of epithelium in the absence of the mesenchymes which normally induce them. We have also, in the case of gizzard mesenchyme, succeeded in demonstrating an inhibitory activity not previously detected. Lastly, we hope to be able to characterize the factors responsible for lung and stomach morphogenesis in chick embryo.

References

MARIN, L. (1962). Migration cellulaire sur un substrat modifié par une culture préalable. *C.R. Acad. Sc.*, **255**, 171.

MARIN, L. (1965). Contribution à l'étude de la migration de cellules embryonnaires de poulet cultivées *in vitro*. *Mémoires de la Société Zoologique de France*, **35**, 1–85.

MARIN, L., and SIGOT, M. (1963). Evolution d'une ébauche épithéliale au contact d'une surface ayant porté un mésenchyme inducteur. *C.R. Acad. Sc.*, **257**, 3475–3478.

MARIN, L., and SIGOT, M. (1965). Induction d'ébauches épithéliales au contact de surfaces conditionnées par une culture de mésenchyme. *Compt. Rend. Soc. Biol.*, **159**, 98–101.

ROSENBERG, M. D. (1960). Microexsudates from cells grown in tissue culture. *Biophs. J.*, **1**, 137–159.

WEISS, L. (1961). Studies on cellular adhesion in tissue culture. IV: the alteration of substrata by cell surfaces. *Exp. Cell Res.*, **25**, 504–517.

WOLFF, Et., and HAFFEN, K. (1952). Sur une méthode de culture d'organes embryonnaires *in vitro. Texas Rep. Biol. Med.*, **10**, 463.

CHAPTER IX

APPLICATION OF IMMUNOCHEMICAL TECHNIQUES TO THE STUDY OF CERTAIN PROBLEMS ARISING FROM TISSUE INTERACTIONS DURING ORGANOGENESIS

Yvon Croisille

Laboratoire d'Embryologie expérimentale, Collège de France and Centre National de la Recherche scientifique, Nogent-sur-Marne

THE FOREGOING chapters clearly show that the genesis of an organ is the result of a chain of interactions—often lengthy and complicated—between tissues. When these interactions take place between adjacent tissues, in such a way that at least one of them is orientated towards a new pathway of differentiation, they are referred to as inductions. In certain cases, induction appears to be a unidirectional phenomenon, while in others reciprocal interactions are observed; in the latter, each tissue participating in the formation of a structure alternately plays the role of inducer and reactor. What are the chemical modifications during induction, and what happens at the point of contact between inductive and reactive tissues? Are the morphological, cytological and chemical changes, observed after contact between two tissues, the result of a simple surface effect, without exchange of material between cells, or is there a transfer of substances? Both points of view have been put forward to explain the nature of tissue interactions during induction and these two concepts have been analysed and commented on by many researchers (for a review see SAXÉN and TOIVONEN, 1962). It should be noted at this point that, under various circumstances, identical or different cells can come into contact without there being a change in the differentiation pathway of any one of them; there must thus be more than a simple surface effect during inductive interactions. In this context,

EBERT (1965) states: "We see no convincing evidence that inductive interactions, which by definition result in an alteration of the developmental
course of the interactants, are mediated through surface contacts without
an exchange of material." Following the demonstration that certain inducers
act at a distance, and that intimate contact between the inductive and
competent tissues is not necessary, it now seems generally accepted that
the inductive stimulus is transmitted by diffusible substances. However,
although under certain experimental conditions contact between cells may
not be essential (inductions across porous membranes or in the presence
of tissue extracts), it does not necessarily follow that the same is true in
normal development. Here the establishment of an intimate contact between
inductive and reactive tissues seems to create optimal conditions for an
exchange of material. In an attempt to clarify certain aspects of these
difficult problems in the sphere of inductive interactions, such as the role
of surface interactions or the nature of the substances transferred, some
authors have used immunochemical techniques. Most of the results in this
field have been analysed by SAXÉN and TOIVONEN (1962) and CROISILLE
(1963). We shall therefore give only a brief summary in the two first sections
of this account.

Another important problem arising from inductive interactions concerns
the synthesis of specific proteins in the reactive tissue in response to the
inductive stimulus. After inductive interactions between two tissues, at
least one of them begins to differentiate along new lines. Thus, under the
influence of inductive tissues such as the chorda-mesoderm or the optic
vesicle, the ectoderm is determined to differentiate into nervous tissue or
lens respectively; inducers such as the Wolffian duct or the ureter determine
the differentiation of the meso- and metanephrogenic mesenchymes into
secretory tubules of the mesonephros and metanephros. If we look at the
problem in terms of protein composition we find, in the adult organism
which has reached the final stage of development, that each organ, in
addition to the proteins common to other tissues, possesses its own specific
proteins. It is immediately apparent that one of the embryologist's main
problems is to define at what period in development both the common
and specific proteins appear. It would be of particular interest to know
exactly when the first organ-specific protein is synthesised—at the stage of
determination, during the very early stages of differentiation, or later. The
synthesis of new proteins during development can be investigated by
various methods, but the specificity and sensitivity of immunochemical

methods have led to their increasing use in this sphere of research. The results obtained have already been the object of several detailed reviews (EBERT, 1955, 1958, 1959; NACE, 1955; SCHECHTMAN, 1955; WOERDEMAN, 1955; TYLER, 1955, 1957; EDDS, 1958; CLAYTON, 1960; BRACHET, 1960; FLICKINGER, 1962; RANZI, 1965; SOLOMON, 1965; TEN CATE, 1965; VAN DOORENMALEN, 1965; CROISILLE, 1958, 1963, 1965). Most of the evidence available shows that the constituents common to all tissues in the adult can generally be detected at a very early developmental stage, whereas the specific constituents appear progressively as the various cellular types become specialized. However, apart from a few exceptions, we have very little information on a possible correlation between induction and the initiation of specific protein synthesis. Much research work has, in fact, dealt mainly with the later phases of differentiation and has clearly indicated the progressive character of chemical differentiation. The absence of experimental data on the synthesis of specific proteins during the first stages of differentiation can be attributed to the techniques applied, since their limits of sensitivity would rarely enable specific constituents to be detected at early stages. However, the immunofluorescence techniques in particular have made it possible, in certain cases, to detect the presence of organ-specific proteins in the reactive tissue only a few hours after induction—or, more precisely, a few hours after the establishment of contact with the inductive tissue. In the third section of this account, we shall first deal with the progressive appearance of various common and organ-specific constituents during embryonic development. Next, we shall attempt to define the precise moment when the first organ-specific constituent appears during differentiation, and to establish a correlation between induction and the initiation of specific protein synthesis.

I TRANSFER OF SUBSTANCES FROM THE INDUCTIVE TISSUE TO THE REACTIVE TISSUE

Generally speaking, little is known about the chemical nature of inducers. However, as regards primary induction, it has been shown that the substances with inductive capacity are protein in nature (cf. BRACHET, 1957; YAMADA, 1958; TIEDEMANN and colleagues, 1960, 1961). Thus it is easy to see why various authors have turned to immunochemical methods, hoping to be able to demonstrate the passage of macromolecular substances from the inductive tissue to the reactive tissue.

In 1958, ROUNDS and FLICKINGER showed that antigenic substances passed from the chorda-mesoderm of the frog (*Rana pipiens*) into the competent ectoderm of the salamander (*Taricha torosa*) if the two tissues were cultured in association for 4 to 5 days. Extracts of salamander ectoderm from such associations show a higher degree of reactivity (titre 1/32) towards an antiserum against frog gastrulae, than do control extracts of *Taricha torosa* gastrulae or neurulae (titre 1/8). The authors conclude from these results that antigenic substances have passed from the inducer to the reactor. However, ectodermal contamination by a few cells of the dorsal mesoderm cannot be entirely excluded. In 1959, FLICKINGER, HATTON and ROUNDS confirmed the previous results, and in addition, by carrying out a detailed histological study of 40 chimeric explants, they were able to exclude the possible migration of frog chorda-mesodermal cells into the salamander ectoderm. It thus seems established that antigenic substances pass from the inductive tissue to the reactive tissue. CLAYTON and ROMANOVSKY (1959) cultured the ectoderm of *Triturus alpestris* in the presence of heterogenous inducers, such as alcohol-treated guinea pig liver and bone marrow. Using fluorescein-labelled antisera, they showed that where the inducer is in direct contact with the ectoderm, a relatively intense fluorescence can be observed in the cytoplasm of a few ectodermal cells. In two instances, fluorescence did not remain confined to a few cells in the immediate vicinity of the inductive tissue, but extended to the whole ectoderm. Thus there actually seems to have been passage of antigenic substances from the inductive to the reactive tissue, with penetration of guinea pig type constituents into amphibian tissue. VAINIO, SAXÉN and TOIVONEN (1960) cultured preparations of alcohol-treated guinea pig bone marrow, sandwiched between layers of *Triturus vulgaris* presumptive ectoderm. After 1 to 3 hours culture, the explants were opened and the inducer removed. After repeated washing, the ectoderm explants were homogenized and the supernatant after centrifugation used for precipitin tests in the presence of antiserum against guinea pig bone marrow. If the inducer is removed after 3 hours, a greater degree of guinea pig type antigenicity can be demonstrated in the extracts of newt ectoderm than after only 1 hour of culture. Transport of guinea pig constituents into amphibian tissue is thus more marked after 3 hours contact. Using fluorescein-labelled antisera, SAXÉN and TOIVONEN (1962) show that after 3 hours contact with a heterogenous inducer, fluorescent granules can be observed in the ectodermal cells, whereas such granules are not seen after only 1 hour's contact. However, despite frequent histological checks, the authors do not believe that possible direct contamination of the ectoderm by cells of the inducer can be completely excluded.

All the results so far described indicate that a transfer of antigenic substances from the inductive tissue to the reactive tissue really has taken place. But, as we have just seen, it appears that contamination of the reactive tissue by inducer tissue cells cannot be completely excluded. Furthermore, it is difficult to say anything definite about the nature of the substances transferred. It should be remembered that while the term "antigenic substances" usually implies proteins, other components can be antigenic. The conclusion that macromolecules—especially proteins—are transferred from the inductive tissue to the reactive tissue thus seems somewhat premature.

In another system namely that of lens induction, WOERDEMAN (1950) showed that extracts of optic vesicle or presumptive ectoderm from axolotl neurulae did not react individually with an antiserum against adult lens. However, if the two extracts are mixed and incubated at 37° for 24 hours before testing with adult lens antiserum, there is a specific precipitation reaction. DE VINCENTIIS (1954, 1957) obtained the same results with *Rana esculenta*; while extracts of optic vesicle and presumptive ectoderm did not react individually with antiserum against adult lens in double diffusion, a mixture of both extracts gave a very distinct precipitation band. These results suggested that precursors present in the optic vesicle could react with precursors in the presumptive ectoderm and thus play a role during lens induction. In 1961, PERLMANN and DE VINCENTIIS showed that during chick embryo development, at least one of the specific lens proteins (α-crystallin) is present in microsome extracts well before it can be detected in the soluble phase. Microsomal extracts from embryos of 44 to 46 hours incubation gave a positive precipitation reaction with anti-lens sera, while the supernatant (soluble fraction) of the same stages did not react. The same results were obtained with 60 hour old embryos, but extracts of older embryos showed a positive reaction with both microsomal and soluble fractions. In the light of these observations, the authors proposed that, during lens formation, inductive substances could determine the solubilization of pre-existing specific proteins from the microsomes, this phenomenon being accompanied by activation of the synthesis of these same proteins at the ribosomal level. The experiments of WOERDEMAN and DE VINCENTIIS could perhaps be similarly interpreted: it is possible that substances capable

12*

of reacting with anti-lens sera are present in the ectoderm extract, but in a microsome-bound form, and hence inaccessible to antibodies; there could be substances in the extract of optic vesicle which produce solubilization of specific components, thus rendering them detectable by immunoprecipitation tests. However, as we shall see subsequently (section IIIB), most authors have been unable to confirm the existence of specific proteins prior to induction, and agree that in the chick embryo, specific lens proteins first appear between 50 and 60 hours incubation, i.e. shortly after induction. Furthermore, PERLMANN and DE VINCENTIIS observe a positive precipitation reaction in the presence of anti-lens sera not only with cephalic extracts, but also with microsomal extracts from the trunks of young chick embryos. VAN DAM and coworkers (1963) and ZWAAN (1963) also observe a reaction between anti-adult lens sera and extracts of chick embryo trunks. But according to these investigations, the antibodies responsible for these reactions can be absorbed by a liver extract, and therefore correspond to components common to all tissues, and not to specific lens proteins.

CLARKE and FOWLER (1960) treat histological sections of chick embryos between the 7 somite stage and 5 days incubation with anti-adult lens sera labelled with fluorescein isothiocyanate. On the 5th day of incubation, they observe very marked fluorescence of the lens. The intensity of fluorescence is much less in younger embryos. At the 19 somite stage, when induction is almost complete, the optic vesicle and lens ectoderm fluoresce with equal intensity. At the 12 somite stage, i.e. shortly after contact has been established between optic vesicle and ectoderm, optic vesicle fluorescence is distinctly more intense than that of the presumptive ectoderm. In the 7 somite embryo, i.e. before establishment of contact, only the optic vesicle and brain fluoresce; no specific fluorescence is observed in the ectoderm (FOWLER and CLARKE, 1959). Thus, prior to induction, the optic vesicle contains substances capable of reacting with anti-adult lens sera. During the phase of contact and subsequently, the reactivity of the optic vesicle diminishes; simultaneously, the reactivity of the ectoderm increases so that by the 5th day, fluorescence is localized specifically in the lens. How can these observations be interpreted? Some consider that the results are compatible with a transfer of substances from the optic vesicle to the ectoderm during the phase of contact. Others in turn believe that these results merely reflect quantitative variations in the metabolic activity of the cells themselves. It has also been shown that, during the contact phase, the RNA level of the optic vesicle diminishes, while increasing in the lens ectoderm (MC KEEHAN, 1956). In 1961, HUNT observed that in the chick embryo at stages 11 to 13, the optic vesicle contains more ribonucleoprotein particles, while at stage 14, the ectoderm contains the larger amount. Other authors have shown that at the beginning of the interaction phase, the activity of certain enzymes is higher in the inductive tissue, while towards the end of induction, these activities are higher in the reactive tissue (TURCHINI, 1968). Despite the fact that all these results appear to indicate a transfer of substances from the inductive tissue to the reactive tissue, they can equally well be explained by changes in the metabolic activity of the two tissues. In the inductive tissue, this activity is high at the beginning of induction and subsequently diminishes, while in the reactive tissue it increases progressively during the phase of tissue interaction. In the third section, we shall see that in response to the inductive stimulus, new components are synthesised in the reactive tissue; this involves a greater activity at various cell levels.

With respect to the question posed at the beginning of this chapter, we can see that the results described indicate, but do not prove, a transfer of macromolecules—proteins in particular—from the inductive to the reactive tissue. In fact substances other than proteins are antigenic, and other interpretations, apart from the transfer of substances, are often equally plausible. In a similar context, FICQ (1954) and SIRLIN and BRAHMA (1959) show that there is transmission of radioactive material from a labelled inductive tissue to the reactive tissue; but again, the nature of the transferred material is not known. To summarize, although these results are very suggestive, they do not definitively demonstrate that macromolecules pass from the inductive tissue to the reactive tissue, nor that the substances transferred, whatever their nature, play a determining role in the process of induction.

II EFFECT OF ANTISERA ON THE INDUCTIVE CAPACITY OF A TISSUE

Since surface effects seem to play an important part in the process of induction, and antibodies react primarily with cell surface components, VAINIO (1957) wondered to what extent a known inducer could be affected by an antiserum. He concentrated on two main points: 1) can the inductive capacity of an organ be influenced by its homologous antiserum; 2) can an antiserum against the dorsal lip of the blastopore of newt gastrulae affect the inductive capacity of organs possessing a known inductive specificity, such as certain heterogenous inducers? Many experiments conducted by TOIVONEN and coworkers (1949, 1950, 1953, 1954) have shown that alcohol-treated guinea pig liver induces mainly archencephalic structures. Under the same conditions, guinea pig bone marrow induces mesodermal formations, and guinea pig kidney induces mesodermal and sometimes neural structures. Vainio experimented with these three heterogenous inducers, whose inductive capacity has been demonstrated on many occasions; treatment with either normal rabbit sera or with various antisera was followed by exposure to 70% alcohol and subsequent implantation into the blastocoele of young gastrulae. The results clearly showed that antisera affected the inductive capacities of all the heterogenous inducers studied, while the control rabbit serum had no effect. Thus liver implants treated with a rabbit antiserum against guinea pig liver lost their activity in 43% of cases; 27% of kidney implants treated with a homologous antiserum lost inductive capacity, as did 70% of bone marrow implants treated with a rabbit antiserum against guinea pig bone marrow. In general, homologous antisera—and to a lesser extent heterologous antisera—have an inhibitory effect on the inductive capacity of the implanted tissues. This inhibitory effect is particularly marked with bone marrow; when this tissue is treated with its homologous antiserum, histological observation reveals the presence of the inductive fragment without induction having taken place in 40 out of 57 cases. Control rabbit serum in no way affects the inductive capacity of marrow and kidney. Liver inductive capacity is, however, modified and sometimes inhibited by control rabbit serum, but this inhibition is much more marked after treatment with various antisera. It should be added that inhibition of heterogenous inductive capacity is also obtained with antisera against the dorsal lip of the blastopore of newt gastrulae. As antibodies react primarily with cell surface constituents, these results suggest that surface antigens play a fundamental role in the processes of induction.

The observation of WOERDEMAN (1955), suggesting that optic vesicle precursors might play a part in lens induction by reacting with ectodermal precursors, prompted FOWLER and CLARKE (1959) and CLARKE and FOWLER (1960) to investigate whether the inductive activity of the optic vesicle could be blocked by treatment with an antiserum against adult lens. The procedure was as follows: the optic vesicle is removed from chick embryos at the 4 to 7 somite stage, and cultured on a synthetic medium containing either control rabbit serum, or a rabbit antiserum against adult fowl lens. After 18 hours in culture, the explants are washed, covered with ectoderm from 4 to 7 somite chick embryos, and placed on a serum-free medium. In several experimental series, the control cultures differentiated a lens in 53% of cases (35/66), 81% of cases (35/43) and 73% of cases (36/49). Cultures where the optic vesicle had previously been treated with anti-lens serum differentiated a lens in only 3% of cases (2/61) (FOWLER and CLARKE, 1959), 6% of cases (2/34) (CLARKE and FOWLER, 1960), and 27% of cases (16/59) (CLARKE and FOWLER, 1961). Even in the controls no real lens vesicle formation was observed, only a thickening of the ectoderm to form a placode; nevertheless the absence of this transformation is sufficient to evaluate the inhibition of inductive capacity. The anti-lens serum does not affect the inductive capacity of the otic vesicle; the inhibitory effect on the optic vesicle thus appears to be specific. Furthermore, if the optic vesicle is treated with an anti-lens serum previously absorbed by an extract of adult lens, placode formation is observed in 75% of cases (59/78); the inhibitory effect is thus due to antibodies reacting with constituents normally present in the lens (CLARKE and FOWLER, 1961). According to CLARKE and FOWLER (1960), the inhibitions observed suggest that substances present in the optic vesicle and capable of reacting with anti-adult lens antibodies, play an essential role in the process of induction.

The previous results show irrefutably that the inductive capacity of an organ can be inhibited by antisera. But how can the inhibitory effects observed be interpreted? It might first be considered that antisera exercise their effects at cell surface level. It is well known that antibodies react primarily with cell surface components (BITENSKY, 1963; BECK, 1963); it is also known that antisera inhibit the reaggregation of dissociated cells (SPIEGEL, 1954, 1955; MOSCONA and MOSCONA, 1962); as we shall see in section III C the presence of antiserum inhibits cellular movements and regroupings in explants of chick embryo organs cultured *in vitro* according to the technique of WOLFF and HAFFEN (1952). The inhibition of inductive capacity by antisera could thus be explained by an effect on certain cell surface components which prevents the establishment of direct contact between the inductive and reactive tissues. From this it might be concluded that an intimate contact is indispensable during the interaction phase, and in particular that surface effects play an essential role during induction. However, various experiments have shown that intimate contact between the inducer and the competent tissue is not necessary (NIU and TWITTY,

1953; GROBSTEIN, 1956; McKEEHAN, 1958). How, then, can we explain
the inhibitory effects observed after antiserum treatment? A second interpretation is to consider that, after the reaction of antibodies with certain
cell surface components, material is no longer free to diffuse out of the
inducer tissue cells; in this case, the inhibitions observed would be in favour
of a transfer of material from the inductive tissue to the reactive tissue. But
there is a third possibility, namely that antibodies combine with components
which in fact play an essential role during induction, thereby inactivating
them. If this interpretation is correct, the results observed by VAINIO could
point the way to some extremely interesting and valuable developments.
Since the inductive capacity of heterogenous inducers is inhibited both by
homologous antisera and by an antiserum against the dorsal lip of the
blastopore of newt embryos, it could be deduced that the heterogenous
inducers (guinea pig liver, kidney and bone marrow) and the dorsal lip of
the blastopore of newt embryos (natural inducer) contain components
possessing similar or identical reactive groupings. If this is true, we should
expect to find immunochemical cross-reactions between material from these
two species, which are phylogenetically far apart. Such reactions have in
fact been demonstrated (VAINIO, 1957). These observations could provide a
better understanding of why, particularly in primary induction, agents of
such varied origin possess inductive capacity; this common property could
be manifested by the existence of common reactive sites on each of them.
However, the way in which these reactive sites participate in induction
remains to be elucidated. Before ending this discussion, it should be stressed
that the antisera used in the experiments just described are prepared
against extracts of complex tissues, and hence contain a large number
of different antibodies. This very complexity makes the explanation
of the results difficult and to some extent unreliable, so that any
attempt to interpret the significance of these observations is still rather
speculative.

   Although immunochemical methods have not provided definitive an-
swers to the questions raised earlier—namely, what part is played by surface
effects on the one hand, and by transfer of substances on the other, during
inductive interactions—they have indicated the possibility that structural
analogies exist between certain heterogenous inducers and the natural
inducer. We shall now approach the problem of the synthesis of specific
proteins by the reactive tissue in response to the inductive stimulus. Considerable advances have been made in this field in recent years and with

the use of immunochemical techniques it has been possible to detect the presence of organ-specific constituents in the reactive tissue, only a few hours after the establishment of contact with the inductive tissue.

III STUDY OF THE TIME OF APPEARANCE OF SOME ORGAN-SPECIFIC PROTEINS DURING DIFFERENTIATION OF BRAIN, LENS, KIDNEY AND SKIN IN THE CHICK EMBRYO

We saw at the beginning of this account that one of the embryologist's main problems is to determine at what point during the differentiation of an organ, the various specific proteins appear. We shall consider this problem successively with respect to the differentiation of brain, lens, kidney and skin in the chick embryo.

A) Immunological study of brain constituents

As regards the appearance of specific brain constituents during embryonic development, we shall refer first to the work of SCHALEKAMP. In 1963, this author showed that, in presence of an antiserum against adult fowl brain, immunoelectrophoretic analysis permitted the demonstration of at least 15 different constituents in extracts of adult fowl brain. Certain of these are blood constituents, others are common to nearly all other organs, and lastly others are specific for nervous tissue. When absorbed by an extract of adult fowl liver or kidney, the anti-brain serum gives only 3 precipitation bands with extracts of adult fowl brain in immunoelectrophoretic analysis. These 3 precipitation bands correspond to the specific nervous tissue constituents. Using the absorbed serum, SCHALEKAMP (1963) was able to show that the first specific constituent is detectable in the embryo at 2 days incubation, the second at 7 days and the third at 14 days (figure 1).

In a more recent study, MC CALLION and LANGMAN (1964) used the double diffusion technique and observed 9 precipitation bands between extracts of adult fowl brain and the homologous antiserum. Out of these 9 bands, 6 correspond to serum constituents or constituents common to other organs, while the remaining 3 correspond to specific nervous tissue components. According to these authors, the 3 specific constituents can be detected on the 5th, 9th and 12th days of incubation respectively.

How can the differences between the results of SCHALEKAMP and those of McCALLION and LANGMAN be explained? The most usual explanation given for such discrepancies is that there are differences in the titres of the antisera used. This is clearly relevant in many cases; however, it assumes that both authors were necessarily dealing with the same constituents, whereas there is no evidence that this was so. They could very well have been dealing with different components. Still, both investigations show that most of the common constituents are present at a very early stage, while the specific constituents appear progressively as the nerve cell matures. The first specific constituent is detectable at stage 14 (about 48 hours incubation) (SCHALEKAMP, 1963), i.e. about 30 hours after induction (figure 1). We shall see that in other organs, such as lens and kidney, it is possible, by the use of immunofluorescence techniques, to detect specific constituents at even earlier stages, about 15 hours after induction.

B) Determination of the time of appearance of the first specific constituent during lens differentiation

In the chick, lens formation is exclusively dependent on inductive influences of the optic vesicle. At the level of the optic cup, the cephalic ectoderm thickens to form a placode. The placode invaginates progressively giving rise to a lens vesicle. For induction to take place, direct contact between the cup and the presumptive ectoderm seems to be essential, during a period from the 9 somite to the 20 somite stages (MCKEEHAN, 1951, 1954). To ascertain when the first specific lens protein appears, various researchers have used immunochemical methods, such as interface precipitation, double diffusion, immunoelectrophoresis, immunofluorescence, and the study of effects of antisera *in vivo* and *in vitro*. Most of the literature has been reviewed by CROISILLE in 1963. More recently, TEN CATE (1965) and VAN DOORENMAALEN (1965) have reconsidered the question in the light of new data.

Figure 2, taken from VAN DOORENMAALEN (1965), shows that there was much confusion regarding the exact determination of when the first specific constituent appeared during lens development. Certain authors had found that specific constituents were only detectable at a rather late stage. Others, on the contrary, had observed positive reactions with anti-adult lens sera at very early stages (between 30 and 40 hours incubation), well before the lens rudiment could be distinguished from the surrounding cephalic ectoderm.

Figure 1 Diagram summarizing the order of appearance of the three specific constituents of nervous tissue, demonstrated by SCHALEKAMP (1963), (after TEN CATE, 1965).

Table I Demonstration of specific constituents of adult kidney in extracts of embryonic kidney at different stages of development

Organ-extracts studied	Precipitation bands observed in double diffusion in the presence of rabbit antisera against adult fowl kidney (AR 234 and AR 345) previously absorbed by serum and liver extract from adult fowl		
	1	2	3
Extract of 4-day embryo	—	—	—
Mesonephros of 6-day embryo	+	—	+
Mesonephros of 8-day embryo	+	+	+
Mesonephros of 10-day embryo	+	+	+
Mesonephros of 12-day embryo	+	+	+
Mesonephros of 14-day embryo	+	+	+
Mesonephros of 16-day embryo	+	+	+
Mesonephros of 18-day embryo	+	+	+
Metanephros of 12 day embryo	+	+	+
Metanephros of 16 day embryo	+	+	+
Metanephros of 20 day embryo	+	+	+
Adult kidney	+	+	+
Adult liver	—	—	—

the spinal cord, notochord, somites and part of the lateral plates from 30 somite stage embryos on to culture media containing non-absorbed anti-adult kidney serum. In this way, we hoped to test the specific cytotoxic properties of the anti-kidney serum, and possibly inhibit the differentiation of secretory tubules in the explants. Histological sections showed that at the time of explantation, no secretory tubules had yet differentiated; only the Wolffian duct and mesonephrogenic blastema were visible. On control culture media (standard medium of Wolff and Haffen, where Tyrode's solution is replaced by serum from non-immunized rabbits), the explants cicatrize and contract to form a homogeneous spheroidal mass in the first 24 hours, exactly as on the standard medium (CROISILLE, 1958); during the following days, several secretory tubules differentiate from the mesonephrogenic mesenchyme. On media containing anti-kidney serum, an inhibition of cell movements is observed, as shown by the delay in cicatrization and the absence of fusion and contraction of the explants; throughout the culture period they maintain exactly the same appearance as at the time of explantation. On the other hand, differentiation of secretory tubules is not inhibited. We did not thus observe any specific effect of the anti-kidney serum on mesonephric differentiation in explants cultured *in vitro*. However, it must be stressed once again that this absence of a specific effect does not prove that specific constituents are absent at the early stages of differentiation.

Using the direct immunofluorescence technique, OKADA (1965) did in fact succeed in detecting the presence of specific adult kidney constituents at very early stages, shortly after induction. He prepared antisera against the soluble protein fraction obtained by extracting microsomes of adult fowl kidney in presence of sodium deoxycholate. In double diffusion, the antiserum used in the experiments to be described here, gives one strong band of precipitation and one of weaker intensity only with the kidney microsomal extract; no reaction is observed with the supernatant (the fraction which is non-sedimentable at 100,000 g), or with the various cellular fractions from liver or lung. The globulin fraction of this antiserum, obtained by precipitation with ammonium sulphate at 45% saturation, and conjugated with fluorescein isothiocyanate, is used to treat either histological sections of chick embryos between stages 16 and 30 of HAMBURGER and HAMILTON, or cell smears from the nephrogenic zone. Immunofluorescence studies show that the antiserum reacts specifically with kidney (meso- and metanephros); no reaction is observed with other tissues, such as liver, lung, stomach, intestine or spleen. At stage 28 ($5\frac{1}{2}$ to 6 days incubation), when the mesonephros is already well differentiated, only the cells of the proximal secretory tubules fluoresce after treatment with the antiserum. Furthermore, the reaction is specifically localised in the apical cytoplasm. The cells of the Wolffian duct and collecting tubules, and similarly the glomeruli, mesenchyme and endothelium do not fluoresce. At stages 24 to 25, the results are similar to those observed at stage 28, although fluorescence is less intense. Stage 20 (41 somites, $3\frac{1}{2}$ days incubation) is the first at which OKADA (1965) observed fluorescent cells on histological sections of embryos after fixation and embedding in paraffin. At this stage establishment of the epithelial arrangement has started from the condensations of nephrogenic mesenchyme in antero-posterior order. Fluorescence is observed along the inner border of these early epithelia. A few cells in the mesonephrogenic condensation show a small, weakly fluorescent spot. At stage 18, (33 somites, 67 hours incubation), OKADA observes no specific fluorescence on histological sections. However, on cell smears, after dissociation with trypsin, he observes specific fluorescence in 6% of the cells from the mesonephrogenic cords of the mid-abdominal region. Fluorescence generally appears as a small spot or dot per single cell; in 33% of the positive cells, the fluorescent dot appears in the central part of the cell rather than the apical cytoplasm, presumably in the nucleus. At stages earlier than stage 17 (31 somites, 64 hours incubation), no specific fluorescence could be observed, either on histological sections or on cell smears. Pronephros was negative throughout its development.

In recent experiments (CROISILLE, 1969), we also applied the immuno-fluorescence techniques using our anti-kidney sera AR 234 and AR 345. It should first be recalled that, in double diffusion, these antisera previously absorbed with serum and liver extract from adult fowl, react specifically with 3 constituents of adult kidney. Two of these constituents can be detected in mesonephros extracts from 6 day embryos, while the third is detectable only at 8 days. All 3 are detectable in metanephros extracts at 12 days incubation (table I). Direct and indirect immunofluorescence techniques have shown that in meso- and metanephros, the kidney-specific constituents revealed by the liver-absorbed anti-kidney sera are localized only in the secretory tubules. We treated histological sections of embryos (after fixation with Carnoy's fluid and embedding in paraffin) either with the globulin fraction of AR 234, precipitated by 50% saturation with ammonium sulphate and conjugated with fluorescein isothiocyanate (direct technique), or with antiserum AR 345, followed by a goat anti-rabbit globulin serum, labelled with FITC (indirect technique); by this means, we were able to show that only the secretory tubules fluoresce on microscopic observation under ultra-violet light. We observed no specific fluorescence in the Wolffian duct, the ureter, the collecting tubules and glomeruli, or in any other embryonic tissue. Furthermore, while there is a diffuse fluores-cence throughout the secretory cell, maximum fluorescence is localized in the apical part of the cell, i.e. in the part directed towards the lumen of the secretory tubule (plate I, A and B). In order to verify that fluorescence really was due to an antigen-antibody reaction at the cellular level, we realized 3 types of controls. Firstly, sections were treated with control rabbit serum, conjugated with FITC. In a second control series, sections were treated with a non-fluorescent anti-kidney serum, then with the same anti-kidney serum labelled with FITC. In the third series of controls, sections were first treated with control rabbit serum (pretreated with serum and liver extract from adult fowl), then with a fluorescent anti-rabbit globulin serum (plate I, C). In all 3 instances, no specific fluorescence

13*

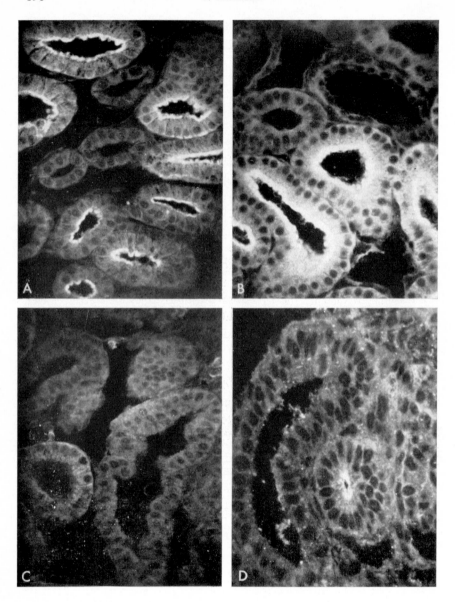

PLATE I

Immunohistological study of the presence and localisation of certain kidney-specific constituents during chick embryo development.

A) Histological section of the mesonephros from a 7-day chick embryo, treated by the globulin fraction of a rabbit antiserum against adult fowl kidney (AR 234) previously absorbed with serum and liver extract from an adult fowl, and labelled with fluorescein isothiocyanate (direct technique). Only the apical part of the secretory tubule cells fluoresces. The collecting tubules are negative.

B) Histological section of the mesonephros from a 7 day chick embryo treated firstly with a rabbit anti-adult fowl kidney serum (AR 345) absorbed by serum and liver extract from an adult fowl, and secondly by a goat anti-rabbit globulin serum, labelled with fluorescein isothiocyanate (indirect technique). The specific fluorescence is localised essentially in the apical part of the secretory tubule cells. There is however, a diffuse fluorescence throughout the cytoplasm of the secretory cell. The cells of the collecting tubules show no specific fluorescence.

C) Histological section of the mesonephros of a 7 day chick embryo, treated firstly with a control rabbit serum, to which has been added fowl serum and a liver extract from an adult fowl, and secondly with a goat anti-rabbit globulin serum labelled with FITC. No fluorescence is observed in the secretory tubule cells.

D) Histological section of a 36 somite chick embryo, at a level immediately anterior to the 20th somite and treated as in B). The only secretory tubule differentiated in this region is fluorescent, and the specific fluorescence is localised in the apical part of the cells. The Wolffian duct is negative (after CROISILLE, 1969).

was observed in the secretory tubules. Using the much more sensitive indirect immunofluorescence technique, we attempted to detect the presence of kidney-specific constituents in the early mesonephros, during its formation in 36 somite stage embryos. By observing serial sections made in a postero-anterior direction, all the steps of differentiation can be observed at this stage, from the blastema up to secretory tubule formation. At a level anterior to the 20th somite the only secretory tubule that has differentiated is fluorescent, and the fluorescence is localized in the apical part of the cells (plate I, D). At a more posterior level (20th to 22th somites) fine fluorescent granulations have been observed in the apical part of the cells that participate in the formation of the early tubules. No specific fluorescence could be observed in the cells of the pretubular condensations. About 20 hours elapse between the time when the Wolffian duct passes, and the time when the first specific fluorescence is detected. By examining the differentiation of the metanephros in the anterior part of the metanephrogenic zone, i.e. at the gonadal level, we observed the first specific fluorescence in embryos at 9 days incubation. At this stage, a few isolated secretory tubules have differentiated, and the apical part of the cells is fluorescent. This specific apical fluorescence is detectable as soon as the lumen of the developing tubule opens. At a slightly more advanced stage, when the primary secretory tubules elongate and become convoluted to form the characteristic S-shape, fluorescence is no longer confined to the apical part but there is also a relatively intense fluorescence throughout the cytoplasm of the secretory cells. These results appear to indicate that at least one of the constituents demonstrated by our antisera can be detected at a very early stage during secretory tubule differentiation, and is localized in the apical part of the cell; another component, distributed throughout the cytoplasm, appears later. The ureter and its ramifications, the collecting tubules, are consistently negative. At earlier stages (8 days incubation), when only the ureter, its ramifications, and a few mesenchymal condensations are visible, no specific fluorescence is observed. It is more difficult, in this instance, to assess the time elapsing between the beginning of the inductive interactions and the point at which specific fluorescence can first be detected; one would think however, that the two events are separated by a period of about 20 hours, as in the differentiation of the mesonephros.

The experiments of OKADA (1965) on mesonephric differentiation nevertheless show that specific constituents can be detected at earlier stages, i.e. in the closely packed cells of the nephrogenic mesenchyme, at the time when the initiation of the epithelial architecture of the cells has just begun. At stage 18, OKADA observes a weak fluorescence in the form of a spot, situated either apically or in the central part of the cell (apparently in the cell nucleus). One may ask if the constituents demonstrated by OKADA and by the author are identical. It is difficult to answer this question with any certainty, but if we compare the methods of preparing the extracts, and the distribution in double diffusion, of the kidney-specific constituents in the various subcellular fractions obtained by ultracentrifugation, it appears improbable that they could be the same. Okada used antisera against the deoxycholate-soluble fraction of microsomes; he observed no reaction with the supernatant, and only the deoxycholate-soluble fraction of the microsomes reacted positively in double diffusion; furthermore, judging from the isolation procedures as well as gross chemical analysis OKADA and SATO (1963) and OKADA (1965) assumed the kidney-specific antigens to be lipoproteins probably constituting the membraneous elements of the cells. In our experiments, on the other hand, we used antisera produced against total kidney homogenate; the three specific constituents identified in double diffusion are present primarily in the supernatant fraction (non-sedimenting at 100,000 g for 1 hour), and only traces of them are present in the mitochondrial fractions, and deoxycholate-soluble and -insoluble microsomal fractions. Furthermore, treatment of immuno-diffusion plates with Sudan Black (URIEL, 1960) has shown that the three constituents revealed by our antisera are not lipoprotein in nature. It thus seems that the constituents demonstrated by OKADA and the author are not the same, although as previously mentioned, no definite conclusions can be drawn.

Nonetheless, the results obtained by OKADA (1965) show that the first specific fluorescence is detectable in the mid-abdominal region at stage 17 to 18, perhaps immediately before the appearance of an epithelial architecture of the cells can be observed; this is some time after the passage of the Wolffian duct or, in other words, some time after induction. But at what precise moment does induction take place, or rather at what point does it begin? Although in normal development the mesonephric blastema is formed shortly after or during the passage of the Wolffian duct, we know from the work of BISHOP-CALAME (1966) that this blastema still forms even if the progression of the Wolffian duct is arrested. Furthermore, in the absence of the Wolffian duct, the blastema disappears by cell dispersion or necrosis (BISHOP-CALAME, 1966). The Wolffian duct is thus responsible for maintenance of the blastema, proliferation of the cells, and finally differentiation of the secretory tubules. Its inductive role seems to be exercised very shortly after its passage into the nephrogenic zone. It is estimated that about 10 to 15 hours elapse between this time, and the time when, according to the results of OKADA (1965), the first kidney-specific antigens can be detected. It may be observed that this interval is approximately the same both for interaction of the Wolffian duct with the mesonephric mesenchyme, and interaction of the optic vesicle with the presumptive lens ectoderm.

To sum up, we have now seen that the various organ-specific constituents appear progressively during development, the first one being detectable about 10 to 15 hours after induction. We shall attempt to discuss the significance of this time lapse at the end of this chapter.

D) Correlation between the time of induction and the appearance of new proteins in chick embryo skin

In the chick embryo, feather germ development results from the interaction of two tissues, one epithelial and the other mesenchymal; these inductive interactions have been elucidated by SENGEL (1958). Several phases can be distinguished in skin differentiation. Firstly, the dermis brings about differentiation of the ectoderm into epidermis. Next, small condensations of cells form in the dermis. Over each of these masses of dermal cells the epidermis starts to thicken; this is the stage of the feather primordium. Skin fragments explanted before the appearance of the first feather primordia do not differentiate feather germs in *in vitro* culture; older fragments, on the other hand, continue their morphogenesis *in vitro* and are able to differentiate feather germs. In 1964, BELL confirmed that skin fragments from embryos of $5\frac{1}{2}$ days incubation or younger, are incapable of differentiating feather germs *in vitro*, while fragments from embryos of 6 days incubation and older, develop their feather germs. The induction which leads to the acquisition, by the skin, of the capacity to differentiate feather germs therefore takes place between $5\frac{1}{2}$ and 6 days incubation.

BEN-OR and BELL (1965) show that proteins which cannot be detected at 5 days incubation or earlier, are detectable in the skin from the 6th day onwards, i.e. shortly after induction. Using antisera prepared against epidermal extracts of 7 day chick embryos, they detect 2 new constituents at 6 days incubation. However, the antibodies reacting with these constituents can be absorbed by liver or brain extracts from 7 day chick embryos; the constituents demonstrated are thus not specific for skin. Using antisera against feathers of 13 day chick embryos, BEN-OR and BELL were nevertheless able to detect the appearance of specific skin constituents at 6 and 13 days. If these antisera are first absorbed by a brain extract from 13 day embryos, they give two precipitation bands in double diffusion with feather extracts from 13 day embryos; one of these bands is given with skin extracts from 12, 11, 10 and 7 day embryos and with extracts of 6 day embryos; extracts of 5, 4 and 3 day embryos give no reaction with the antisera. From these observations, the authors conclude that, at 6 days incubation—i.e. immediately after induction—the presence of 3 new antigens can be demonstrated in the skin, one of which is specific for skin. It is not possible to estimate the time elapsing between the start of induction and the point at which specific constituents can be detected. However, by analogy with the systems previously described, this interval of time can be considered to be of the order of a few hours.

DISCUSSION AND CONCLUSIONS

Our original question concerned the part played by surface effects and/or the transfer of substances in inductive interactions; we saw in the first two sections that, while certain results suggest the participation of cell surface constituents in the establishment of contact, others indicate a transfer of substances during the interaction phase. Sometimes, however, both explanations are equally possible; furthermore, other interpretations are often just as feasible. There is some evidence to suggest that the substances transferred are protein in nature. When a cell suspension or tissue extract is administered to an individual, antibodies are formed primarily against the protein constituents. Thus the specific fluorescence observed in the experiments described in the first section could indicate a transfer of proteins from the inductive tissue to the reactive tissue. Furthermore, in the experiments of VAINIO (1957) the anti-bone marrow serum primarily affects the inductive capacity of bone marrow, which induces mesodermal formations; it has much less effect on guinea pig liver and kidney, which induce neural structures and both neural and mesodermal formations respectively. This suggests that the neural structure-inducing activity is due not only to a protein, but also to the existence of other reactive groups not inhibited by the antibodies. The protein nature of the mesodermal structure-inducing agent seems to be strongly substantiated by these results. However, in interpreting these observations, the antigenicity of substances other than proteins must be taken into account. This reservation also applies to the results discussed in the third section, concerning the synthesis of new proteins during organ differentiation; this is why we have mostly used the terms "antigenic substances" or "constituents". As to the second question—i.e. when do the various organ-specific proteins appear during differentiation—we have seen that the different constituents found in the adult appear progressively as the various cell types become specialized. In no instance was it possible to detect an organ-specific constituent prior to induction. In lens and kidney development, it was found that a certain period elapsed from the time when contact between the inductive and reactive tissues was established, to the time when the first specific constituent could be detected in the reactive tissue; this lapse of time is estimated at about 10 to 15 hours, and could represent the time necessary fo the inductive stimulus to reach a certain threshold, for transcription and translation of genetic information to take place, and particularly for the specific proteins to reach a local concentration which is sufficiently high to be detected. It is generally recognised that induction cannot be considered as a sudden event taking place immediately after contact between tissues has been established. It in fact seems that one of the characteristics common to all inductive interactions is the quite considerable time lapse separating the moment when contact is established, and the point at which the reactive tissue is capable of auto-differentiation in the absence of the inductive stimulus; this time interval is mostly of the order of a few hours (SAXEN and coworkers, 1965; GALLERA, 1965; LEIKOLA and McCALLION, 1967). Now, it is at the very time when the reactive tissue is capable of autodifferentiation, that the presence of organ-specific proteins can first be detected.

This last point naturally leads us to consider the problem of the sensitivity of the techniques used. One important aspect should be stressed here: whatever the titre and specificity of the immune sera used, and whatever the method employed, the absence of a positive reaction does not mean that a particular component is absent. Each technique has its own limits of sensitivity, and the same researcher using the same antiserum may still not obtain the same results when employing methods as different as the ring-test and the immunofluorescence techniques. In the latter technique, the observation of a positive reaction does not depend on the total amount of protein present, but on the local concentration in a restricted zone of the cell. Thus an appreciable amount of protein may be present, but not detectable, if it is distributed uniformly throughout the cell. In the light of these observations, it might appear somewhat futile to ask when the first organ-specific protein is synthesised during differentiation, since the answer depends largely on the sensitivity of the techniques used. However, as it is possible to detect specific proteins in a single cell in the first stages of differentiation, using immunofluorescence techniques, IKEDA and ZWAAN (1967) consider it highly likely that these constituents can be detected very shortly after the beginning of their synthesis.

For greater simplicity and clarity, we shall limit the greater part of the discussion to the problems of induction and differentiation in the chick lens. We have seen that, according to the results of IKEDA and ZWAAN (1966), the first specific lens protein can be detected in the placode of the 23 somite stage chick embryo. However, in an earlier review (CROISILLE, 1963), we examined a number of publications showing the existence of substances capable of reacting with anti-adult lens sera at much earlier stages, particularly in the young optic vesicle, the presumptive ectoderm, extracts of heads or trunks of neurulae,* and even in extracts of young immature frog oocytes. In the past, these results had led to the development of a number of theories concerning induction. Thus the capacity of the ectoderm to differentiate into a lens was attributed to the presence of specific lens proteins in the competent tissue. The demonstration in the young optic vesicle of substances which could react with anti-adult lens sera, suggested a transfer of specific lens substances—or at least precursors—from the optic vesicle to the ectoderm during induction (see discussions of TEN CATE, 1965, and IKEDA and ZWAAN, 1966). However, the results obtained by most researchers, like the results just examined, do not fit in with these hypotheses. The majority of researchers have been unable to confirm the presence of specific lens constituents, either in the optic vesicle or in the competent tissues, and agree that these constituents first appear in the lens ectoderm of chick embryos at 50 to 60 hours incubation, i.e. shortly after induction. Clearly, it might be supposed that one or more molecules exist at earlier stages, and that their presence cannot be detected by most of the techniques employed. But such an argument inevitably raises once again the dispute between the protagonists of preformation and those believing in epigenesis, in this case at the molecular level. In this context, LOVTRUP (1966) states: "I presume that, in contrast to opinions held in earlier times, nobody maintains today that the embryo is preformed in the egg, ready to develop by what may be called a growth process. In

other words, none of the morphological entities, liver, brain ... etc., are
present", and a little further on he adds: "if the various organs are absent
it would seem an obvious inference that no organ-specific proteins can
occur, since the synthesis of these compounds must depend upon the
activity of the respective differentiated cells". In any case, proteins do not
possess the power of reduplicating themselves; what is required for their
synthesis is not a protein prototype, but the genetic code present in the
cell nucleus (LOVTRUP, 1966). The results discussed here, like the observations made by the majority of authors, point to a plausible and logical
scheme of what takes place in the ectoderm at the time of induction. At
present, it seems clear that the presence of specific lens proteins is not an
essential condition for the realization of the inductive phenomenon. It
appears more probable that the synthesis of these proteins follows induction
after a certain time interval. Furthermore, if the lens placode of a mouse
embryo is grafted into the eye of a chick embryo, the crystallins synthesised
are of mouse, not chick type (IKEDA and ZWAAN, 1966). This experiment
shows that the genes of the ectoderm, and not those of the optic vesicle,
determine the type of proteins synthesised; it also contradicts the idea
that pre-existing crystallins, or their precursors, are transferred from the
optic vesicle to the ectoderm. But we must be careful not to overgeneralize
and say that nothing passes from the optic vesicle to the ectoderm. It is
undeniable that the optic vesicle sends a signal to the ectoderm during the
contact phase, and this signal doubtless enables the ectoderm to express
part of its potentialities by activating a specific part of the genome. According to IKEDA and ZWAAN (1966), the optic vesicle factors could act either
directly as derepressors, or indirectly by contributing to the establishment
of changes in the lens ectoderm cell cytoplasm. But the nature of the signal,
and the mechanism of action remain unknown.

By analogy with the mechanisms proposed to explain the regulation of
protein biosynthesis in micro-organisms (JACOB and MONOD, 1961a, 1961b,
1963), various authors have put forward the idea that inductive actions
merely have a releasing or de-blocking character (NIEWKOOP, 1966) and
that embryonic induction can be considered as a derepression (TIEDE-
MANN, 1966). It is true that the explanation proposed by JACOB and MONOD
"sheds so much light on hitherto very obscure phenomena that it cannot
be overlooked" (WOLFF, 1966). But how far can the mechanisms ex-
plaining the regulation of protein synthesis in micro-organisms be applied
to inductive interactions between tissues? It should be noted that the term

"induction" in itself, when applied to one of the mechanisms by which protein synthesis is regulated in micro-organisms, does not have the same significance as when it designates tissue interactions during embryonic development. This difference in the term's interpretation has been stressed by various authors, especially HOLTZER (1963): "Enzyme induction in microbial systems (or even metazoans) is a homeostatic response, a physiological response of a terminally differentiated unit. In contrast, the biological significance of induction in cell differentiation is to insure that the cell, after induction, is engaged in a new activity and does not revert to its pre-induced state". While it seems probable that the fundamental mechanisms recognized in micro-organisms are also utilised by higher organisms (JACOB and MONOD, 1961), it also appears that multicellular organisms present infinitely more complex problems and must be expected to possess mechanisms which are non-existent in unicellular organisms (JACOB and MONOD, 1963). In order to regulate the level of synthesis of different proteins, the embryo doubtless makes use of mechanisms similar or identical to those used by unicellular organisms; it has in fact been possible, particularly in the chick embryo, to observe an increase in the synthesis of certain enzymes in response to the administration of substrate. What are the mechanisms responsible for initiating these *de novo* syntheses, which are seen to follow inductive interactions between tissues? We may well be justified in considering that they are fundamentally the same as those subsequently regulating the production level of the various components elaborated by the cell; however, there is at present no definite evidence on this point.

Before concluding, we should like to raise another problem, relating to the results described in the third section of this chapter. One may ask if, in relation to our knowledge on the mechanisms of cellular differentiation, there is anything to be gained by looking at the time of appearance of the various specific proteins. Using immunochemical methods, it has been possible to show that at least one organ-specific constituent is present at a rather early stage, doubtless before any apparent morphological differentiation, but it has been impossible to detect specific constituents prior to all visible cytological differentiation or before determination. At that point in lens development when the first organ-specific constituents can be detected, the ectoderm, under the influence of the optic vesicle, has already undergone profound transformations; certain of these are visible under the optical microscope (MCKEEHAN, 1951, 1954), or the electron microscope (WEISS and FITTON-JACKSON, 1961; HUNT, 1961; BYERS and PORTER, 1964), while most others, produced at the molecular level, are undetectable. The overall result of these transformations is that when a placode from a 21 somite embryo is transplanted into the coelom of another embryo, it is capable of autodifferentiation giving a small lens with character-istic fibres (MCKEEHAN, 1954). Although the chemical mechanisms under-lying these very first transformations and leading to the determination of the tissues, are in process of being elucidated, they are still poorly under-stood. Like TEN CATE (1965) we shall for convenience use the term "primary chemical differentiation", so as to distinguish this period from the later phases of chemical differentiation, which are easier to study and which have been the main subject matter of this chapter. According to TEN CATE (1965), the study of the appearance of proteins during development is nothing more than descriptive chemical embryology. It is still not certain whether these constituents are merely a consequence or an index of differen-tiation, or whether they play an effective role in differentiation processes. It appears that when we detect the various proteins, we are in fact detecting the end products of gene activity and hence the end products of an earlier chemical differentiation. The mechanisms initiating the synthesis of these constituents are largely, if not entirely unknown. Doubts have sometimes been expressed as to the value of making an inventory of the various proteins appearing at different stages of embryonic development, but we do not consider these doubts to be justified. Before studying the mechanisms responsible for initiating and regulating protein synthesis during develop-ment, it is wise to possess definite information on the time of synthesis and the quantitative variations in the different proteins. Immunochemical methods should prove very valuable in this sphere of experimental embryol-ogy. We should like to end by quoting a relevant comment of EBERT (1965): "there is merit in making an inventory of proteins and describing changes in them during development, not only because we want to learn all we can about differentiation, but also because we must constantly be on the lookout for systems in which the entire range of reactions may be studied".

References

BECK, J. S. (1963). Antibodies as cytological tools. *Brit. Med. Bull.*, **19**, 192–196.

BELL, E. (1964). The induction of differentiation and the response to the inducer. *Cancer Res.*, **24**, 28–34.

BEN-OR, S., and BELL, E. (1965). Skin antigens in the chick embryo in relation to other developmental events. *Develop. Biol.*, **11**, 184–201.

BISHOP-CALAME, S. (1966). Etude experimentale de l'organogenèse du système urogénital de l'embryon de poulet. *Arch. Anat. Microscop. Morphol. Exp.*, **55**, 215–309.

BITENSKY, L. (1963). Cytotoxic action of antibodies. *Brit. Med. Bull.*, **19**, 241–244.

BRACHET, J. (1957). *Biochemical Cytology*. Academic Press, New York.

BRACHET, J. (1960). *The Biochemistry of Development*. Pergamon Press, London, New York, Paris.

BURKE, V., SULLIVAN, N. P., PETERSEN, H., and WEED, R. (1944). Ontogenetic change in antigenic specificity of the organs of the chick. *J. Infect. Diseases.*, **74**, 225–233.

BYERS, B., and PORTER, K. R. (1964). Oriented microtubules in elongating cells of the developing lens rudiment after induction. *Proc. Nat. Acad. Sc.*, **52**, 1091–1098.

CLARKE, W. M., and FOWLER, I. (1960). The inhibition of lens-inducing capacity of the optic vesicle with adult lens antisera. *Develop. Biol.*, **2**, 155–172.

CLARKE, N. M., and FOWLER, I. (1961). The nature of the toxicity of adult lens antisera. *Anat. Record*, **139**, 216–217.

CLAYTON, R. M. (1960). Labelled antibodies in the study of differentiation. In *"New Approaches in Cell Biology"* (Ed. Walker P.), 67–88, Academic Press, New York.

CLAYTON, R. M., and ROMANOVSKY, A. (1959). Passage of antigenic material between inductor and ectoderm. *Exp. Cell. Res.*, **18**, n° 2, 410–412.

COONS, A. K., and KAPLAN, M. H. (1950). Localization of antigens in tissue cells. Improvements on a method for the detection of antigens by means of fluorescent antibody. *J. exp. Med.*, **91**, 1.

CROISILLE, Y. (1958). Les méthodes immunochimiques appliquées à l'étude du développement embryonnaire. *Ann. Biol.*, **34**, 331–351.

CROISILLE, Y. (1958). Action de différents extraits d'organes sur l'embryon de poulet et sur des organes embryonnaires cultivés *in vitro*. *Arch. Anat. Microscop. Morphol. Exp.*, **47**, 359–400.

CROISILLE, Y. (1962). Etude immunochimique de quelques constituants caractéristiques de l'adulte dans le rein embryonnaire du poulet. *Compt. Rend. Soc. Biol.*, **156**, 1221–1225.

CROISILLE, Y. (1963). Application des méthodes immunochimiques à l'étude des problèmes de l'induction et de la différenciation. *Ann. Biol.*, **2**, 155–177.

CROISILLE, Y. (1965). Synthèse et distribution des protéines contractiles, myosine et actine, pendant le développement des muscles cardiaque et squelettique chez l'embryon de poulet. In *"Méthodes nouvelles en Embryologie"*. Séminaire 1964 de la Chaire d'Embryologie expérimentale du Collège de France publié sous la direction de Et. Wolff. Hermann, Paris, 175–199.

CROISILLE, Y. (1965). Etude, par les méthodes immunochimiques, de l'apparition de quelques constituants caractéristiques du foie et du rein adultes pendant le développement embryonnaire du poulet. In "*Méthodes Nouvelles en Embryologie*". Séminaire 1964 de la Chaire d'Embryologie Expérimentale du Collège de France publié sous la direction de Et. Wolff. Hermann (Paris), 203–231.

CROISILLE, Y. (1969). Détection et localisation de constituants spécifiques de rein adulte à des stades précoces de la différenciation chez l'embryon de poulet. *Compt. Rend. Acad. Sc.*, **268**, 375–378.

DE VINCENTIIS, M. (1954). Alcune indagini sui meccanismi che presiedono la morfogenesi del cristallino. *Boll. Zool.*, **21**, 379.

DE VINCENTIIS, M. (1957). Sui fattori che presiedono al differenziamento dell' abbozzo oculare con particolare riguardo alla morfogenesi del cristallino. Extrait de: "*Attualità zoologiche*" suppl. *Arch. Zool. Ital.* (272 pages).

EBERT, J. D. (1955). Some aspects of protein biosynthesis in development. In "*Aspects of synthesis and order in Growth*" (Ed. Rudnick D.), 69–112, Princeton University Press.

EBERT, J. D. (1958). Immunochemical analysis of development. In "*A Symposium on the chemical basis of development*". (Ed. McElroy W. et Glass B.), Johns Hopkins Press Baltimore, 526–545.

EBERT, J. D. (1959). The acquisition of biological specificity. In *The Cell*, Vol. I (Ed. J. Brachet and A. Mirsky), 619–693. Acad. Press. N.Y.

EBERT, J. D. (1965). *Interacting systems in Development*. Holt, Rinehart and Winston. New York, London.

EDDS, M. V. (1958). *Immunology and development*. (Ed. Edds M. V.), University of Chicago Press.

FICQ, A. (1954). Analyse de l'induction neurale chez les Amphibiens au moyen d'organisateurs marqués. *J. Embryol. Exp. Morphol.*, **2**, 194–203.

FLICKINGER, R. A. (1962). Embryological development of antigens. In "*Advances in Immunology*", **2**, 310–366 (Taliaferro W. H. and Humphrey J. H. eds), Academic Press, New York.

FLICKINGER, R. A., HATTON, E., and ROUNDS, D. E. (1959). Protein transfer in chimaeric Taricha-Rana explants. *Exp. Cell Res.*, **17**, n° 1, 30–34.

FOWLER, I, and CLARKE, N. M. (1959). The inhibition of lens-inducing capacity of the optic vesicle with adult lens antisera. *Anat. Record*, **133**, 217.

GALLERA, J. (1965). Quelle est la durée nécessaire pour déclencher des inductions neurales chez le poulet? *Experientia*, **21**, 218–219.

GRABAR, P., and WILLIAMS, C. A. (1953). Méthode permettant l'étude conjuguée des propriétés électrophorétiques et immunochimiques d'un mélange de protéines. *Biochim. Biophys. Acta.*, **10**, 193.

GROBSTEIN, C. (1956). Transfilter induction of tubules in mouse metanephric mesenchyme. *Exp. Cell Res.*, **10**, 424–440.

HOLTZER, H. (1963). Comments on induction during cell differentiation. In "*Induktion und Morphogenese*", Springer-Verlag (Berlin).

HUNT, H. H. (1961). A study of the fine structure of the optic vesicle and lens placode of the chick embryo during induction. *Develop. Biol.*, **3**, n° 2, 175–209.

IKEDA, A., and ZWAAN, J. (1966). Immunofluorescence studies on induction and differentiation of the chicken eye lens. *Invest. Ophtalmol.*, **5**, 402–412.

IKEDA, A., and ZWAAN, J. (1967). The changing cellular localization of α-crystallin in the lens of the chicken embryo, studied by immunofluorescence. *Develop. Biol.*, **15**, 348–367.

JACOB, F., and MONOD, J. (1961). Genetic regulatory mechanisms in the synthesis of Proteins. *J. Mol. Biol.*, **3**, 318–356.

JACOB, F., and MONOD, J. (1961). On the regulation of gene activity. *Cold Spring Harbor Symposia on Quantitative Biology*, **26**, 193–211.

JACOB, F., and MONOD, J. (1963). Genetic repression, allosteric inhibition and cellular differentiation. In *"Cytodifferentiation and macromolecular synthesis"* (M. Locke Ed.), Academic Press, 30–64.

LEIKOLA, A., and McCALLION, D. J. (1967). Time required for heterogenous induction in chick embryo ectoderm. *Experientia*, **23**, 869.

LOVTRUP, S. (1966). The chemical basis of sea urchin embryogenesis. *Bull. Swiss. Acad. Med. Sc.*, **22**, 201–276.

MAISEL, H., and LANGMAN, J. (1961). An immuno-embryological study on the chick lens. *J. Embryol. Exp. Morphol.*, **9**, n° 1, 191–201.

McCALLION, D. J., and LANGMAN, J. (1964). An immunological study on the effect of brain extract on the developing nervous tissue in the chick embryo. *J. Embryol. Exp. Morph.*, **12**, 77–88.

McKEEHAN, M. S. (1951). Cytological aspects of embryonic lens induction in the chick. *J. Exp. Zool.*, **117**, 31–64.

McKEEHAN, M. S. (1954). A quantitative study of self differentiation of transplanted lens primordia in the chick. *J. Exp. Zool.*, **126**, 157–175.

McKEEHAN, M. S. (1956). The relative ribonucleic acid content of lens and retina during lens induction in the chick. *Am. J. Anat.*, **99**, 131–156.

McKEEHAN, M. S. (1958). Induction of portions of the chick lens without contact with the optic cup. *Anat. Record*, **132**, 297–303.

MONOD, J., and JACOB, F. (1961). Teleonomic mechanisms in cellular metabolism, growth and differentiation. *Cold Spring Harbor Symposia on Quantitative Biology*, **26**, 389–401.

MOSCONA, A., and MOSCONA, M. H. (1962). Specific inhibition of cell aggregation by antiserum to suspensions of embryonic cells. *Anat. Record*, **142**, 319–320.

NACE, G. W. (1955). Development in the presence of antibodies. *Ann. N.Y. Acad. Sci.*, **60**, 1038–1055.

NIEWKOOP, P. D. (1966). Induction and pattern formation as primary mechanisms in early embryonic differentiation. In *"Cell differentiation and Morphogenesis"*. North Holland Publ. Co. (Amsterdam), 120–143.

NIU, M. C., and TWITTY, V. C. (1953). The differentiation of gastrula ectoderm in medium conditioned by axial mesoderm. *Proc. Nat. Acad. Sc.*, **39**, 985–989.

OKADA, T. S. (1962). Tissue specificity in the soluble antigens in kidney microsomes. *Nature G. B.*, **194**, 306–307.

OKADA, T. S. (1965). Development of kidney-specific antigens, an immuno-histological study. *J. Embryol. Exp. Morphol.*, Vol. **13**, fasc. 3, 285–297.

OKADA, T. S., and SATO, A. G. (1963). Soluble antigens in microsomes of adult and embryonic kidneys. *Exp. Cell Res.*, **31**, 251–265.

OUCHTERLONY, O. (1948). Antigen-antibody reactions in gels. *Arkiv. Kemi Mineral. Geol.*, **26** B, nº 14.

PERLMANN, P., and DE VINCENTIIS, M. (1961). Lens antigen in the microsomal fraction of early chick embryos. *Exp. Cell Res.*, **23**, 612–616.

RABAEY, M. (1962). Electrophoretic and immunoelectrophoretic studies on the soluble proteins in the developing lens of birds. *Exp. Eye Res.*, **1**, 310–316.

RANZI, S. (1965). Problèmes d'immunochimie et de la différenciation protéique dans le développement des Oursins, des Batraciens et d'autres animaux. In *"Méthodes Nouvelles en Embryologie"*. Séminaire 1964 de la Chaire d'Embryologie expérimentale du Collège de France publié sous la direction de Et. Wolff. Hermann (Paris), 37–73.

ROUNDS, D. E., and FLICKINGER, R. E. (1958). Distribution of ribonucleoprotein during neural induction of the frog embryo. *J. Exp. Zool.*, **137**, 479–500.

SAXEN, L., and TOIVONEN, S. (1962). *Primary embryonic induction.* Logos Press, Academic Press (London).

SAXEN, L., TOIVONEN, S., and VAINIO, T. (1964). Initial stimulus and subsequent interactions in embryonic induction. *J. Embryol. Exp. Morphol.*, **12**, 333–338.

SAXEN, L., WARTIOVAARA, Y., HÄYRY, P., and VAINIO, T. (1965). Cell contact and tissue interactions in cytodifferentiation. *Fourth Scand. Congr. Cell Res.*, 21–36.

SCHALEKAMP, M. A. (1963). *Immunologische aspecten van de orgaanontwikkeling.* Doctor Thesis, Utrecht University (Meijer-Woormerveer, Amsterdam).

SCHECHTMAN, A. M. (1955). Ontogeny of the blood and related antigens and their significance for the theory of differentiation. In *"Biological specificity and Growth"* (ed. E. Butler). Princeton Univ. Press., 3–31.

SENGEL, Ph. (1958). Recherches expérimentales sur la différenciation des germes plumaires et du pigment de la peau de l'embryon de poulet en culture *in vitro*. *Ann. Sc. Nat. Zool.*, **20**, 432–514.

SIRLIN, J. L., and BRAHMA, S. K. (1959). Studies on embryonic induction using radioactive tracers. *Develop. Biol.*, **1**, 234–246.

SOLOMON, J. B. (1965). Development of non-enzymatic proteins in relation to functional differentiation. In *"Biochemistry of Animal Development"*. (R. Weber ed.). Academic Press, 367–440.

SPIEGEL, M. (1954). The role of specific surface antigens in cell adhesion. I) The reaggregation of sponge cells. *Biol. Bull.*, **107**, 130–148.

SPIEGEL, M. (1954). The role of specific surface antigens in cell adhesion. II) Studies on embryonic amphibian cells. *Biol. Bull.*, **107**, 149–155.

SPIEGEL, M. (1955). The reaggregation of dissociated sponge cells. *Ann. N.Y. Acad. Sci.*, **60**, 1056–1076.

TEN CATE, G. (1965). Considerations on the problem of differentiation and a review of immunochemical studies on the embryonic brain and ocular lens. In *"Méthodes nouvelles en Embryologie"*. Séminaire 1964 de la Chaire d'Embryologie expérimentale du Collège de France publié sous la direction de Et. WOLFF. Hermann (Paris), 77–148.

TIEDEMANN, H. (1966). The molecular basis of differentiation in early development of amphibian embryos. In *"Current Topics in developmental Biology"* (Moscona AA Monroy A, Eds.). Acad. Press N.Y., London. Vol. I, 85–112.

TIEDEMANN, H., TIEDEMANN, H., and KESSELRING, K. (1960). Versuche zur Kennzeichnung von Induktionsstoffen aus Hühnerembryonen. *Z. Naturforsch.*, **15** *b*, 312–319.

TIEDEMANN, H., KESSELRING, K., BECKER, U., and TIEDEMANN, H. (1961). The chemical nature of organ determining substances in the early development of embryos. *Biochim., Biophys. Acta.*, **49**, 603–605.

TOIVONEN, S. (1949). Zur Frage der Leistungsspezifität abnormer Induktoren. *Experientia*, **5**, 323–325.

TOIVONEN, S. (1950). Stoffliche Induktoren. *Rev. Suisse Zool.*, **57**, 41–56.

TOIVONEN, S. (1953). Bone-marrow of the guinea-pig as a mesodermal inductor in implantation experiments with embryos of Triturus. *J. Embryol. Exp. Morphol.*, **1**, 97–104.

TOIVONEN, S. (1954). The inducing action of the bone-marrow of the guinea-pig after alcohol treatment in implantation and explantation experiments with embryos of Triturus. *J. Embryol. Exp. Morphol.*, **2**, 239–244.

TURCHINI, J. (1968). Recent research on enzymatic induction. In "The Relationship between Experimental Embryology and Molecular Biology". Gordon & Breach, New York.

TYLER, A. (1955). Ontogeny of immunological properties. In *"Analysis of Development"*. (Ed. B. H. Willier, P. Weiss, V. Hamburger.) W. B. Saunders Co., 556–573.

TYLER, A. (1957). Immunological studies of early development. In *"Beginnings of embryonic development"*. (Ed. Tyler, Von Borstel, Metz), A.A.A.S. (Washington), 341–382.

URIEL, J. (1960). Les réactions de caractérisation des constituants protéiques après électrophorèse et immunoéletrophorèse en gélose. In *"Analyse immunoélectrophorétique"*, P. Grabar, P. Burtin, Masson (Paris), 33–56.

VAINIO, T. (1957). An experimental study of the complementariness of heterogenous efflbryonic inductive agents. *Ann. Acad. Sci. Fennicae, Ser. A IV* (Helsinki), IV, **35**, 1.

VAINIO, T., SAXEN, L., and TOIVONEN, S. (1960). Transfer of the antigenicity of guinea pig bone marrow implants to the graft tissue in explantation experiments. *Experientia*, **16**, n° 1, 27–29.

VAN DAM, A. F., SCHALEKAMP, M. A., SCHALEKAMP-KUYKEN, M., and TEN CATE, G. (1963). Immunoelectrophoretic studies on adult and embryonic ocular lenses. VIth. Internat. *Embryol. Conf.* (Helsinki), 22–25, VII 1963.

VAN DOORENMAALEN, W. Y. (1965). Immunohistological studies of proteins during the development of chick lens. In *"Méthodes nouvelles en Embryologie"*. Séminaire 1964 de la Chaire d'Embryologie expérimentale du Collège de France publié sous la direction de Et. Wolff. Hermann (Paris), 151–171.

WEISS, P., and FITTON-JACKSON, S. (1961). Fine-structural changes associated with lens determination in the avian embryo. *Develop. Biol.*, **3**, 532–554.

WOERDEMAN, M. W. (1950). Over de toepassing von serologische methods in de experimental embryologie. *Proc. Acad. Sci. Amsterdam*, **59**, 5.

WOERDEMAN, M. W. (1955). Immunological approach to some problems of induction and differentiation. In *"Biological specificity and Growth"*. (Ed. E. Butler). Princeton Univ. Press., 33–53.

WOLFF, Et. (1966). General factors of embryonic differentiation. In *"Cell differentiation and Morphogenesis"*, International lecture Course, Wageningen, IV-1965, North Holland Publ. Co. (Amsterdam), 1–23.

WOLFF, Et. (1966). Recherches récentes sur la différenciation embryonnaire. *Scientia*, III, IV-1966, 1–11.

WOLFF, Et., and HAFFEN, K. (1952). Sur une technique permettant la culture *in vitro* des gonades embryonnaires des oiseaux. *C.R. Acad. Sc.*, **234**, 1396–1398.

YAMADA, T. (1958). Induction of specific differentiation by samples of proteins and nucleoproteins in the isolated ectoderm of Triturus gastrulae. *Experientia*, **14**, 81–87.

ZWAAN, J. (1963). *Immunochemical analysis of the eye lens during development*. Thesis, University of Amsterdam.

CHAPTER X

GENERAL CONCLUSIONS

Etienne Wolff

Laboratoire d'Embryologie expérimentale, Collège de France, and C.N.R.S.,
Nogent-sur-Marne

IN STUDYING differentiation mechanisms, it is possible to detect a general process known as embryonic induction. One embryonic *rudiment* acting on a neighbouring one, as yet undetermined, orientates the latter towards a precise differentiation. The first *rudiment* is termed the *inducer*, the second the *competent* tissue. The concept of embryonic induction is very different from that of induction as applied to enzymology. Enzymatic induction is the enhancement of a pre-existing process, the stimulation of an activity already functioning at a low level. It is not a case of *de novo* creation, or the first appearance of a differentiation. On the contrary, embryonic induction causes an embryonic *rudiment* to pass from an undifferentiated (but pluripotential) state to a differentiated state. This is creation in the true sense, after which a tissue exhibits new properties, characterized by a precise structure or the synthesis of well-defined chemical substances.

Induction phenomena have been especially fully studied in vertebrates. But they have been demonstrated in many other animal species, such as arthropods, echinoderms, worms and molluscs. They are known to occur both in embryonic development and in the regeneration of organisms.

The question arises as to whether all differentiation involves a preliminary induction. This concept is not wholly applicable to the first determined anlage of an organism, since an organ must be determined in order to provoke induction in another anlage. Thus the primary inducer, i.e. the chorda-mesodermal anlage of Amphibia, is determined by a process other than induction. Let us suppose that a first anlage is determined: do all the others then become determined by a series of chain reactions, where one anlage induces another, which in turn can become an inducer and possibly affect the destiny of the first? Although a logical inference, it cannot strictly be laid down that the process of induction alone can initiate differentiation. Apart from the first determination just mentioned, it is possible that other determinations come about through mechanisms other than induction. It must not be forgotten that many ova manifest some degree of preformation, that some areas are already determined in the unsegmented egg or during the early stages of segmentation (molluscs, annelids). The non-uniform distribution in the egg of certain substances, such as reserves or pigments, often determines the position of future organs (Ascidia). The localization of differentiated anlage thus comes about by mechanisms other than induction.

Even in embryos as isotropic as those of birds and mammals, is there any certainty that most differentiations result from induction phenomena? We only have to think of the very early determination of cardiac rudiments in the chick embryo, and the simultaneous determination in these rudiments of the various parts—sinus, atrium, ventricles—with their electrophysiological characteristics, as shown by LE DOUARIN and coworkers (1966) using *in vitro* culture methods and intracellular electrodes.

At the primitive streak stage, i.e. the stage of primary induction, a whole complex of anlage arises rapidly and simultaneously; and yet no induction phenomena can be demonstrated between the many anlage acquiring their determination at this stage and which almost instantaneously form a mosaic of areas whose destiny is ordained. The hypothesis cannot be excluded that certain tissue complexes, having undergone the action of the primary inducer, become specialized spontaneously into a mosaic of anlage without individually requiring a particular induction. This is what happens when parts of an embryo are removed, explanted, and then differentiate into numerous organs, possibly forming more or less complete embryos. Such is the fate, for example, of the chorda-mesodermal anlage of amphibian embryos; despite their general determination, these anlage can differentiate many more organs in culture than they would normally (HOLTFRETER, 1938). To say that these anlage possess the power of regulation, that they constitute equipotential systems or morphogenetic fields, does not explain the fact that all these areas become determined spontaneously, and not through the agency of classical inductions. The latter can, however, play a subsequent part in the overall process, for example, in differentiation of the nervous system. It may be envisaged that an anlage with multiple potentialities, such as the chorda-mesoderm, can manifest all these potentialities when not inhibited by factors from neighbouring anlage.

These reservations apart, induction is a general phenomenon encountered both in primary development and in organogenesis. The first consequence of an inductive action is to make a competent tissue pass from the undetermined to the *determined* state. Determination is a transitory state, generally of short duration, during which an anlage is orientated towards a particular differentiation without the latter being visible. It is a sort of predifferentiation, not manifested by morphological characteristics but which remains in the latent state. Chemical and ultrastructural analysis could certainly provide valuable information on this stage of transition towards morphological differentiation. As regards biochemical modifications, let us simply recall the transformations observed in RNA and DNA synthesis at the stage of primary induction in the gastrula of amphibia.

Again, there is the appearance of fibrillae, visible by electron microscopy, in the cardiac rudiments of chick embryo at a stage where no differentiation can yet be discerned under the optical microscope (LE DOUARIN, 1965). There can thus be no doubt that something happens in the embryonic rudiments at the time of determination, and that a close study of the chemical modifications produced at the time of induction and immediately afterwards would be of great interest. The research of Hadorn, discussed in chapter I of this book, throws new light on our understanding of the state of determination. We have seen that the transplantation of imaginal disks into the abdomen of adult *Drosophila* prolongs the state of determination, and that successive transplantations can maintain it indefinitely. At the same time, the tissues multiply actively; the quantity of utilisable determined tissues becomes considerable, and can be studied by many available techniques. It is not so much the prolongation of the phase of determination which is remarkable, but rather the increase in quantity of determined tissue; under normal conditions of development, the imaginal discs are determined at a very early stage of embryonic development and remain so throughout larval life until metamorphosis. Hadorn's method should make it possible to clarify the differences between undetermined, determined and differentiated tissues. The phenomena of transdetermination indicate that certain determinations are not irreversible, and that while determination prepares the way for chemical and morphological differentiation of certain tissues, there may be more than one possible end result. There must therefore be fundamental biochemical differences between the

14*

determined and the differentiated state—the former allowing a *rudiment* to differentiate in a number of possible ways.

From a detailed study of certain induction processes, we have gained some information on the nature of this phenomenon, and the way it comes about. These findings have removed the mystery from a concept considered somewhat obscure and metaphysical by certain authors; it has been given a concrete content, open to experimental study. For the concept of induction, we have substituted that of interaction between tissues: an embryonic *rudiment* induced by another tissue, often exercises a reciprocal inductive action on this tissue, thus specifying its determination. In this way, the mesodermal *rudiment* has a determinant action on nervous system differentiation, but is subject in turn to the influence of this nervous system: the mesenchyme, arising from the somitic mesoderm, becomes organised into cranial bones and vertebrae through the inductive action of the neural tube—brain and medulla. Those organs formed initially from two associated rudiments show interactions which are often complex, in which each rudiment orders the differentiation of its partner. In limb differentiation, we see a succession of complex actions and reactions between the mesodermal axis and the "ectodermal cap", ending in differentiation of the various parts of the limb (KIENY, 1960; SAUNDERS, 1948; SAUNDERS, GASSELING and GFELLER, 1958; HAMPE, 1957, 1959; ZWILLING, 1955, 1956). But the very recent research of PINOT (1969) shows that the phenomena involved are even more complex than had been thought; limb morphogenesis cannot result from interactions between the two components of the *rudiment* unless the bud has also undergone induction by neighbouring organs, the somites, situated exactly at the level of one or other limb bud.

Heterogenous associations between two *rudiments* not belonging to the same organ provide clearer information on the nature of inductions contributing to the differentiation of an organ. The combination of lung or liver epithelium with metanephric mesenchyme, or of a ureter with various mesenchymes, makes it possible to clarify certain aspects of induction. Inducers can be said to exercise a specific action on other tissues in two possible ways:

1. They may impose their differentiation on the competent tissue. This is what happens when a ureter is associated either with its own (metanephric) mesenchyme, or with lung or gizzard mesenchyme. In all three cases, secretory tubules form in the mesenchyme (BISHOP-CALAME, 1966).

2. They may be the only inducers which can produce *normal* and *complete*

differentiation of the competent tissue. Here the inducer does not always have a strict specificity, as tissues other than the normal inducer can orientate the differentiation of the competent tissue. Thus metanephric mesenchyme can provoke differentiation of pulmonary or hepatic epithelium. But these differentiations are incomplete, either morphologically (Dameron, chapter VII) or biochemically (Le DOUARIN, chapter III). In mouse metanephros, it appears that other tissues such as the neural tube (GROBSTEIN, 1955) can be substituted for the ureter, the natural inducer of the convoluted tubules. Differentiation appears to be normal, but it has not been possible to observe subsequent development long enough to confirm this. In many other cases, the natural inducer is the only one which can produce differentiation of the competent tissue. This is true for different parts of the neural tube and brain, which cannot replace one another in inducing differentiation of the cranial bones and vertebrae.

The reaction of a heterogenous tissue is often remarkable: two types of response may be seen.

1. It may impose a differentiation on the inducer, in conformity with its own nature. Thus the mesenchymes of lung, proventriculus, and intestine of chick embryo transform the ureter wall into a mucosa resembling that of lung, proventriculus and intestine, respectively. This shows that these tissues have already undergone a first determination, and that they can impose it on a heterogenous inducer, while still being subject to its influence.

2. In other cases, the heterogenous component undergoes the influence of the associated inducer, but does not obey its orders—and develops those structures which it would normally have differentiated. Thus the pulmonary rudiment, in presence of metanephric mesenchyme, induces renal secretory tubules and not pulmonary structures. The pulmonary epithelium can be considered as a weak inducer, initiating the phenomenon of differentiation but not imposing the nature of this differentiation. It is relevant to note here that it does not have an inductive role in normal development; on the contrary, it undergoes induction by its own mesenchyme, following which it acquires its histological structure and ramifies. Under the abnormal conditions of association with the metanephric mesenchyme, it acts as a stimulant of differentiation; however, since it cannot impose the nature of the differentiation, the metanephric mesenchyme expresses its own innate potentialities.

Having demonstrated the precise action of inductive tissues, it is possible to reject the hypothesis that they merely initiate reactions in a non-specific way, without influencing the nature of the differentiation. We need only recall that an inducer such as the chorda-mesoderm or medulla has no action on limb or liver morphogenesis, to be convinced that the inducers cannot be considered as mere non-specific stimulants.

One main problem remains to be discussed: how do the inductive tissues act? It can no longer be doubted, from the results of many authors, that something passes from the inductive to the competent tissue. There are two points of view:

a) Substances from the inducer pass into the competent tissue and modify the chemical composition of its molecules.

b) The inductive action is due to surface interactions between the two tissues, without a transfer of substances from one to the other taking place.

The results of many experiments accord with the first hypothesis. It has been possible to separate the inducer from the reactive tissue by filters (millipore) or dialysing membranes, which allow no contact between the two tissues (GROBSTEIN, 1956; DAMERON, 1968). Experiments where the medium was conditioned by a diffused substance (NIU and TWITTY, 1953), where crude or purified extracts of inductive organs had the same action as the primary inducer (TOIVONEN, 1954; TIEDEMANN, 1959; SAXÉN and TOIVONEN, 1961), demonstrate that soluble substances, fractions with known chemical affinities belonging to the protein group, are capable of effectively replacing living tissues with respect to their inductive properties. The research of MARIN and SIGOT (1963, 1965) provides proof that inductive tissues leave a structureless exudate on the supporting material, which has the same properties as the inductive tissues themselves. Lastly, it should be remembered that sexual differentiation in birds can be determined or reversed by steroid hormones possessing the same properties as the gonadal medulla (WOLFF and HAFFEN, 1952). There is thus no doubt that the concept of inductive tissue can be replaced by that of substances responsible for differentiation. Are these results sufficient to exclude the possibility that surface interactions between molecules of the two tissues, of antigen-antibody type, could play some part in induction? We must refer back to the account of Croisille (chapter X) for a detailed study of this problem. Certain results show that antigenic substances present in the inductive tissue can be found in the competent tissue shortly after induction. These results can easily be interpreted by the hypothesis of a transfer of macro-molecules from one tissue to the other.

However, other results do not exclude the hypothesis of contact phenomena. The inductive activity of tissues such as the primary inducers, or the optic vesicle, can be blocked by their respective antibodies (VAINIO, 1957); this indicates that surface antigens play a fundamental role in induction, since the effect of antisera is exercised at cell surface level. However, the two hypotheses are not mutually exclusive, and it must be recognised that, in both interpretations, the action of the inducer determines chemical modifications either at the cell surface or within differentiating cells.

These chemical modifications have been revealed principally by immunochemical techniques. The appearance of specific proteins shortly after the action of the inducer is evidence of the transformations which induction has brought about in the competent tissue. The formation of specific antigens has been demonstrated by many authors at the beginning of brain, lens, liver, kidney and skin differentiation in chick embryo. It can thus be stated that a chemical differentiation is synchronous with the first manifestations of differentiation. It would be logical to consider this chemical differentiation as the primary effect of induction, but we can only state one thing with certainty, i.e. that specific antigens appear at the same time as differentiation begins.

We now see that the process of induction can be expressed in chemical terms: elaboration of chemical substances by the inductive tissue, transfer of substances or contact reactions between the inducer and the receptor, synthesis of new substances in the differentiating tissue. Certainly, very little is known about the nature of inducers. But in the case of the primary inducer, Tiedemann has succeeded in extracting two proteins with different properties: one having a neural-inducing action, the other a mesodermal-inducing action on the undifferentiated ectoderm. Although their composition is not yet fully elucidated, their physical and chemical properties are known; it is possible to estimate and combine their activities in such a way that the undifferentiated ectoderm can be induced to give embryonic head or trunk formations, and, under certain conditions, a quasi-normal embryo (TIEDEMANN and TIEDEMANN, 1964). This surely proves that we can control the factors of induction and their effects, since the competent ectoderm cultured alone is incapable of differentiating any formation, and that all ectodermal differentiation arises from the action of inducers. This remarkable result thus enables us to construct an embryo, with the aid of a tissue incapable of differentiating on its own, and two inert substances which, when applied in the correct proportions, can impose on it every embryonic differentiation.

Refinements in biochemical techniques will perhaps provide more precise data on the nature of the inducing substances which produce differentiation of different organs. Such an analysis is at present limited by the technical means at our disposal, as the inducers represent only minimal quantities of tissue—a few µg, or even less. Similarly, only infinitesimal amounts of active substances can be extracted. Embryologists do not generally have at their disposal heterogenous inducers such as guinea pig liver and kidney, or chick blood serum, which can functionally replace the chorda-mesoderm of amphibia. With the increasing miniaturisation of biochemical techniques, the chemical composition of inducers may well be resolved in years to come.

Shall we then have solved all the problems of differentiation? One essential question remains to be clarified: where and how do the inducers act in the cycle of intracellular processes, in the transmission of information from the nucleus to the cytoplasm? It is essential to know at what level and in what way the inducers act in this chain. This problem has been dealt with in an earlier work of the same series*. Let us see briefly how it appears in terms of genetics and cellular biology. In the light of recent discoveries in molecular biology, the differentiation of a cell can be considered as the result of a transmission of information from a determined gene to the cytoplasm. This structural gene or cistron C_1, characterized by a specific DNA, DNA_1, is transcribed into a messenger RNA m_1. This carries the information to the cytoplasm, where it is translated at the level of polyribosomes by a transfer RNA into a sequence of amino acids, S_1, which is responsible for the composition of a certain specific protein, P_1. All differentiations are accomplished through analogous chains, involving a whole series of cistrons, $C_1, C_2, C_3, ..., C_n$. But all the cistrons are not activated at the same time. They only act at distinct stages of development and in specific embryonic areas. What we want to know is how this selection is made and what factors are responsible for releasing gene activity. Are they activators in the strict sense of the term, or agents regulating cell cycles, which remove an inhibition, i.e. derepressors of the type demonstrated in bacteria? This is how it may be considered that inducers act in cellular

* Seminar of the Chaire d'Embryologie expérimentale du Collège de France 1967: "The relationship between experimental embryology and molecular biology" (Gordon and Breach 1967).

cycles. Certain experimental results based on the action of metabolic inhibitors, such as actinomycin D, suggest that the inducers act at the point of messenger formation, i.e. transcription of a specific DNA into the corresponding RNA. It could act directly or indirectly as a specific derepressor. Each chain of reactions, starting with a given cistron, $C_1, C_2, C_3, \ldots$ etc. would be initiated by a specific inducer, $i_1, i_2, i_3, \ldots$ etc., ordering a specialized differentiation.

This could be a profitable field for future research: the embryological problem of differentiation—which has made great progress during the last 30 years, owing to the demonstration of inducers and their properties—would link up with cytogenetic problems at a cellular and biomolecular level.

References

BISHOP-CALAME, S. (1966). Etude expérimentale de l'organogenèse du système urogénital de l'embryon de poulet. *Arch. Anat. Microscop. Morphol. Exp.*, **55**, 215–309.

DAMERON, F. (1968). Etude expérimentale de l'organogenèse du poumon: I. Nature et spécificité des interactions épithélio-mésenchymateuses. *J. Embryol. Exp. Morphol.*, **20**, 151–167.

GROBSTEIN, C. (1955). Inductive interaction in the development of the mouse metanephros. *J. Exp. Zool.*, **130**, 319–340.

GROBSTEIN, C. (1956). Transfilter induction of tubules in mouse metanephrogenic mesenchyme. *Exp. Cell. Res.*, **10**, 424–440.

HAMPE, A. (1957). Recherches sur la régulation des déficiences et des excédents du bourgeon de la patte de poulet. *Arch. Anat. Microscop. Morphol. Exp.*, **46**, 265–281.

HAMPE, A. (1959). Contribution à l'étude du développement et de la régulation des déficiences et des excédents dans la patte de l'embryon de poulet. *Arch. Anat. Microscop. Morphol. Exp.*, **48**, 345–478.

HOLTFRETER, J. (1938). Differenzierungspotenzen isolierter Teile der Urodelengastrula. *Arch. Entwicklungsmech. Organ.*, **138**, 522–656.

KIENY, M. (1960). Rôle inducteur du mésoderme dans la differenciation précoce du bourgeon de membre chez l'embryon de poulet. *J. Embryol. Exp. Morphol.*, **8**, 457–467.

LE DOUARIN, G. (1965). Etude au microscope électronique de la structure du mésenchyme précardiaque et des cellules du tube cardiaque avant le stade de la formation des myofibrilles. *C.R. Acad. Sc.*, **260**, 973–976.

LE DOUARIN, G., OBRECHT, G., and CORABŒUF, E. (1966). Déterminations régionales dans l'aire cardiaque présomptive mises en évidence chez l'embryon de poulet par la méthode microélectrophysiologique. *J. Embryol. Exp. Morphol.*, **15**, 153–167.

MARIN, L., and SIGOT, M. (1963). Evolution d'une ébauche épithéliale au contact d'une surface ayant porté un mésenchyme inducteur. *C. R. Acad. Sc.*, **257**, 3475–3477.

MARIN, L., and SIGOT, M. (1965). Induction d'ébauches épithéliales au contact de surfaces conditionnées par une culture de mésenchyme. *Compt. Rend. Soc. Biol.*, **159**, 98–101.

NIU, M. C., and TWITTY, V. C. (1953). The differentiation of gastrula ectoderm in medium conditioned by axial mesoderm. *Proceed. Nat. Acad. Sc.*, **39**, 985–989.

PINOT, M. (1969). Le rôle du mésoderme somitique dans la morphogenèse precoce des membres de l'embryon de poulet. *J. Embryol. Exp. Morphol.*, (in press).

SAUNDERS, J. W. (1948). The proximo-distal sequence of origin of the parts of the chick wing and the role of the ectoderm. *J. Exp. Zool.*, **108**, 363–403.

SAUNDERS, J. W., GASSELING, M. T., and GFELLER, M. D. (1958). Interactions of ectoderm and mesoderm in the origin of axial relationships in the wing of the fowl. *J. Exp. Zool.*, **137**, 39–74.

SAXEN, L., and TOIVONEN, S. (1961). The two-gradient hypothesis in primary induction. The combined effect of two types of inductors mixed in different ratios. *J. Embryol. Exp. Morphol.*, **9**, 514–533.

TIEDEMANN, H. (1959). Neue Ergebnisse zur Frage nach der chemischen Natur des Induktionsstoffes beim Organisatoreffekt Spemanns. *Naturwissenschaften*, **22**, 613–623.

TIEDEMANN, H., and TIEDEMANN, H. (1964). Das Induktionsvermögen gereinigter Induktionsfaktoren im Kombinationsversuch. *Rev. Suisse Zool.*, **71**, 117–137.

TOIVONEN, S. (1954). The inducing action of the bone-marrow of the guinea-pig after alchohol and heat treatment in implantation and explantation experiments with embryos of Triturus. *J. Embryol. Exp. Morphol.*, **2**, 239–244.

VAINIO, T. (1957). An experimental study of the complementariness of heterogenous embryonic inductive agents. *Ann. Acad. Sci. Fennicae*, **35**, 1–94.

WOLFF, Et., and HAFFEN, K. (1952). Sur l'intersexualité expérimentale de gonades embryonnaires de canard cultivées *in vitro*. *Arch. Anat. Microscop. Morphol. Exp.*, **41**, 184–207.

ZWILLING, E. (1955). Ectoderm-mesoderm relationship in the development of the chick embryo limb bud. *J. Exp. Zool.*, **128**, 423–442.

ZWILLING, E. (1956). Reciprocal dependence of ectoderm and mesoderm during chick embryo limb development. *Am. Naturalist*, **90**, 257–265.

AUTHOR INDEX